GUITAR ERGONOMICS

A Wholistic Perspective of Technique Through Repertoire

Martín Pedreira

© 2021 by Mel Bay Publications, Inc. All Rights Reserved.

WWW.MELBAY.COM

ACKNOWLEDGMENTS

I wish to express my immense gratitude for the important support received from institutions, researchers, health professionals, colleagues, students, family and friends, especially to:

Doctors Rafael Alvisa (School of Psychology), Norma González and Humberto Olivera (Faculty of Medicine) at the University of Havana.

Doctors Beatriz Moreno, Lino Neira, Alina Ponsoda, Efraín Amador, Dolores Rodríguez, Miriam Escudero and Claudina Hernández at the University of Arts of Havana.

Dr. Carlos Rubén Gómez (psychiatrist and guitarist), Dr. Jaume Rosset (Institute of Physiology and Medicine of Art of Barcelona), Dr. Stephen Mattingly (University of Louisville), Dr. Mesut Özgen (Florida International University), and René Izquierdo (Wisconsin State University).

National Center of Artistic Education, National School of Music, Music Museum of Cuba, National Library "José Martí," Victoria Eli (Complutense University of Madrid) and María Antonia Virgili (University of Valladolid).

Lidia Pedreira, David Pedreira, Carlo Calcines, Joseph Urshalmi, Alfredo Escande, Flores Chaviano, Lester and Carmen Carrodeguas, Jorge Triana, Pedro Enrique Peña, Ana Lilian Báez, Claudia Pírez, Rafael Dávila, Roxana Castro, Francisco Alava, Austin Audu, Roberto la Rosa, Christopher Kilday, Eduardo Martín, and Walfrido Domínguez.

Special thanks to Silvia Santamaría, Ana María Rosado (New Jersey City University), Roberto Rodríguez, Rossini Hayward and Stephen Rekas (Mel Bay Publications) for their invaluable help and suggestions in the translation of this book.

To Leyda and David, my vital circle.
To my teachers, from whose remembrance I am still learning.
To my students, from whom I never cease to learn.

CONTENTS

FOREWORD

Why do we need this book? The need for another technique book, even one with a fancy title like "Guitar Ergonomics" might be questionable, until we consider the long tradition to which this text belongs, and discover the many ways in which it renews that tradition: by presenting a new approach to effective technique, by including a unique survey of the repertoire, and by incorporating important multidisciplinary ideas.

As far back as the sixteenth century, plucked string instrument players of the cultured style –vihuelists and lutenists– have been grappling with the problem of teaching through print the many enthusiasts they could not reach personally; they were already too busy teaching at court. The title of *El Maestro* by Luis Milán (c.1500-1560) proclaims its central mission, and many other music texts of the time also aimed to instruct through a tablature repertoire that would both entertain and develop the abilities of the player. We could continue with a long list of titles by guitarists from the seventeenth century to our own days that prolong this quest for enlightenment through the written word, and by printed scores in modern notation, for the many aspiring players of the world.

In his outstanding *Guitar Ergonomics,* Martín Pedreira has added an innovation to this old tradition via a book which not only helps players improve their technique, but provides them with a thorough understanding of the principles of correct posture and application of technique use and educates them in repertoire.

While some interesting texts have appeared in recent years that present good ideas about technique, their reliance on text alone can make them a bit intimidating for young people; visually oriented as they seem to be, *Guitar Ergonomics* has a wealth of musical samples and images that make it very inviting to the eyes as well. To illustrate technical aspects, this book relies on the use of fragments of pieces by an impressive variety of composers that can help a young player learn of the riches that lie in the guitar repertoire. In lieu of just exercises, although he includes a few, Pedreira utilizes short sections of masterpieces and lesser-known works to illustrate the technical points the text is addressing.

To enumerate the composers represented would add much baggage to this page. Suffice to mention the names of stalwarts such as Bach, Sor, Tárrega, Barrios, Brouwer, Ponce, and Villa-Lobos, with lesser known names such as Foscarini, Fortea, and Camargo Guarnieri, to some modern stars such as Sergio Assad, Roland Dyens, and Jorge Morel, while spicing the mélange with Cuban voices such as Eduardo Martín, José Antonio ("Ñico") Rojas, and Joaquín Nin-Culmell, etc., and we catch a glimpse of the 54 composers included, and the variety of styles represented within. While studying the musical excerpts, players can better understand the principles espoused, and select pieces they might like to add to their repertoires.

"Ergonomics" is a relatively new term that describes the dynamic between the body and its environment, in this case - the guitar. This book provides a primer to the ideas that guide this newer approach to body function: how to use our "mechanism" in a manner that is to our best advantage and in turn leads to optimum results. Pedreira supports his explanations with the theory of ergonomics: the best way to sit with the instrument, how to breathe, and how to play and interpret music as an integrated activity that is governed by the laws of healthful body motion.

Quotes from the writings of M. Alexander, Stanislavski, Feldenkrais, and other personalities from the worlds of acting, dance, and science, who have explored the connection between successful performance and correct body use, are used to buttress the text, and allow the curious-minded to further pursue their rich paths.

To presume to be educated in music without

knowing about other art forms is a fallacy, and as fast as the fingers may move, the ignorant player will still have nothing to say. Pedreira aims to inspire us to fill this essential gap by sprinkling the text with a myriad of quotes from poetry to the wisdom of players such as Andrés Segovia and John Williams, which underscore the need to become a well-rounded individual with a cultivated mind. In this aspect, Pedreira leads by example, possessing a vast culture and an inquisitive mind that enjoys the world of thought, all the while demonstrating a deep knowledge of music and a mastery of the intricate art of performance.

Going back to the initial question of why we need this book, playing an instrument is a physical and intellectual endeavor; one without the other is a prescription for failure and possible injury. Instrumental and vocal areas have a long tradition of books that aim to educate performers in the best way to use their mechanisms, and to avoid self-inflicted harm in the process. Any performer who does not continue their education after formal lessons is courting disaster, and diminishing their ability to continue growing. It is even more important for teachers to stay current on the ideas that propel technique forward by consulting methods and texts that promote new ways of thinking in that regard.

A lesson is a crisis management situation in which we try to evaluate how to best help the student develop. Oftentimes, in this short interaction our choices leave out pressing concerns for which the time frame does not allow room. The assistance of a text like this one can help teachers better guide the development of their charges.

While many technique books contain an excess of exercises, precious few present an in-depth explanation of the mechanics, and even fewer offer a precise and concise way to develop and improve a player's command of the instrument. This book is very much needed.

Guitar Ergonomics follows the lead of the most important thinker of guitar pedagogy in the twentieth century, Abel Carlevaro (1916-2001), who, in his seminal *Escuela de la Guitarra (School of Guitar)* (1979), laid down principles of correct use that have not been challenged by any other approach since. Pedreira's text elaborates on the ideas of Carlevaro, and filters them through the perspective of ergonomics to make them more in tune with our technology-driven times. In the process, he enriches the presentation with the wisdom accumulated in his decades of teaching, and with many strategies that he has developed for the technical and musical improvement of his students. In my opinion as an educator with many years of experience as well, this book should be required reading for any performance student, aspiring teacher or serious aficionado, let alone professional players and instructors.

Finally, it has been a pleasant challenge to contribute in the translation of this text from the original published in Havana, Cuba in 2011 (*Ergonomía de la Guitarra. Su técnica desde la perspectiva corporal*), and not just for its innovative ideas; I was well acquainted with many of them as I make it my practice to stay current on guitar technique, but rather because of the new "ergonomic" angle.

Martín Pedreira's prose is sophisticated, his vocabulary expansive and precise, and his ideas are highly original. This book has been very inspiring to me on many levels: as a Spanish speaker, as a professional guitarist, as a teacher, and as a lifelong learner! Readers are sure to enjoy and benefit from this wonderful book.

Ana María Rosado, D.M.A.
Associate Professor - Retired
New Jersey City University

INTRODUCTION

La Guitarra, al lector:
Yo soy aquella que todo lo canto,
soy Reyna de los tonos delicados,
soy la que alegro à todos los estados,
y soy la que condena al triste llanto...
Joan Carles Amat
Guitarra española de cinco órdenes.
Barcelona, 1596

The Guitar, addressing the reader:
I am the all-singing one,
I am the Queen of delicate tones,
I am the one who cheers all moods,
and I am the one who condemns to a sad crying...
Joan Carles Amat
Spanish Guitar of Five Courses.
Barcelona, 1596

Shortly after a successful graduation, and at the onset of my professional career, I began to experience functional difficulties with the guitar, which gave way to a severe motor blockage. Focal dystonia in my right hand prevented me from executing even the simplest arpeggio and, for almost three years, this frustrating condition was the reason for endless soul searching. I doubted the first-rate instruction received from excellent teachers was at fault, and up to this moment, my dedication as a student of the instrument had led to predictably positive results... So, what could be the origin of this seemingly insurmountable barrier?

During my pilgrimage through medical consultations, I encountered new knowledge that in other circumstances, I would have considered foreign to my artistic requirements. Instead, this newly-found knowledge allowed me to realize that I needed to: revise my work strategy, redefine means and concepts and, in sum, rethink my general approach to the instrument.

Adopting the ergonomic approach turned out to be a key element, not only for a gradual recovery, but for a revitalized development of my playing skills much further beyond the peak reached before the onset of my dystonia.[1] Throughout this process –continuously enriched by my teaching interactions– I began to outline didactical resources that I have successfully put to use for almost three decades. The desire to share the essentials of this experience was the main motivation behind the writing of this text, for which I found inspiration in a cardinal thought expressed by Heinrich Neuhaus in *The Art of Piano Playing*:

> Any improvement of technique is an improvement of art itself and consequently helps to reveal the "content," the hidden meaning; in other words it is the material, the real body of art (Neuhaus, 1973:2).

The Instrumental Evolution

The development of instrumental families, in so far as repertoire and technique are concerned, has relied to a great extent on relatively stable designs. The first keyboards (organs) date back to the Middle Ages and in the seventeenth century underwent changes prefiguring the present piano. Toward the early 1700s, the Italian luthiers Amati, Guarneri and Stradivari converged on a violin design that has lasted essentially until the present.

With a millennial prehistory, we find in the thirteenth century the first reference to the guitar –as *Guitarra Latina* (Latin) or *Morisca* (Moorish)– in the *Cantigas de Santa María*, a book compiled by King Alfonso X, *el Sabio* (*the Sage*), although only since the Renaissance can we establish a trajectory of the instrument with relative certainty.

Since the late seventeenth century – the period of the evolution toward the six single strings– the guitar has experienced remarkable transformations, a process that reaches a significant moment towards the mid-nineteenth century. Its current prototype is due to the work of the Andalusian Antonio de Torres Jurado (1817-1892), known as "The Father of Modern Lutherie," who made possible an increment of volume and tonal possibilities with

[1] *Ergonomics* is a scientific discipline formed through the confluence of psychology, physiology, work hygiene and technical sciences which is dedicated to studying the reciprocal adaptation of human beings to their work environment, or human beings to their work with machines, vehicles or instruments. The criteria elaborated through ergonomics are applicable to any sphere of human activity, both in work and in daily life.

his innovations and craftsmanship. Since Torres, the guitar has become an even more versatile instrument for music performance.

The nineteenth century was bountiful in virtuosi: including the Spaniards Fernando Sor and Dionisio Aguado; Mauro Giuliani, heading an outstanding group of Italian interpreters and composers –Niccolò Paganini among them– and the masters of Romanticism, who following the path of splendor laid down by their predecessors, had in Francisco Tárrega Eixea (1852-1909) their most significant exponent. An exceptional artist, and precursor of the modern guitar, the Spanish maestro notably enriched guitar technique, apart from composing and transcribing numerous works of classic and contemporary composers for the instrument.

Among the later most outstanding performers, it was undoubtedly Andrés Segovia (1893-1987) who made a transcendental contribution to the universality of the guitar. During his long and legendary career he had an active influence on many excellent guitarists, and also inspired numerous composers to write new music for the guitar, thus expanding the horizon of the instrument.

Embraced by the common people and played by kings, admired or despised, the guitar finally conquered the great stage scenarios and began its academic life in conservatories.

1, 2. Vihuela and Renaissance guitar; 3. Baroque guitar; 4. Six-course guitar (late eighteenth century); 5. Classic-Romantic guitar (first-half nineteenth century); 6. Antonio de Torres' guitar (1892).

Body Awareness and Perception

Despite the important legacy of great masters of the past, the guitar does not yet have a primary didactical consensus. Still prevalent among many teachers is an approach mainly based on the physical aptitudes of the students, from whom a questionable virtuosity is demanded, oftentimes more akin to gymnastics than to art. It is not surprising then that some health statistics place guitarists among the most vulnerable musicians to performance-related injuries, also known as "occupational diseases."

One way or another, all the aspects of an artist's life are related to his or her creative projection. Along with a demanding theoretical training, each instrumentalist should seek the widest knowledge of his corporal resources and use them consciously, something that will not only prevent injuries but also achieve greater qualitative results in one's continuous growth as an active performer.

A special combination of talent, culture, and intuition has characterized extraordinary performers who, while aiming for artistic expression as their goal, have achieved a highly efficient use of the entirety of their psychophysical resources. Disregarding this evidence, many instrumentalists persist in working as if the sole framework of performance were the hands, starting at the fingertips, and ending at the wrists.

Each individual has an image of his body, built on the basis of sensations. This scheme, usually linear and fragmented, defines how he or she perceives and acts. The corporal concept has been defined from multiple perspectives, and expresses essentially the way in which we perceive and use our body. According to Le Boulch it is...

> ... the immediate and continuous knowledge that we have of our body, at rest or in movement, in relation to its different parts and, above all, in relation to space and the objects that surround us. (Le Boulch, 1986:17)

Physiology is one of the most objective aspects in the context of instrumental technique. Let us have in mind that *the body is the primary vehicle* through which we perform the miracle of art, in our case with the help of a musical instrument.[2]

For the musician, the corporal concept should embrace an acute consciousness of his or her body (body awareness) in terms of tension, relaxation, and posture with the instrument –including hand positions– and the application of these elements with optimal energy and motion efficiency.

The understanding of the muscular functioning and of the most effective motion allows the player to reach an optimal and sustained performance. Nevertheless, deriving the practical benefits of this information depends on the scope of our perceptions, since all artistic realization implies a dynamic sensorial interaction.

Oscar Ghiglia reminds us that music is not only understood with the intellect but with the body:

> Likewise, it is necessary to understand the instrument with the hands, with our sensations.[3]

For the artist, the emotional context has a fundamental role in every instance. Emotions are the driving force for creativity, and they promote intuition. It is senseless, however, to demand from this source solutions to the problems of instrumental execution. Tackling complex musical works requires us to seek the higher road of technical excellence, which in turn needs a conscious application of physiology.

A Didactic Approach Based on Perception

Thanks to sensations, we know the qualities of objects and phenomena, and perception is the integral reflex of these sensory messages, determining their properties in our consciousness.

Perception has a voluntary and selective character, since from the set of stimuli that surround us, only those in which we focus our attention are properly detailed. It is a complex phenomenon in which, in addition to sensations, we find implicit mnemonic evocation, idea associations, and even various judgments. Its purpose is the understanding of what is received. Therefore, *to perceive* means *to understand.*

Simply put, *perceiving* is equivalent *to connecting mind and body.*

Corporal awareness is an essential requirement for verifying what Konstantin Stanislavski called "inner scenic delight," a state of mind favorable to the spiritual understanding of the work and its enjoyment in performance. *Developing an ergonomic (physiologically functional) bond with the instrument is one of the keys to this realization.* Can the performer "experience the music" without a pleasant bodily sensation in a balanced interaction with the instrument?

Pepe Romero affirms that:

> The soloist has to sing inwardly at every moment, and enjoy the music as one more spectator instead of trying to control the performance, letting it take its own form and pass freely through our mind and our own body, bathing our ears with its potent and purifying power, always maintaining an inner silence.[4]

Among the various disciplines of body work developed from art contexts since the nineteenth century are the acting techniques proposed by K. Stanislavski, the Alexander Technique, and the *Eurhythmics* of Emile-Jacques Dalcroze, as well as more recent methodologies such as *Sensoperception* in dance, a discipline that has

---

[2] "This body, as a translator of a musical idea to movements, and from them to sounds, requires a particular attention that exceeds the intellectual understanding of the passage to be performed or work on the technique itself. Precisely the act of playing an instrument implies a solid plot that articulates perception, sensitivity, knowledge, intellect, memory, creativity and expressiveness, as well as a specific instrumental technique." (Alejandra García Trabucco and María Alejandra Silnik: "El plano corporal en la enseñanza de instrumentos musicales," http://eutonicamendoza.blogspot.com/p/investigacion.html)

[3] Alain Riou: "Rencontre avec Oscar Ghiglia," *Les Cahiers de La Guitare*, No. 33, Paris, 1990.

[4] Pepe Romero: "La preparación del guitarrista ante el concierto," http://www.orfeoed.com/guia/guia20.asp.

much potential given its results in music practice.[5]

Like any other artistic expression, musical performance must be essentially a pleasant experience. The artist needs to perceive beauty to recreate it as a free projection of his spirit, which nevertheless requires specific informative references.

The process of learning a score resembles the staging of a play, for which the actor begins by a simple revision of the script without yet displaying all its richness and complexity. His first actions will be limited to the spontaneous and the ordinary; to look, walk, open a door, etc., actions that will gradually yield to a dramatically enriched projection of the character.

From the subjectivity of sounds, the performer also works from the external to the internal. The first reading and score analysis sets up the initial stimuli for the expression of its content through a physical as well as intellectual and emotional action. This process depends substantially on the communicative force of an act which involves not only his knowledge, but his whole being. What would be the role of perceptions in this context?

Mobility deployment on the instrument is linked to two aspects: the *postural frame*, essential for balance during performance, and the *proprioceptive sensations* that allow the handling of effort according to the functional efficiency of our actions.

Amos Comenio states in his *Didactica Magna* (1628): "There is nothing in understanding that was not in the sense before," recognizing thus the importance of perceptions for learning. We are now aware that acquired knowledge conditions the manner in which we assimilate new information.[6] Thus, taking into account the "sensory progression" in the learning process is a crucial element for the most effective development of *mechanism*, a set of reflexes that make the execution possible.[7]

Let's take as an example the teaching progression for a basic articulation procedure – slurs.

Once a balanced left-hand position is established, the teacher should indicate the practice of a simple pattern that later will be used in a reduced musical context (a sketch), then in a study, and finally in a musical piece. This scheme, practiced on variations of increased difficulty (mordents, trills, etc.) allows the acquisition of mobility habits by means of gradual tactile and auditory perception development. The absence of this progression generally limits the mechanism of students. Ricardo Iznaola states:

> The belief that technique can be acquired through work on the repertoire alone is a common fallacy. Since good technique relies on a physically fit playing mechanism, and since artistically conceived works do not have a pre-designed formative technical purpose, technical equipment built on the study of the repertoire alone will always have many weak areas. Its physical component will not be thoroughly trained. (Iznaola, 2000:11)

A deficient mechanism is comparable to an "acquired incapacity" –negative learning whose artificial limits to effective actions are clear to the eye. If we neglect our physical perceptions, how can we really know how efficiently we are performing, and how much more we can still improve?

It is necessary to not only think *about* the body, but *to think **from** the body, to be always open to its messages* in a language of sensations framed in opposite pairs: pleasure/pain, comfort/discomfort, plenitude/dissatisfaction, etc. As a sort of dialog, during practice it is advisable to continuously alternate the "wanting to do" with the "allowing to do." Fedora Aberastury, who saw a wise manifestation of energy in natural body motion, said: *Letting do is a conscious doing*.[8]

---

[5] *Sensoperception* is part of the necessary adaptive mechanism of every living being. Individuals actively regulate the information gathered through the sensitive threshold of their "receivers." The sensory receivers are strategically located in such specific ways that the stimuli gathered are transformed into electrical signals sent to the brain, where the information is then processed.

As its name indicates, sensoperception consists of two parts: *sensation* and *perception*. *Sensation* is a neurophysiological process that involves the reception of information (from sensory receptors distributed throughout the organism) that comes from our own body and the environment.

Perception is developed in three phases: first, sensory information is received; second, there is a process of discrimination and selection of sensory data, which access our consciousness; and third, the areas in charge of sensory processing are responsible for interpreting and processing.

[6] With the establishment of playing habits, the action is modified, and therefore the way in which we perceive the environment and elaborate new adaptation responses. (See Hilgard, 1961:17)

[7] See Eduardo Fernández (2001:3). Mechanism is a primary component of technique.

"Technique means the power of expressing oneself musically. It embraces all the physico-mechanical means through which one's musical perceptions are expressed." (Tobias Matthay, 1947:3)

[8] Fedora Aberastury (1914-1985) developed a "Conscious System for Movement Technique" from pianistic execution, an approach applicable to all individuals, musicians or not. The method relies basically on developing correct perceptual attention for the ordering of motor function.

Technique at the Service of Art

We can only gain security in playing by comprehensively tackling problems in the study of each score. For this purpose a diaphanous perception of tasks in performance and a consistent theoretical-aesthetic formation are essential aspects. Let us quote once more Neuhaus, this time referring to the necessary unity of technical and artistic work:

> ... While you are learning the E-flat major scale it is a prefabricated part; when you play it, let us say, at the end of Beethoven's *Fifth Piano Concerto,* it is the finished article, because it is music. (Neuhaus, 1973:114)

In regard to this subject, Isaac Nicola, an exceptional guitar pedagogue comments:

> How much work do we need to do to assimilate each technical procedure? Only the necessary time to establish the basic habits associated with the mechanism before implementing it in studies and pieces. *The actual and only purpose of technique is to facilitate the realization of a musical idea.*[9] Technique work must be approached in the right proportion, and with a clear sense of its objective, according to the individual needs of the student. This way, it will not become an obstacle for the student, but a valuable means of development together with an indispensable theoretical and aesthetic formation.[10]

Although corporal awareness is continually on high alert during study, our use of technical resources depends substantially on the artistic conception of the score. Andrés Segovia synthesizes this apparent duality with a poetic vision of the instrument:

> The guitar demands, of whoever is devoted to her, very heterogeneous natural gifts: the finest sensibility, so fine that it can be disturbed by a shadow as fine as a hair; subtle hearing to perceive, with inner audition, the tenuous resonances that form like the halo of her delicate sound; flexible and strong hands to shape the sonorous body of music with tenderness and energy, impetus and precision. But these gifts, to be fruitful, must receive the solar heat of Culture.[11]

Engraving from the title page of a score by Ferdinand Carulli (1770-1841).

[9] I. Nicola, M. Pedreira (2002:8). This is a principle that Francisco Tárrega had as a rule. Emilio Pujol thus characterizes the essence of the Tárrega School: "Tárrega's pedagogical sense, supported on his faith in work, consists of solving beforehand any problems that might arise from the elements that contribute to the performance of a score: instrument, hands and spirit." (E. Pujol: "Pedagogía de Tárrega," *Guitarra*, II No. 2, Havana, 1941).

[10] I. Nicola, M. Pedreira, ob. cit.

[11] From an article published in the newspaper *El Día*, Montevideo, November 8, 1942 (see Escande, 2005:99).

I. POSTURE, INSTRUMENT PLACEMENT AND BREATHING

The primary objective that requires the attention of singers and instrumentalists is to assume a graceful body posture without affectation; therefore, those who play the guitar should hold it in a way that results in composure *and* comfort.

Federico Moretti
Principios para tocar la guitarra de seis órdenes..., Madrid, 1799

Posture determines the elasticity and agility of the fingers.

Fernando Sor
Méthode pour la Guitare, Paris, 1830

Because of its portable nature, we can hold the guitar in many ways, but assuming a balanced posture is a primary condition to ergonomically interact with the instrument and achieve an optimum and healthy use of our natural biomechanical resources in performance.[12]

The amount of time devoted to practice is in itself a powerful reason to study the best options –those that combine functionality and wellness– a task which demands the review of specific aspects of physiology.

Normal Posture and Mobility

A fundamental requirement for efficient development of mechanism is to observe our body. It is advisable that teachers examine the postural habits of students *before* holding a guitar in order to help them to perceive what Matthias Alexander called Primary Control: *the inherent and intrinsic mechanism for balance and support in the body* (Conable, 1995:1), which ensures that musculoskeletal alignment is achieved effortlessly, and that movements will be stable and flowing.

Normal posture in a biped stance is characterized by:

> ... the symmetrical distribution of body parts in relation to the spinal column. In a normal posture the vertical position of the head is established when the chin is slightly raised and the shoulders are at the same height; the thorax is neither protruding nor sunken in its front or back, having a symmetrical alignment with the mid-section. The shoulder blades are tight against the trunk, and at equal distance from the spine, with their angles following a horizontal line.
> From the side, the thoracic cavity is slightly raised, and the abdomen is lightly sunken; the lower extremities will be extended and a moderate manifestation of the physiological curvature of the spine, with its undulated line, will be noticeable. (Popov, 1992:107)

Regarding the instrument, performance requires the attainment of a *flexible postural platform* from which the necessary changes will occur during execution. Our balance and the mobility of our extremities are conditioned by the axial skeleton: body structure formed by the spinal column, the scapular girdle (neck and shoulders), the pelvis girdle (hips), and different muscle groups.

> Movement begins in the center of the body and unfolds through it in a wave-like manner; it is individual, expressive, and beautiful, and acts freely and confidently; it is not linked to time or fashion, ... it is a "law" of all exercises, whether they are functional, educational or artistic.
> The natural movement is not stylized, neither artificial nor angular, but fluid; it is not measured but rhythmic; it is adapted to the body, physiologically adjusted, ... economic, materially authentic and simple in the attainment of intentions. (Meinel, 1977:42-45)

There is a close relationship between *Postural Balance, Functional Relaxation, Economy of Effort,* and *Fluency of Movements.*

Any distortion of the joints results in a chain reaction throughout the body, a reason why assuming a physiologically adequate posture is of particular importance for the player.

Faulty posture causes unnecessary contractions

[12] Let us call "natural" any posture, technical resource or mobility, that in accordance to our psychophysiological possibilities, allows for the most efficient fulfillment of any task in performance. Likewise, the word "posture" is here used as synonym of balanced body; a conjunction of attitudes perceptive-focused, therefore, neither rigid nor static, since permanent muscle tension tends to generate an excessive effort.

and blockages in the joints, altering balance. As a result, "compensatory responses" appear, disrupting the fluidity of motion and producing fatigue and deformation –both structural and practical– to a greater or lesser extent. (See C. Hernández, 2009:67)

Traditional Placement of the Guitar

In the so-called "traditional placement," the guitar rests on the left thigh, lying flat on the curve of its lower side. This seemingly stable position introduces a postural asymmetry that leads to adverse muscle contractions and various functional limitations.

Viewed from above, this placement produces a right angle between the thigh and the soundbox, forming a parallel line with the shoulders (Fig. A). In this way, placing the forearm over the side forces the right shoulder to move forward in a permanent rotation of the upper part of the back (Fig. B), sometimes tilting the torso towards the fingerboard.

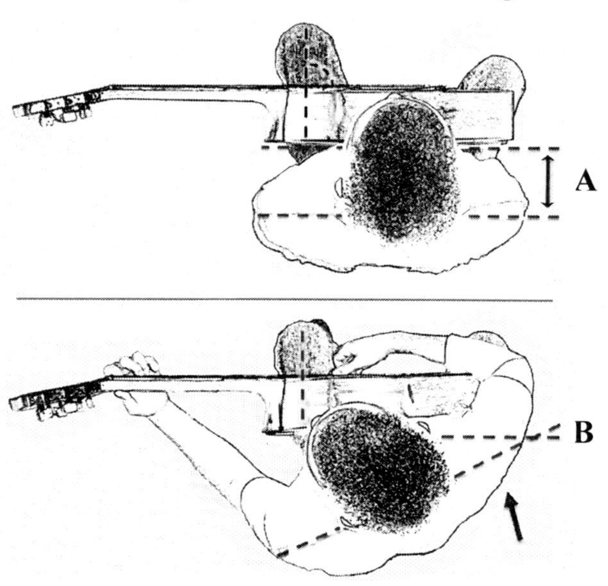

Traditional, less advantageous sitting position.

This position tends to reduce breath capacity and generates zones of tension that gradually spread to adjacent areas, with a more marked effect on individuals of medium size with short limbs.

From the placement described, moving the left hand to the fingerboard requires moving the arm and back out of its more comfortable and efficient scope of action, which is forward. Furthermore, this position places the back of the soundbox flush against the chest, which hinders any adjustments of the torso. Using the standard-size guitar for adults with a string length of 65 cm or the smaller ones for children –about 53 cm or less– the effect will be proportionally the same.

Another questionable practice regarding the traditional sitting position is the use of a foot stand, which makes the hips uneven, strains the lumbar region with a resulting lateral compression of the intervertebral discs, and hinders blood circulation. As an alternative, a variety of ergonomic attachments have been created to promote a balanced seated posture, leading to an approximately 90° angle between legs and hips.

Other immediate benefits include less back tension and freer breathing, particularly if you sing as well as play.

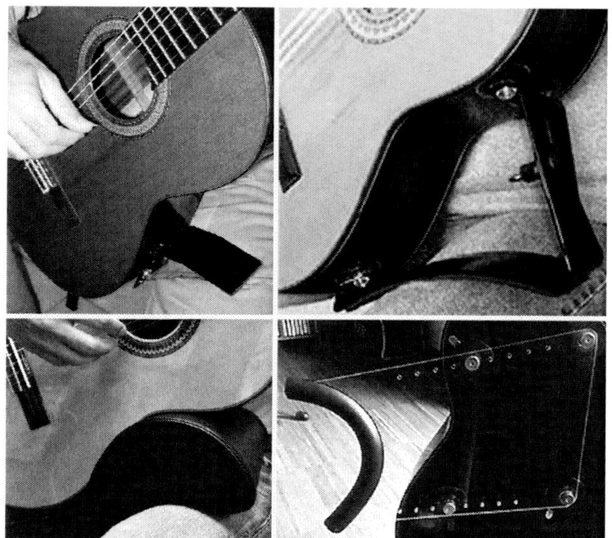
Ergonomic alternatives to the traditional foot stand.

Psychophysical Effects

Excessive muscular tension tends to have negative repercussions on both the technical mechanism and the emotional state of the performer.

Given the extensive innervation of the *scapular girdle* –an area where the central nervous system branches out towards the whole body (peripheral system)– stimuli in this zone are perceived more intensely, as in the first sensation of a cold shower.

On the other hand, neck muscles in connection with the shoulders reflect psychic tension, something that happens frequently without our realizing it. (See Schultz, 1969:20-40)

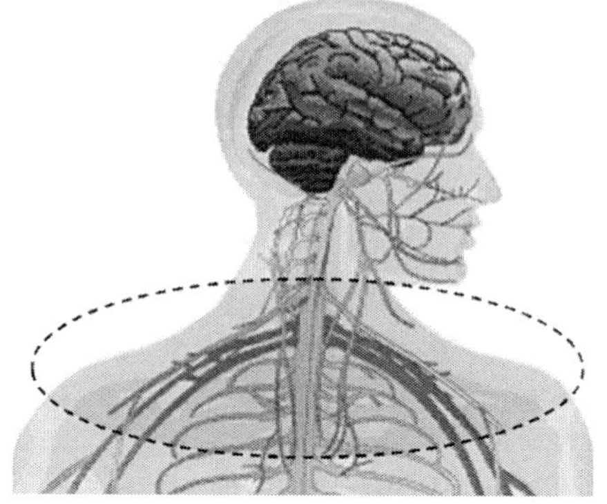
The scapular girdle.

If risky situations or worries prompt spontaneous physical reactions (heartbeat acceleration, sweating, skin reddening, muscle tension, etc.), conversely, body tension caused merely by posture can provoke or exacerbate certain kinds of behavior, especially in events of a sensitive nature: a category in which musical performance undoubtedly belongs.

When posture is a source of superfluous tension, the possibility that our natural anxiety prior to a concert will lead to an unexpected lack of control when on stage also increases. Rightly so, common nervousness of young students during exams is emphasized by an awkward instrument position.[13]

Slanted Placement

As the very beginning of his innovative contributions, Abel Carlevaro emphasized the importance of *adapting the guitar to the body* (Carlevaro, 1984:2), and to realize this cardinal goal he proposed a slanted placement. This is accomplished by moving the guitar neck forward until the shoulders become aligned. This way, the soundbox contacts the chest from its center toward the right side, allowing for the natural position of the player's upper back. The balance attained allows us to distribute the weight of the arms, so that they remain stable during performance (See Annex II).

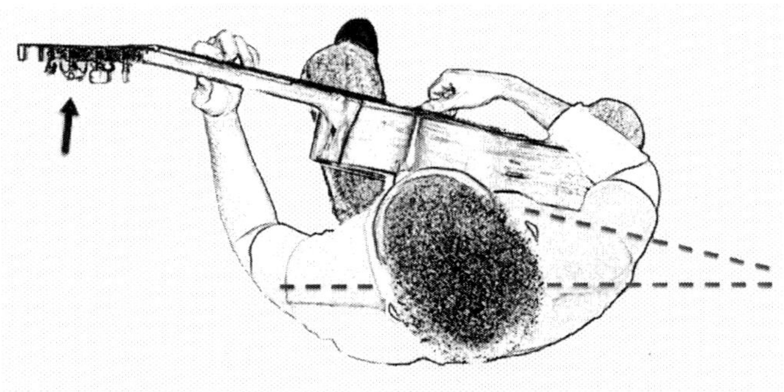

Preferred position prescribed by Abel Carlevaro.

In addition to promoting postural symmetry, the slanted placement favors greater freedom of movement and, as a result, allows for the use of a wider range of technical resources.

[13] On a psychological level, our expectations and aspirations, filtered by constraints such as fear of making mistakes, desire for approval, or high self-demands can reinforce the problems arising from an inadequate mechanism.
What do I wish to achieve (or demonstrate) by performing this piece (or concert program)? Do I truly enjoy what I do? Do I play for myself or for others? Answering such questions helps to define and enrich our goals, in addition to stimulating self-observation and a positive critical attitude during study.

This placement presents four points of contact with the body:

- Left thigh
- Chest (toward the right side)
- Inner edge of the right thigh
- Right forearm support

Tilting of the Soundbox

To slightly recline the soundbox towards the chest brings about a series of additional benefits:

- Reduces pressure on the forearm point of support, which is now more lateral, less incisive, and more suitable for soundbox adjustments without the need to disrupt the balance of the instrument or press it to the thigh.
- Favors a more vertical plucking (without the need to raise the wrist), which increases sound volume. Moreover, the tilting allows for a better acoustic refraction (See *Physical-Acoustic Phenomena and Sound in Performance*).
- Reduces the need to raise the elbow toward the first positions.
- Allows space for abdominal breathing –whose regularity is highly beneficial– as well as for the breasts of female players.
- Ensures that adjustments of the torso maintain the right hand-forearm alignment, especially from fret IX onward. (Tilting of the torso forward and

slightly to the left can be achieved by shifting the weight of the body toward the left foot. A tilt in the opposite direction is accomplished by shifting the weight to the other foot).[14]

• Promotes better fingerboard visibility.

Visual orientation is critical in the shaping of our kinesthetic sense (*proprioceptive perceptions* of movement), which receives and decodes the sensorial stimuli to guide us through space. The tilted position also allows us to look at the fingerboard with less neck torsion, not an insignificant benefit considering the harmful effects on the cervical area that this sustained posture could lead to.

The use of ergonomic supports favors the tilting of the instrument, but when using a footstool, we can add a non-slip material on the thigh, such as a rubber mat – to improve the tilt angle.

Other Issues Related to Posture with the Instrument

• The seat must have a stable and solid surface, and must be of a suitable height for the player.

• On a standard chair, it is advisable to sit toward the front half, leaving a small space on the left side, so that the edge of the chair does not interfere with the placement of the soundbox.

• In a standing position, the alignment of six joints forms an axis of fundamental balance that distributes the weight along the bone structure. These joints include the atlanto-occipital (upper part of the neck), shoulders, back, hips, knees and ankles.

• In a sitting position, body balance is centered on a tripod-like structure formed by the feet and the ischiums (lower part of the hips). Sitting at the center of the chair with the guitar, most of the weight is displaced towards the spine, affecting balance.

• The headstock should be approximately level with the player's forehead to ensure the natural position of the right shoulder and less supination of the left hand on the fingerboard.

• The music stand should be placed just ahead of the neck of the instrument at a convenient height for sight reading.

• As a general rule, do not sit for much more than thirty minutes at a stretch. While taking breaks, it is advisable to do stretching exercises.[15]

Martha Graham (1894-1991), an outstanding dancer and choreographer, described posture *as a moment of apparent calm that precedes the most intense action; the body at its peak potential efficiency* (Boucier, 1981:17). Likewise, musicians who adopt a balanced and dynamic postural framework will enjoy more options for a freer display of their abilities.

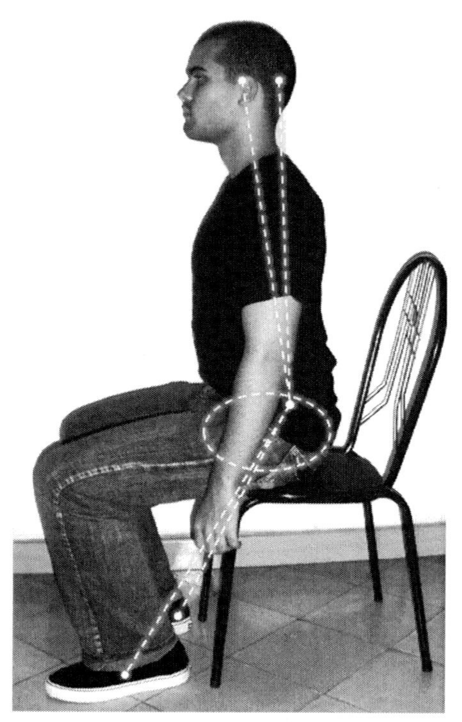

Weight distribution along axis of balance.

Remodeling Instrument Placement

Students with poor posture and guitar placement should seriously consider *remodeling* their sitting position with the instrument.

Any modification of postural habits or acquired mechanisms implies a process that is different from the one used when learning something new, although both cases require voluntary modifications at the sensory-system level.

[14] Carlevaro described the feet as *motor elements.*
"Each foot is then a lever which uses the ground like a platform in order to transmit a force that will directly act on the movements of the body. The body itself need not make any effort whatsoever." (Carlevaro, 1984:8)

[15] A practice system based on short periods of 20-30 minutes (the approximate duration of an efficient period of concentration), with breaks of 5 to 10 minutes or more –depending on the intensity of the work– allows the achievement of a sustained performance without the need for overexertion. Pauses serve two purposes: to release the accumulated tension during a brief physical and mental recovery, and to favor the synthesis of the stimuli received by the brain, which lead to conditioned reflexes.
The previous proposal is based on *Periodization*, a scientific method of sports training (also applicable to the study of musical instruments) that promotes an effective response to the stimulus of the exercises to achieve better results in a shorter time.

An important rule to accelerate redesigning is to put aside our active performance repertoire during this period, a temporary renouncement that does not exclude "putting away" the guitar for a few days. Pieces already known respond to the group of reflexes (mobility and perceptual stereotypes) that we want to transform, and are also conditioned by the previous positioning of the instrument.

In the absence of sustained reinforcement, less than functional movement schemes –emphasized by bad fingering or lack of musical understanding– weaken more quickly. This neurophysiological regularity also explains why we experience greater ease when replaying a "hostile passage" after setting it aside for a few days, clearly a long pause. Likewise, a deficient mechanism requires greater effort to achieve its limited results.

If you try to force such changes, an absurd "battle against ghosts" will take place since conditioned reflexes (habits or *automatism*) are the sole response of a nervous system configuration structured by the repetition of different stimuli categories.

It is fundamental to interact systematically with these "corporal responses" during the implementation of new approaches throughout study, not only to optimize the mechanism but to overcome critical blockages such as focal dystonia, whose causes in instrumentalists commonly have their origins in dysfunctional practice.

Consciously or not, *we learn continuously from our sensations; the body teaches us*. Observing ourselves in front of a mirror is helpful, but assuming a posture with no apparent tensions does not guarantee good assimilation. To achieve the desired control, each posture or technical procedure (movement) should also be verified with our corporal sensations. Correctly placing the instrument will be an incomplete task if we omit this basic requirement.

The first maneuver *to adapt the guitar to the body* consists of sitting normally and positioning the instrument repeatedly, ensuring that our most natural and comfortable perception remains unchanged.

A balanced posture can be achieved with a progressive exercise based on identifying the bodily supports through the sensations of weight and contact. It is essentially an exercise in relaxation with the instrument:

• Hold the guitar at a slanted angle and take a few slow, deep breaths to begin relaxing.

• Lean your head forward, and relax your shoulders until you feel their weight.

• Because of their importance for a wholistic perception of relaxation, verify that the jaw and facial muscles are loose, and subsequently, the abdomen, pelvis and buttocks as well.

• Gradually focus on the sensations of heaviness on the seat, the feet on the floor, the right forearm on the side of the guitar, and the left arm as it hangs loose and dangles. During this exercise it is possible to identify previously unnoticed tension areas that influence mobility in performance.

• The next step consists of progressively integrating these partial perceptions until we feel the body as a whole. An immediate result of this exercise is a readjustment of the muscle tone with a sedative effect (psychic distension reflex) that improves blood circulation, which favors a slight increase of temperature in the limbs.[16]

• Now start plucking open strings, softly and slowly, trying to retain the previous feeling of wholistic body unit. At this point you can incorporate the left hand with some easy tasks or just place it on the fingerboard.

• The final step consists of playing something simple, at a slow tempo at first, and with minimal volume.

A possible temporary symptom at the beginning of the remodeling period will be to experience a slight discomfort in the back which will disappear in a short time.

The exercise described improves *muscle tone flexibility*, that is, the ability to specify the muscular effort required for every action and "know where to return" in terms of relaxation.

The beginning of study is the ideal moment for practicing sensory-perceptive exercises: a "first look" at the body that will regulate all further work. A few minutes of this practice will be enough before starting the daily routine of warming up, to help adjust our tension status *through a dialogue with the body*, as suggested by Joseph Urshalmi (2006:17). This willingness to become self-aware implies *a mental state of*

[16] "The experience of weight leads to vasodilation, which in turn stimulates blood circulation, and therefore, body heat. These effects go hand in hand with muscular strains, which as a partial phenomenon of sleep encourage mental relaxation." (Schultz, 1969:38)

openness, flexibility and experimentation, ... curiosity and enthusiasm. (Ristad, 2009:21)

In the renovative process of the mechanism, there comes a moment when we experience a secure connection with this new way of working. This "point of no return" is encouraged by persevering in a conscious perception of all our actions during study.

Experiencing postural comfort is the first step towards a positive psychological approach to the instrument; at that point, the guitar will no longer be a *daily challenge* but will instead become a pleasant source of artistic development.

•

From outstanding masters of the nineteenth century, the following engravings suggest the placement of the guitar as a common subject among the pioneers of instrumental technique, whose evolution has had significant moments in Dionisio Aguado, Fernando Sor, Francisco Tárrega, and more recently, in Abel Carlevaro, and others.

1. Dionisio Aguado, *Escuela de Guitarra.* Madrid, 1825. Aguado and Sor used to rest the guitar on the right thigh.
2. Fernando Sor, *Méthode pour la Guitare.* Paris, 1830.
3. Matteo Carcassi (1793-1853). Observe the tilted position of the guitar.
4. Aguado with his tripod. *Nuevo Método para Guitarra,* Madrid, 1849.

BREATHING

Posture, thought of in itself, seems a static situation. This is by no means the case. Not only is it the result of a continuous balance of opposing forces, but at the same time it is imbued with pulse and rhythm, the pulse of our heart and the rhythm of our breathing...

Yehudi Menuhin
Violin. Six Lessons with Yehudi Menuhin

Actors use breath to invoke the mood of their characters. Wind instrument players and singers study phrasing and add breath marks to the score, but the rest of us musicians care little or nothing about this vital function despite its decisive influence on performance.

Breathing is not simply inhaling and exhaling. It is the process that takes place inside each cell by means of which assimilated food radiates its energy to the entire body.

Respiration involves the chest, the intercostal muscles and the diaphragm, a wide transversal muscle that separates the chest cavity from the abdominal area.

As you inhale, the diaphragm contracts downward and the ribcage expands, thereby increasing the space in the lung cavity, which is rapidly occupied by air. When the diaphragm relaxes, it rises and the ribs are brought downward and inward.

The nearly 100 billion nerve cells of the human brain demand a huge amount of metabolic energy. This organ constitutes only 2% of the total body weight but consumes 20% of its energy resources, including approximately 50 cm3 of oxygen per minute (Sánchez, 1991:14). If the air supply ceases, functional changes occur that in a few seconds can produce unconsciousness, and in a few minutes the death of cells. With this evidence we can deduce how the quality of breathing affects our daily activities, especially those of an intellectual nature.

A relaxed posture is required to breathe freely. Breathing while out of balance or when lifting a heavy object is more difficult. Hence the custom of holding our breath during a strenuous physical effort, something we also do while performing activities that require special precision.

Gerda Alexander suggests that breathing is normalized in an indirect way, relaxing the tensions that impede its fullness (1986:28). These tensions are located in the above-mentioned muscle groups, the cervical region and the shoulders.

Moshe Feldenkrais details the influence of respiration on our postural condition and vice versa:

> Most of the muscles of the respiratory system are connected to the cervical and lumbar vertebrae; as a result, breathing affects the stability and posture of the spinal column. At the same time, and for the same reason, the position of the spinal column influences the quality and speed of the breath. Consequently, good breathing also means good posture, as one is dependent on the other. (Feldenkrais, 2005:121)

Abdominal Breathing

The lungs have their greater capacity towards the abdomen, where the expansion of the lower (floating) ribs allows easy ventilation.

From lowest to highest order of capacity, there are three types of ventilation: 1. *high* or *collarbone breathing*, 2. *middle* (also called *gymnast breathing*), and 3. *lower*, *abdominal* or *diaphragmatic breathing*, which provides the greatest amount of oxygen and requires the least effort. This last modality is innate (easily seen in little children) and the first link in so-called *complete breath* which includes the middle and high lung areas (*Dirga Pranayama* in yoga practice).

The benefits of diaphragmatic ventilation are multiple. It has a positive effect on health (circulation, abdominal organs, nervous system) and recent studies confirm that it favors the development of fine motor skills (including finger dexterity), which materialize in a broader tactile perception during performance.

After assuming a comfortable position with the instrument, to familiarize ourselves with abdominal breathing, we can use suggestions such as imagining that we breathe through our belly or through the guitar.

The first attempts must be made gently, avoiding forcing the air down. This modality of breathing should become smooth, continuous and imperceptible. From a preliminary phase

–not playing but just holding the instrument– you must implement abdominal breathing by playing something simple. You will probably face a persistent "divided attention" that will gradually diminish until it becomes effortless and automatic. Abdominal breathing should be practiced quietly and constantly from the beginning of the workday.

Breathing Rhythm

It is easy to verify that irregular breathing or hyperventilation always tend to confuse us during any activity. The frequency and intensity of the inhale-exhale cycle is directly related to the type of actions we engage in. An orchestra conductor, a pianist, and a guitarist may breathe at different rates, even while performing the same score.

Nevertheless, no matter how ideal it may seem, excessive synchronization of our breathing with the musical narrative is not a condition for achieving expressive results. On the contrary, it can be completely dysfunctional.

Perhaps our temperament inclines us to mark phrasing with sudden breath intakes, but in any case, we must verify whether our breathing is free or forced, and how it affects the handling of our instrument in general.

Abdominal breathing is a secure platform for the subtle inflections of the inhale-exhale rhythm, while larger air intakes can be made in breaks or score section changes, and between pieces.

Menuhin tells us that to play, we need continuous breathing; that is, *we must never hold our breath* (1972:17). He also states that:

> Good breathing requires the ability to inhale and exhale softly, taking the same amount of time for inhalation as for exhalation. The time for each phase should be as long as possible.

Meanwhile, Jane Kember and Thérèse Wassily Saba recommended paying close attention to breathing when studying a new piece:

> Remember that memorization encompasses more than the mere learning of digital patterns. Your tension, state of mind and breathing patterns are imprinted in memory simultaneously with the movement of your fingers. When you work on a difficult passage, breathe slowly and rhythmically with a relaxed posture.[17]

Breathing versus Excitement

A relaxed body disposition engenders an attitude of mental calm. At the same time, breathing is not just a reflection of one's psychic or emotional state. Breathing can also influence it, a quality that makes it a key device in moderating excitement or excessive emotional reaction in public appearances.

The outstanding pianist and professor Carola Grindea advised students to begin exhaling gently *before* difficult passages (whispering *haaaa...* with the jaw relaxed and the mouth slightly open), instead of suddenly inhaling and holding one's breath. This strategy promotes concentration and both physical and psychic relaxation.

> Exhalation is a performer's greatest ally; it is the antidote to nervous and physical tension. (Grindea, 2000:25)

Besides acting as a regulator of psychic tension, and as a support to our concentration, appropriate breath control leads to an "isolation on stage" that stimulates a free unfolding of technique and enjoyment of the performance.

At this point, we can suggest a more comprehensive *sensory-postural model*, which consists of linking breathing to the set of perceptions experienced previously upon positioning the instrument (balance, weight, relaxation). This practice allows us to create a convenient association reflex (*anchoring*); simply position the guitar, and then allow your respiration to quickly focus on the activity at hand.[18]

The common expression, *The performer seemed to be as one with his instrument*, is an allegory of the special and almost magical feeling we can experience through effective diaphragmatic breathing.

•

[17] "You and Your Guitar," *Classical Guitar*, Vol.14, no. 5, U.K., 1996.

[18] *Anchoring* is a technique proposed by Neuro-Linguistic Programming (NLP) to shape behavior through association of external stimuli with certain mental states or moods (See Robbins, 1987:365).

II. THE RIGHT HAND

... Over there screaming comes the Moorish guitar
in voices shrill and rough in tones;
the potbellied lute with its playful sounds;
the Spanish guitar is joined with them.
JUAN RUIZ (ARCHPRIEST OF HITA)
Book of Good Love, Spain, 1330

The guitarist must be the master of the strings...
DIONISIO AGUADO
Nuevo Método de Guitarra. Madrid, 1849

The Aristotelian conception of the hand as an "instrument of instruments" can be perfectly illustrated with guitar performance at the concert level, which demands an extremely versatile technique. We will begin this chapter with a study of the postural attitudes that affect the right hand's ability to pluck the strings.

THE POSTURAL FRAME

FOREARM SUPPORT POINT

While held up by the shoulder muscles, a portion of the weight of the entire arm rests on the support point where the forearm meets the lower bout of the guitar. The remaining weight is supported by the muscles that maintain the hand over the strings. We will briefly study the leveraging action exerted on the forearm by the support point, and its management as a factor of balance.

About 200 bones and 400 muscles make up the musculoskeletal system, a fantastic framework with more or less rigid structures that facilitate mobility through the use of different types of levers. This basic mechanism plays a part in the simplest of actions, economizing their efforts. In a first order lever, the fulcrum (support point) is located between the effort and the load. This is the model that closest represents the action of the forearm support point, where the force vectors consist of the weight of the hand and forearm at one end, and the upper arm and shoulder at the other. The forearm support point must be adjusted according to performance demands (as when playing artificial harmonics, pizzicato, etc.). We can experience the effect of these changes on plucking perception by moving this support point or by resting the upper arm on the guitar, as it usually happens when placing the guitar on the right thigh (See Iznaola, 1998:31-53).

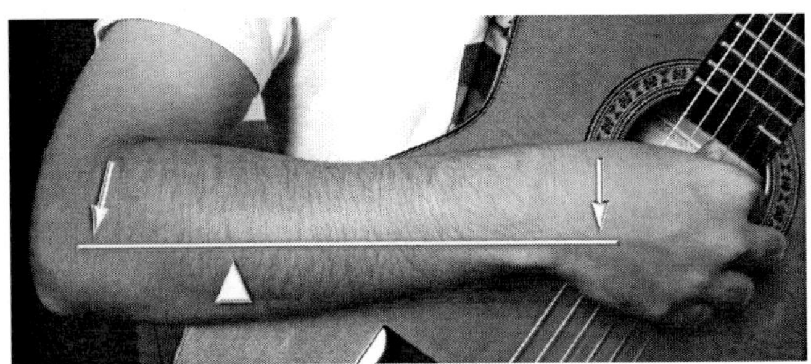

Recommended forearm support point.

Some aspects to consider:

- The forearm should rest on the muscle bulge without additional pressure. If this prominence is shifted sideways, it will result in a stretching of the forearm muscles near their insertion into the elbow joint, which will bring about negative consequences in the short term.
- A slight tilting of the guitar makes contact with the forearm less incisive. Nevertheless, it is advisable to wear a sleeve to ease forearm adjustments. With this goal in mind, many luthiers have begun to add a rounded armrest to the side (Photo A) or a bevel cut from the top ("carved-out" armrest, Photo B) that does not interfere with the soundboard vibrations. These ergonomic refinements contribute to a better perception and control of plucking.

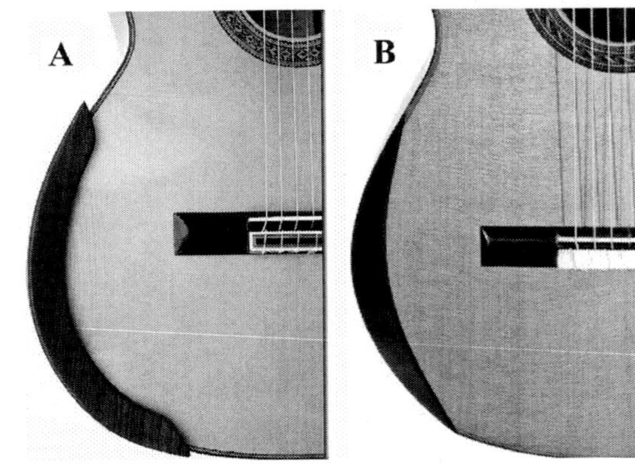

Hand-Forearm Placements

The position of the plucking hand relative to the forearm is a determining factor in effective plucking. Let's examine the features of three biomechanical models that have a direct influence on sound production: *Aligned, Intermediate,* and *Curved Placement.*

Aligned Placement

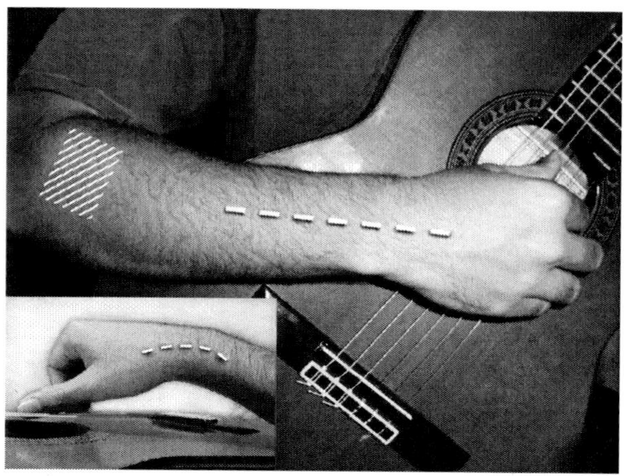

The back of the hand is aligned with the forearm, and the wrist arches slightly to facilitate fingertip/nail contact with the strings. This position causes the least friction of the nine tendons with the carpal tunnel ligaments, through which they pass along with the median nerve, which is in turn responsible for the sensitivity of almost half of the hand (See Appendix I).

As the upper arm-forearm angle is reduced (depending on the height of the headstock), maintaining this alignment will induce greater tension in the forearm, which can be felt by touching the area next to the elbow joint.

Strumming requires aligned placement to produce the needed rotation *(pronosupination).*

Intermediate Placement

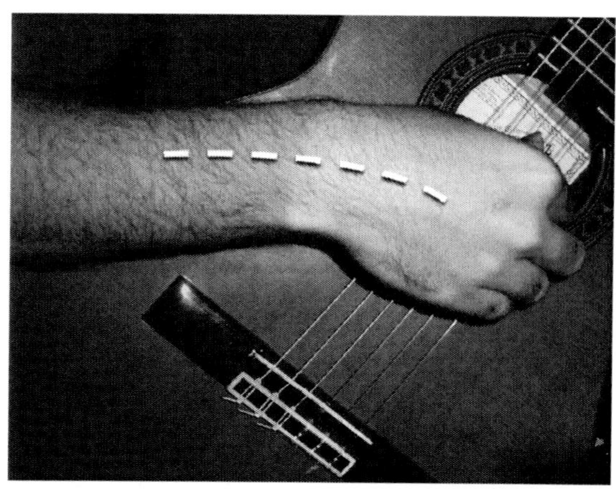

As a flexible alternative, the intermediate disposition is achieved with a slight loosening of the hand from its alignment. This reduces forearm tension and allows a lateral use of the thumb in opposition to the other fingers.

Both the intermediate and the aligned dispositions are conducive to an oblique fingertip/nail attack of *i-m-a-e*.[19]

Curved Placement

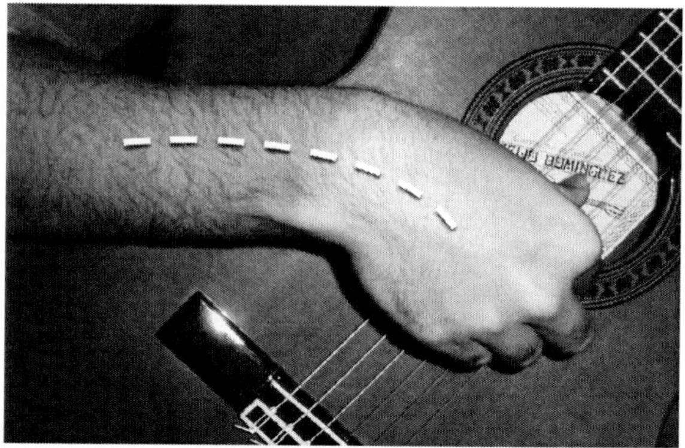

A typical position seen in old photographs, the uncomfortable, overly bent wrist –more awkward in individuals with short limbs– can lead to carpal-tunnel injury in the short term.

Plucking the bass strings with *i-m-a* requires a frontal attack (knuckles parallel to the strings). In this instance, adjusting the forearm support point is advisable to avoid excessive bending of the wrist.

Alignment of the Fingers and Roundness of the Hand

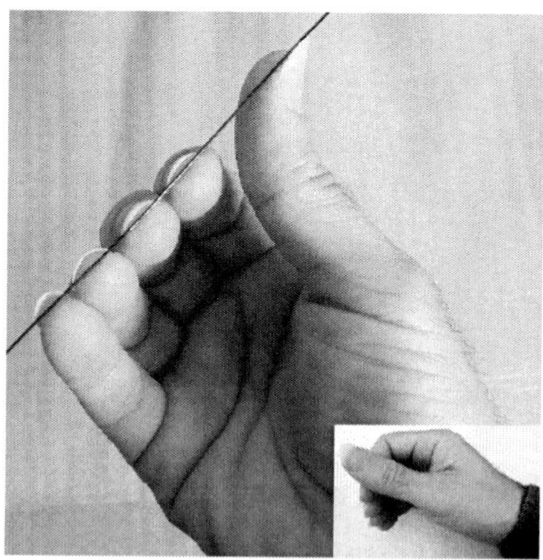

When we close our fingers together and lightly curl them in towards the palm, we can observe that their disproportions seem to even out as the fingertips align, with the index and little finger slightly curved toward each other (oblique flexion).

[19] The little-finger *(e)* is part of the physiological complex linked to plucking mobility. Later, we will discuss different possibilities for its direct or indirect use.

Once placed on the strings, this rounded shape makes it possible to relax the hand more quickly, contributing to fluent mobility, and consequently to greater accuracy and economy of effort in playing. The opposite shape, achieve by flattening the natural hand concavity (metacarpal arch), or by separating the fingers laterally (abduction) produces superfluous tension that hampers plucking agility.

The musculoskeletal alignment is conditioned by the structure of the joints. The alignment of the fingertips suggests areas of activity; the thumb moves "on the outside" from its wrist (carpal joint), closing the semicircle outlined by the *i-m-a-e* curvature.

A functional parallel between finger alignment and the *unity through contact* concept described by Carlevaro can be established (1984:59). It would be a blunder to try to induce this pleasant disposition by means of external devices, such as tying the fingers or holding coins between them while playing; such measures distort mobility and inhibit the natural perceptual training needed by the instrumentalist.

Our mastery as performers increases as we progressively adopt the most spontaneous bodily dispositions *as the source of the easiest movements, which turn out to be the most effective.* Hence, we can consider the rounded shape with aligned fingertips a natural model for plucking.

Sensopostural Patterns

One of the most effective strategies for expanding our body's awareness of the instrument consists of defining the *sensopostural patterns* (sensations linked to postures) to be activated, preferably at the beginning of each practice session – taking a moment to specify our goals for the improvement of fundamental performance skills: coordination, functional relaxation, fluent motion, etc. Based on a flexible physiological adaptation, these patterns are continuously developed by a permanent perceptive attitude, thus becoming a psychomotor remodeling mechanism.

Let's consider the following proposition for defining a sensopostural pattern linked to the placement of the right hand:

1. While leaning your head forward and relaxing your shoulders, let your right arm hang loose for a few moments until you feel its full weight.

2. Then, slowly raise the relaxed hand without moving the fingers, and observe how they are almost aligned without any extra effort. Focus on that perception, which should be maintained for as long as possible after placing your hand above the strings.

At this moment, two forms of stable positioning can be practiced:

a) With *i-m-a-e* relaxed (in the air, not on the strings) and with the thumb in playing position on a bass string. This is the optimal position for finger alternation in scales. While playing, the unused fingers should be perceived as completely free.

b) Place all the fingers on the 1st string, and then transfer that "line" to a four-note chord position on adjacent strings, maintaining the previous sensation of unity derived from relaxation. Obviously, this placement is also related to the execution of arpeggios and simultaneity of *i-m-a* with thumb.

Regular practice of these maneuvers without the guitar in-hand will lead to greater plucking control. Here's why:

> ... By working without the instrument, movements can be evaluated for what they are. Once we are free of that transparent barrier of habit that disguises them when we have the guitar in our hands, we then have the possibility of understanding and changing them at will. (E. Fernández, 2002:10)

The sensopostural approach allows us to identify the systemic character of all actions in performance; in other words, we can understand how apparent "finger difficulties" are related to the hand as a whole, or how left-hand shifts influence fingering accuracy, just to mention two examples. It is within this "body logic" that an effective renovation of our mechanism can occur.

•

Before studying the plucking mechanism, we will briefly review the physical-acoustic phenomena on the instrument, and its connection with tone production in performance.

A vibrating string is best represented schematically by partitioning its multidimensional motion into two planes: longitudinal and transverse. The longitudinal vibration is bounded by the nut and the saddle, between which bounce at high speed wave-trains created by plucking the strings.

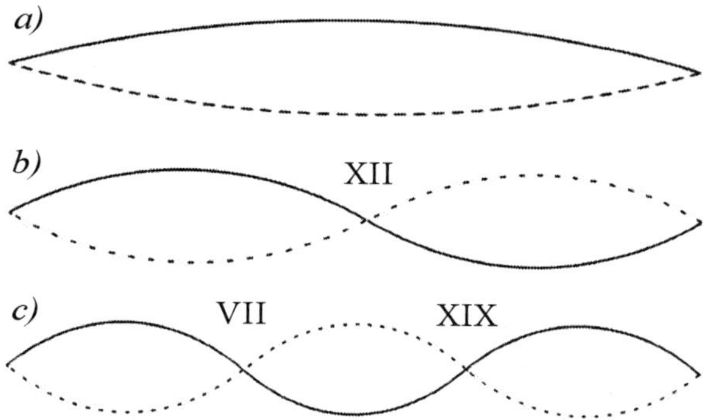

Longitudinal vibration: a) Open string; b) Natural harmonic XII; c) Harmonics VII-XIX.

By pressing the strings to frets, our fretting fingers serve as *moveable nuts*, modifying the oscillation frequency with each placement, and therefore, the pitch (See Taylor, 1978:18).

The transverse vibration, a hardly visible band on the bass strings, is wider towards the middle of the vibrating string, and proportional to the plucking energy. If the string is plucked slightly from below (free stroke) or downward (rest stroke), the rebounding area will be more vertical to the bridge, increasing the entry of vibratory energy for a more powerful and rich sound. The slight tilting of the soundbox also contributes to this result.

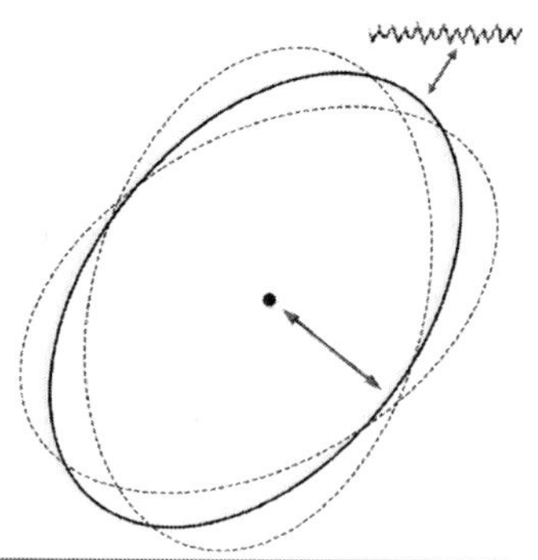

Ellipse of transverse vibration.

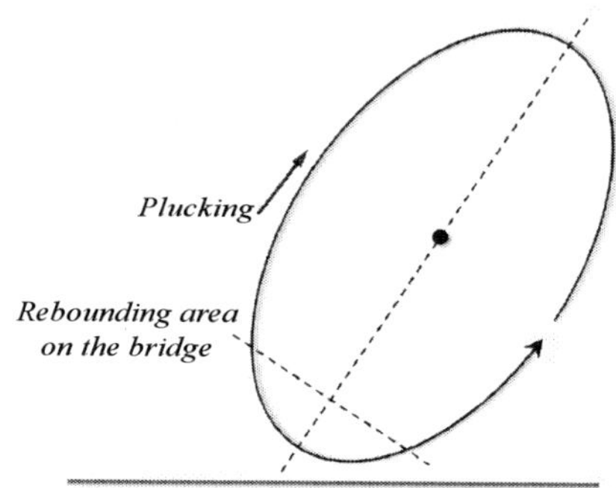

Thumb and *i-m-a* strokes produce transverse oscillations in opposite directions.

Once plucked, the vibration of the strings passes through progressively less dense materials: from the nut-saddle to the wooden bridge, and then to the soundboard, a flexible piece between 2.5 and 4 mm thick, set internally with bracing.

Traditionally arranged in a fan shape, these braces, besides providing enough strength to the guitar top –to withstand the strong pull exerted by the strings– distribute the vibrations throughout its surface. The rapidly fluctuating pressure affects the air inside the soundbox generating the sounds which are projected mainly from the sound hole.

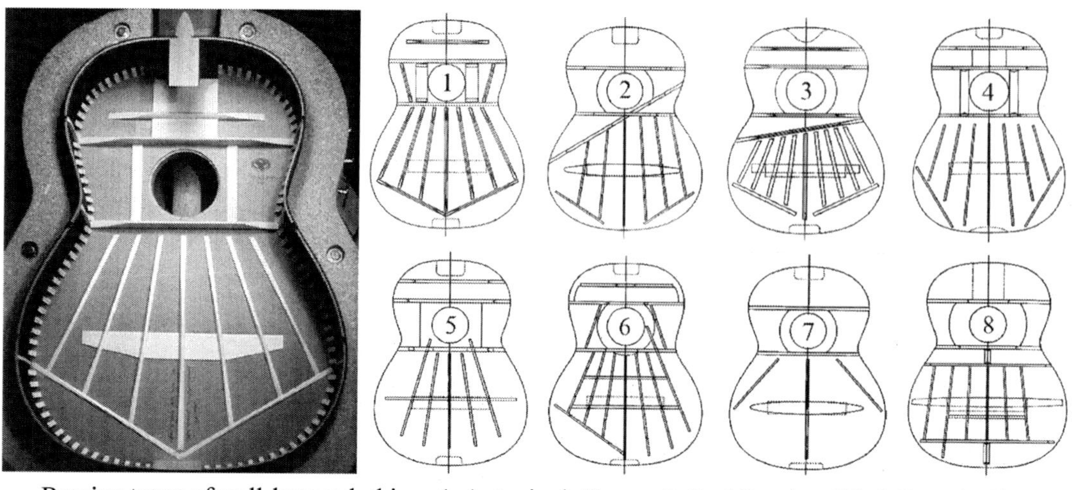

Bracing types of well-known luthiers: 1. Antonio de Torres, 2. José Ramírez III, 3. Ignacio Fleta, 4. Hermann Hauser, 5. Robert Bouchet, 6. Daniel Friederich, 7. Paulino Bernabé, 8. Masaru Khono.

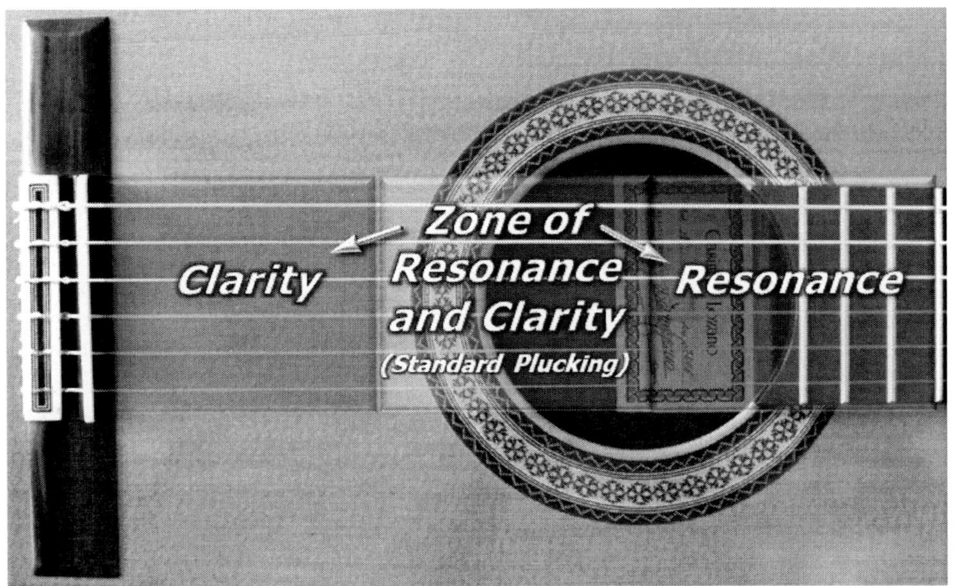

Plucking Zones.

In plucking, *timbre* (or tone color) is determined by multiple factors: the section of the string plucked, width and texture of the contact surface (fingertip/nail), angle of attack, and in general by the set of resources inherent to the plucking mechanism.[20]

The range of nuances in guitar performance is usually described using analogies: bright, harsh or "metallic" near the bridge (*sul ponticello*), and dark, round, warm or *dolce*, from the sound hole towards the fretboard (*sul tasto*). Leo Brouwer describes this variety with acoustic terms: *Zone of Resonance* (towards the fretboard), *Zone of Clarity* (near the bridge), and *Zone of Resonance and Clarity*, for the standard sound located in the intermediate space of this gradation.

The option of producing the same pitch in up to five positions on the fretboard provides us with a wide range of timbric contrast to be exploited by means of left-hand fingering.

From the interpretive perspective, some conventions have been established that place timbre, articulation, and dynamics within a range of possible nuances.

The *forte*-bright sonority is produced by plucking near the bridge, which guarantees a firm purchase because of the higher tension of the strings in this zone.

The dynamic *piano* is complemented by a mellower timbre, typical of the stroke over the sound hole and towards the fretboard. The wide transverse oscillation of the strings in this zone supports legato articulation with a maximum sound duration, whereas the incisive staccato effect is emphasized with an attack towards the Zone of Clarity. (*Piano-ponticello* may suggest "a distant *forte*.")

Quality of sound is also conditioned by the acoustics of space. Even in the most acoustically-responsive concert hall, a perfect transmission of sound is impossible. The sound waves undergo an unavoidable distortion by contacting the walls, ceiling, floor, people, and even the empty seats – elements that reflect them in different ways.

Modern amplification systems can help the performer, but, in any case, the adaptation of performer and audience to a given acoustic environment is of utmost importance.

> The musician registers the sound produced by the instrument-hall complex and, as much as possible, adapts his playing in order to produce the imagined ideal sound. The listener in "good" acoustic conditions (echo, reverberation, reflection, space in the hall, and artistic expectations are the principal factors) will then receive the sound sensation that the artist intended; in other instances, there is the risk of distortion of the musical message...
>
> Antoine Chaigne[21]

[20] The distinctive sonority of each instrument depends mainly on the type and quality of wood used in a specific design (thickness of the soundboard, bracing design, etc.). The spruce *(Picea abies)* soundboard is characterized by its brightness and projection, while the western red cedar *(Thuja plicata)* produces a more muffled and softer sound. Usually, the guitarist's preference for a kind of material or manufacturer label depends on his or her own "sound approach."

[21] A. Chaigne: "Acoustique et guitare," *Les Cahiers de la Guitare*, no. 4, Paris, 1982.

Determined by the composition of upper harmonics, the sound projection (or reach) depends not only on the attack but also on the attributes of the instrument.

With a high-pitch register and a smaller resonance box than the guitar, the violin can be heard in the farthest seat from the stage. This explains why performers of the mid-nineteenth century such as Mauro Giuliani used the *terz guitar* in chamber music: a slightly smaller instrument, higher pitched (G), and with a rather nasal and bright timbre.

The innovations of Antonio de Torres expanded the tone-color palette and volume of the guitar, but its projection was reduced. Since then, luthiers have tried to compensate for this handicap –an endeavor which is still pursued– initially with various modifications and additions such as the *tornavoz*, a cylindrical metal or wooden resonator added to the sound hole (possibly also invented by Torres).

Even though the present construction technology has achieved great results (more effective bracings, Thomas Humphrey's "elevated fretboard," Wagner and Dammann's "double-top," etc.), we often find players who try to increase the projection by forcing the stroke without regard to its consequences. It is a known fact that each instrument has a limit after which the sound becomes distorted, and noise begins to appear.

Conditioned by the physical-acoustic process, and together with other scenic elements, the artistic message invariably passes through the emotional-cognitive filter of the listener. In the same acoustic environment, the player with a powerful sound but poor use of nuances will not arouse the same interest as the one who offers the musical message with a more sensitive mastery (phrase endings, color balance, subtle dynamics, and so on).

Possessing a paradigmatic sound, maestro Segovia used to say that the guitar is a *luminous* rather than a *voluminous* instrument. Indeed, its limited dynamic range is thoroughly compensated by an expressive management of sound.

Characteristic of Romanticism, in the early nineteenth century appear the first intentions of "orchestrating" the guitar sound with suggestive effects and instrument "imitations" of the harp, trumpet, oboe, and flute, the latter through the use of harmonics (then called "fluting sounds").

Dionisio Aguado, comments on the subject in the first paragraphs of his *Nuevo Método de Guitarra* (*New Guitar Method*, Madrid, 1849):

> Who would say that of all [the instruments] that are used today, [the guitar] is perhaps the most adequate to create the illusion of a miniature orchestra? It may seem inconceivable at first; nonetheless, experience leaves no doubt about it.

Let's examine his description of the imitation of the harp:

> By plucking over the fingerboard, and cupping the hand, and therefore the wrist, the sounds produced are similar to the harp's, because the strings are played on a third of their length. In this case, the nearer the sound hole the left hand frets the chords, the more the sounds will resemble those of that instrument, especially if plucked with the fleshy fingertip. Arpeggiated chords are the most suitable for this purpose. (Aguado, 1849:56)

At this point he proposes as an example a passage of *Morceau de Concert Op. 54* by his friend and already renowned composer, the Catalan guitarist Fernando Sor. (Example 2.1)

In his *Méthode*, Sor also discusses the timbric resources of the instrument and the right-hand strokes, considering their mechanics as well as their acoustic peculiarities.

> As the oboe has a quite nasal sound, I not only play the strings as near as possible to the bridge, but I curve my fingers, and use the little nail I possess to set them in vibration… (Sor, 1830:16)

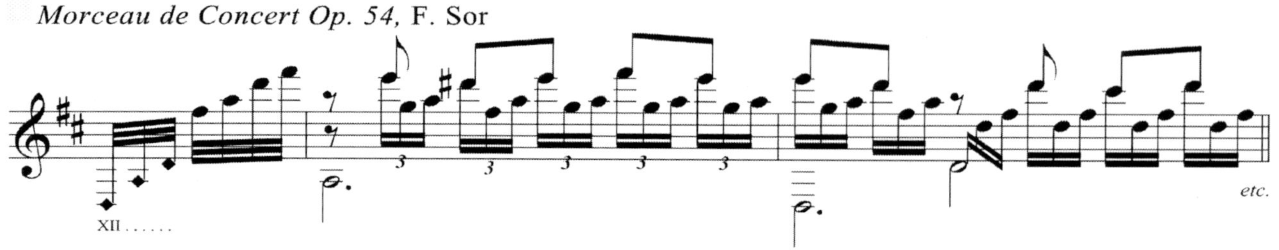

Learning the Sound of the Instrument

Sound is the conducting bridge of the musical essence and the spiritual image of the artist. In its quality, it is the main substance of interpretation.

Emilio Pujol, biography

Since music is a tonal art, the most important task, the primary duty of any performer is to work on tone.

Heinrich Neuhaus. *The Art of Piano Playing*

Musical performance involves the physical, intellectual, and emotional capacities of the performer. This process is centered on tone production, which can be framed in three stages:

- Imagination: Ideal sound in accordance with the interpretative conception of the score. It relates to stylistic elements (character, period and composer), form and phrasing.
- Action: Technical procedures and resources of both hands to achieve the desired sound.
- Auditory control: verifying what is played and how it sounds, in correspondence with the nature of each passage.

Auditory training and the aesthetic application of sound are basic aspects for the musical education of singers and instrumentalists, who develop a particular sound image which becomes embodied in performance and contributes in outlining their artistic identity.[22]

It is of the utmost importance that teachers promote an early knowledge of the sonic capabilities of the guitar to instill in their pupils a taste for expressive performance. At the beginning, minor adjustments to their plucking mechanism to clean up their sound will suffice, but students should progressively develop their mechanism aided by a permanent tactile-auditory control.

The experimental discovery of the rich tonal palette of the guitar is the ideal way to inspire students to focus on their tone production. This perspective will bring forth: faster acquisition of knowledge of the instrument, better inner audition, a creative imagination, and a motivation to build repertoire.

In the early stages, simple exercises like playing the same note on different strings will allow the assimilation of a broader tonal palette. This practice will eventually evolve to the conscious application of color in particular phrases or passages.

Carlevaro meditates on this matter:

> The guitar is privileged with its diversity of colors, but the use of this resource without moderation could give way to something vain and superficial. Seeking timbre for its own sake would be a mistake since the final result could turn out to be merely decorative. A solution can always be found by using timbre within the confines of aesthetics, for when sounds are combined to establish a well-proportioned structural order, timbre will become more than a simple sensation. It will belong to a consciousness, it will be an affirmation. (Escande, 2005:130)

Among the main virtues that an interpreter must have is the ability to reveal the special attributes of their instrument. This involves not only possessing an efficient technique and artistic sensibility, but a solid musical culture, supported by the analytical listening of different styles and musical forms, concert attendance, and the study of a varied repertoire, factors that lead to a broad aesthetic assessment of the expressive contents.

•

[22] Alfredo Escande comments on an interview with María Rosa Puig Madriguera, stepdaughter of Andrés Segovia (Paquita Madriguera's daughter):
"She is a charming lady close to 80 years of age. We talked for more than one hour about the life of Segovia in Montevideo and, on this subject, she told me: *He had three or four guitars that were his favorites, and from all of them he managed to get the same sound. I believe that there is something in the skin, in the vibrations of every person.*" (Correspondence with the author, December 2004)

The Plucking Mechanism

From a comfortable placement of the right hand, even the smallest change is very effective. You have to feel the sound at the tip of your fingers. People ask me what to do with regards to plucking. I say, "Everyone must find how to perform in the most natural way possible..."

John Williams. Masterclass in Havana, May 2000

The expressive handling of sound by the performer is formed by the interaction of two aspects: the emotional-spiritual (interpretation), and the physical (the mechanism or functional options of both hands). In theory, plucking must guarantee control of the sound parameters with maximum plasticity, freedom of movement, and economy of effort. We will address the description of different right-hand procedures framed within the following series of the three events that comprise plucking:

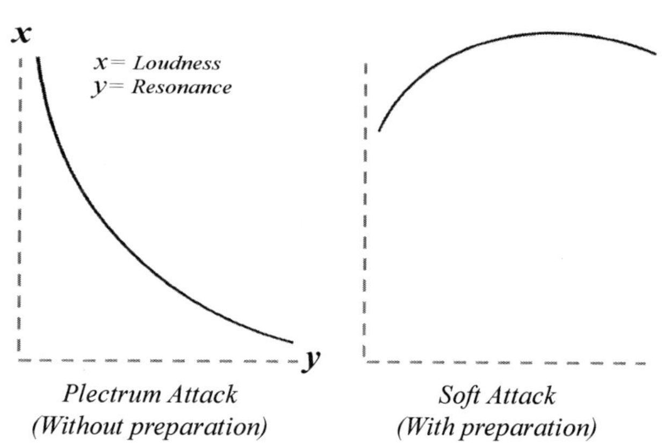

The Plucking Cycle

1. Contact with the strings: String attack. Planting.
2. Grip/Thrust: Free and rest strokes. Use of voluntary fixation.
3. Exit and Relax: Work/Rest cycle.

1. Contact with the Strings

The Archer places the arrow on the bowstring, and aims at his target...

As an expression of fluent mobility, plucking should begin with a soft and brief contact with the string before overcoming its resistance by means of an energy proportional to the desired sound level. This action can be considered a basic form of movement coordination, a subject on which we will expand later when discussing planting procedures.

Given the elasticity of the strings, plucking without preparation *(plectrum attack)* causes a rebound by activating a force vector in opposition to the movement of the finger. This weakened control in plucking leads to an overexertion that also limits the possibilities of nuance; dynamics and tone colors become scarcely contrasted. Perhaps suitable in its use as an *effect*, the plectrum attack produces not only noise but a faster decay of sound than the one produced by plucking from a prior contact with the string or preparation (soft attack), which is favorable in *legato* playing. The following graph shows the beginning and development of sound with both attacks (See Schaeffer, 2006:271).

Besides being physically harmful, the plectrum attack blocks the fine perception of contact with the strings, that induces small movements, which are already facilitated by the round and linear shape of the fingertip. This natural disposition encourages coordination without limiting the possibility of a wide dynamic range, which depends on the pressure applied to strings, rather than the often mentioned "attack speed" characteristic of the piano structural mechanism (hammer).

Let's examine three basic forms of contact with the strings for a variety of results: *Fingernail Attack, Fingertip/Nail Attack*, and *Fingertip Attack* (thumb).

Fingernail Attack

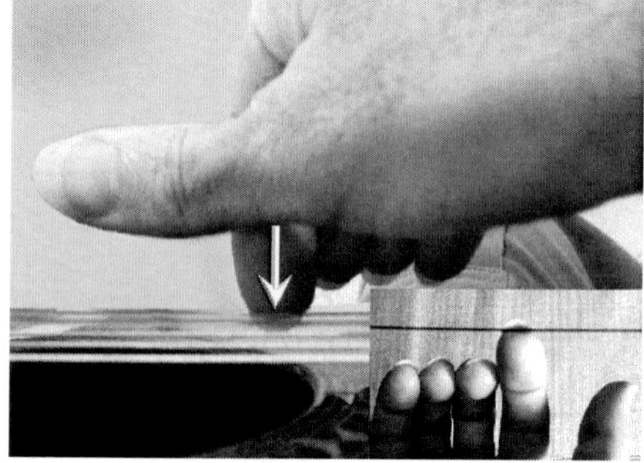

Because of their firmness, we can pinpoint the contact and release points of the fingernails in their transit over the strings, which contributes to precision and lightness. The bright-metallic timbre of the nails-only free stroke is due to the abundance of upper harmonics produced. On the other hand, the fleshy fingertip, with its soft surface and broader area of contact with the string produces a more muffled sound due to a higher abundance of the medium and low-frequency harmonics that are closer to the fundamental tone.

Just as the size and shape of the hands vary from person to person, so do fingernail consistency and quality. Nail shape directly affect the quality of sound that can be achieved by the guitarist. In general, a rounded shape that follows the contour of the fingertip is recommended. The edge of the nail itself should be rounded rather than chisel-sharp, and polished as smooth as glass. Unpolished nails partition the vibration, and thus produce a greater number of dissonant harmonics, giving rise to a shrill or "impure" sound.[23]

The left side of the thumbnail must have a steeper slope than the right side to prevent hooking the strings.

Fingernail attack with *i-m-a* implies a more vertical position where the apex of the nail strikes the strings. This position allows the thumb to play with more ease on the bass strings, and reduces friction with the metal winding, which when plucked diagonally produce an irritating squeak in "walking on the strings."

The inaccuracy of a frontal attack generates a harsh "double-stroke," resulting from the irregular transition of fingertip to nail (a common effect of the plectrum attack).

Fingertip/Nail Attack

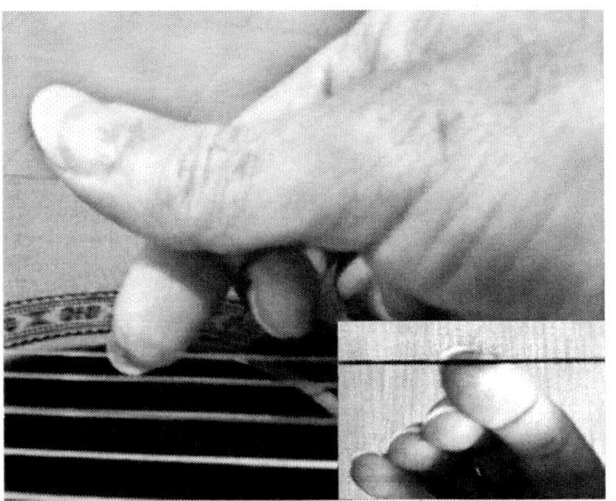

As the standard stroke on the treble strings, the fingertip/nail attack allows a color gradation: the more angled the attack, the larger the surface area of flesh on the string, and the mellower the tone.

The fleshy fingertip, which first contacts the string, adds firmness to the grip and forces the string to slide over the nail with more intensity, producing a warmer and rounder sound that is particularly useful in melodic passages in the mid-to-high register on the treble strings. Nail and fingertip/nail attacks make it possible to modify the sound in different ways without straying from the usual plucking area.

Fingertip Attack (Thumb)

Considering the almost universal use of nails by guitarists, an attack that exclusively utilizes the flesh is only possible with the thumb, whose wide contact surface allows timbric contrast and the implementation of several resources that we will describe later on.

•

[23] Detailed analyses of nail types and suggestions for their shaping can be found in *Learning the Classic Guitar* by Aaron Shearer and *Pumping Nylon* by Scott Tennant.
Essentially made of keratin –a very fibrous and resistant protein– nail health depends on having a balanced diet and avoiding repeated contact with detergents and other corrosive substances. Nowadays, natural products are available to revitalize or correct nail irregularities instead of using acrylic nails, whose weakening effects create permanent dependency.

Planting: Coordination and Synchrony for a Balanced Mobility

Motor coordination is basic to achieve a fluent mobility, and controlling the actions of each hand logically leads to their indispensable synchronization in performance.

To prepare means "to make ready beforehand for some purpose." With regards to plucked-string instrument fingering, preparing or *planting* consists of *placing two or more fingers on the strings at the same time, prior to their simultaneous or consecutive use.*

Planting is essential for mobility balance, which greatly influences accuracy and effort management. In the right hand, it takes place during the brief contact with the string prior to a stroke. There are two basic forms of planting: *simultaneous* and *sequential.*

Simultaneous Planting

Required for the execution of chords and intervals, and suitable for the initial steps of learning arpeggios, simultaneous planting (full or partial) is determined in this case by the order of notes to be played. (Ex. 2.2)

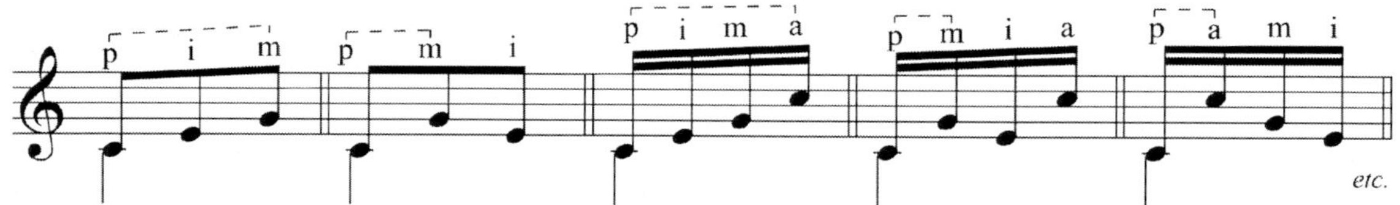

The reiteration of this type of planting in slow to moderate tempi disrupts the resonance necessary for legato, and in fast ones it hinders mobility. Let's examine two examples of positive applications: In *Elogio de la Danza* (Brouwer), the initial planting guarantees a secure displacement of the thumb, while in *La Catedral* (Barrios Mangoré), it can be combined with left-hand planting in linear passages. (Exs. 2.3)

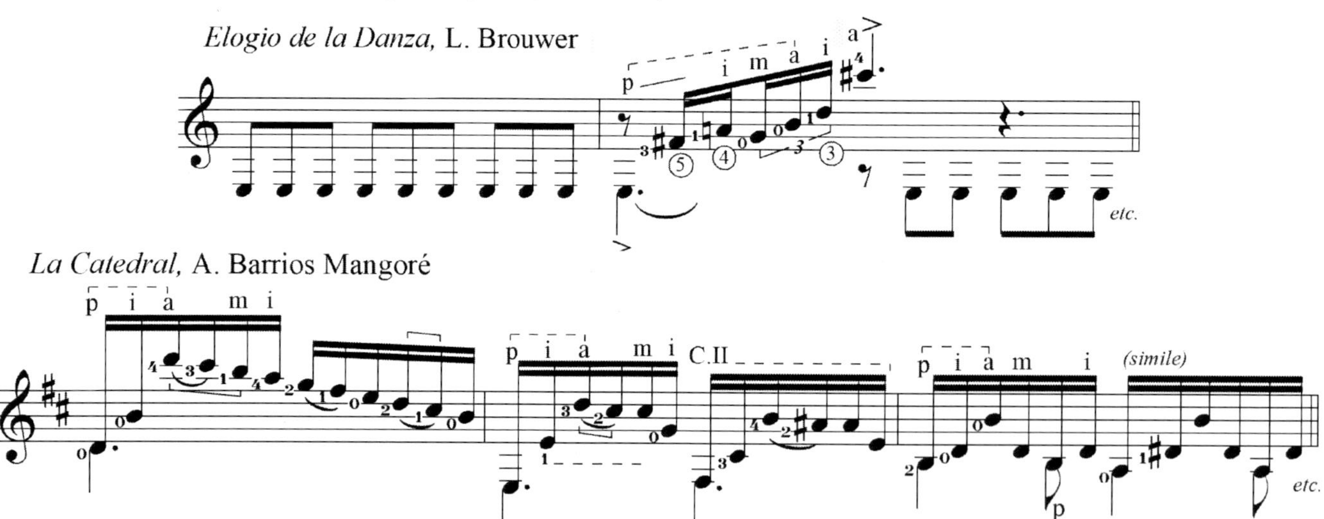

Sequential Planting

With freer mobility, sequential planting is equivalent to "walking on the strings," where one finger plucks one string and is immediately followed by the next finger in the sequence contacting its respective string *(a)*. (Ex. 2.4)

This variant minimizes the need to hold the hand "in the air," an unfavorable situation, especially in conjunction with left-hand shifts by leaps. Sequential and simultaneous planting can be combined in a variety of forms in the execution of arpeggios and fast passages *(b).*

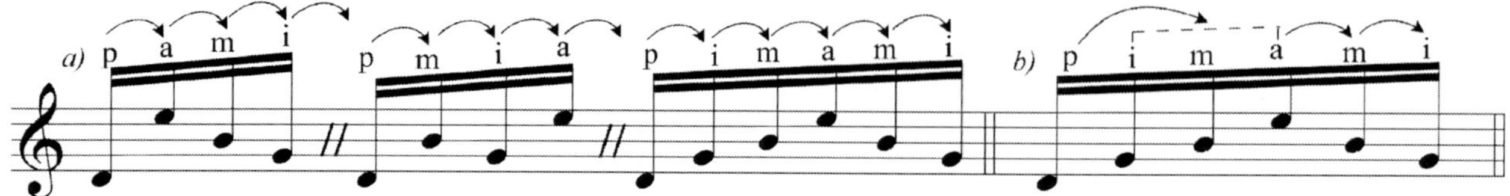

Similar in form to the arpeggio mechanism, cross-string trills and tremolo demand precise coordination. The practice of these procedures with sequential planting helps to balance the succession of continuous free strokes. (Ex. 2.5)

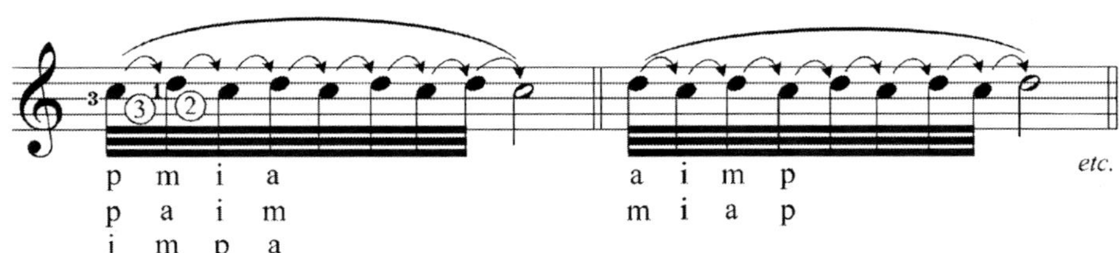

A balance of strokes in tremolo is favored by the sequential preparation from *i* to *p* (if the thumb does not play repeated notes). The simultaneous planting of *p-a* usually works except in rallentando passages or with repeated notes, where it becomes evident that planting the ring finger would shorten the "long note" plucked by the index. It is this long note that accounts for the "sustained-voice" effect characteristic of tremolo, one of the most subtle right-hand guitar techniques. (Ex. 2.6)

Recuerdos de la Alhambra, F. Tárrega

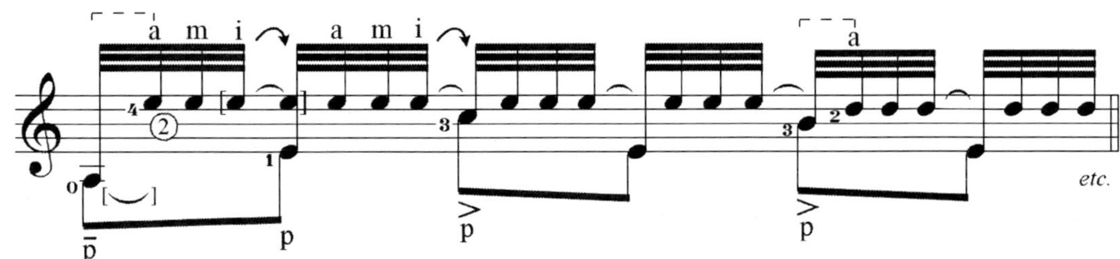

Later on, we will review other forms of planting associated with thumb techniques. Now let's preview one example in which the early placement of the thumb reinforces stability. (Ex. 2.7)

Etude No. 7, H. Villa-Lobos

2. Grip/Thrust

The Archer tenses the bow firmly in proportion to the distance that the arrow must cover...

Looking for analogies with normal hand usage, it can be said that free strokes with *i-m-a-e* engage or "grip" the strings, whereas the rest strokes "thrust" them.

Standard plucking is realized by a progressive grip/thrust that begins at the moment the fingers contact the strings and ends with their release. The energy applied to the strings is directly related to the intensity of sound desired, which requires a complex muscular integration of the whole arm (See *Fixation in Plucking*).

Taking the rounded hand posture as a starting point, we can recognize a direct correlation between security of grip and economy of motion, with the latter influencing the speed of relaxation after each stroke (a sequence of events that is mandatory for realizing the coveted "velocity" in playing).

Free and Rest Strokes

Free and rest strokes have different mechanisms and produce different results. Adding intensity or balanced speed to a melodic passage may require the use of rest stroke (*apoyando*), and the lightness of an ornament may suggests the use of free stroke (*tirando*); using the *alternation* of both forms, however, can lend agility and infuse character to the articulation, and thus enrich the phrasing (See *Rest/Free Stroke Alternation*).

For an obvious functional reason, most strokes must be free, i.e., with an unimpeded path of *i-m-a-e* towards the palm, and of the thumb towards the index. Rest stroke, on the other hand, which naturally favors louder dynamics, is accomplished with a more *inward* motion that ends with a brief "contact/repose" on the adjacent lower string. The resulting stability makes *apoyando* an ideal stroke when first learning to play the instrument.

Rest-stroke with an inward motion.

Let us consider some aspects of the rest stroke:

• Its use does not necessarily imply the accenting of notes, nor is it the only way to intensify sound.

• With a flexible disposition of the phalanges, the rest stroke does not require altering the basic roundness of the hand (Fig. A). Plucking with unnecessarily straight fingers (often due to very long nails) increases tension significantly, particularly with a high placement of the wrist (Fig. B). Besides hindering the sequence of technical procedures, this habit could lead to serious motor dysfunctions.

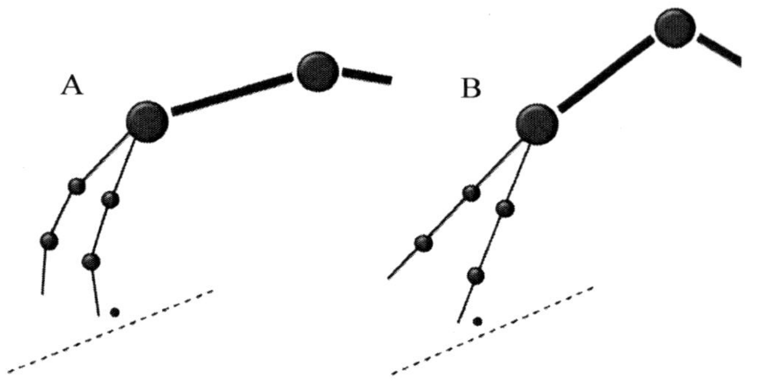

• Unless the rest stroke is executed from an unprepared and abrupt attack, the adjacent string represents the end of motion only if the finger relaxes immediately, action that is conditioned by the postural disposition of the hand and the flexibility of muscle tone achieved (See Appendix I).

• It is more difficult to use the rest stroke in scale passages towards the 1st string, since the movement of the fingers is opposite to the shifting of the hand.

• The rest stroke acts as a balance factor in alternation with free strokes. We will delve deeper into this subject in the section entitled *Right-Hand Articulation Techniques.*

•

Fixation (Muscular Integration in Plucking)

Normally, moving a limb or holding an object requires a linking of muscular tensions, and varying degrees of firmness of the joints for optimal effort management. Similarly, playing the instrument involves complex biomechanical interactions of all segments of the arm: finger, wrist, elbow and shoulder.

Carlevaro defined *fixation* as...

> ... the *voluntary and momentary nullification or immobility* of one or more articulations for the purpose of allowing stronger and more capable elements to perform in a particular way. (1984:22)

The conscious use of fixation in plucking results in a greater functional capacity and economy of effort. We will explore this subject later.

"Free plucking" (without voluntary fixation) used in simultaneity with the thumb, arpeggios and fast scale passages, gives the impression of isolated finger movements. In the case of *i-m-a-e,* movements basically originate at the metacarpal joints, with a spontaneous fixation of the middle and the distal joints that depends on the type of stroke and dynamic level to be applied. (Observe that *forte* strokes require more "firmness" of distal joints and phalanges.)

The optimal thumb free stroke originates at the wrist joint. Plucking that originates from the distal phalanx or from the intermediate joints creates a continuous overexertion and interferes with the movements of *i-m-a-e*, especially of the index.

When playing either rest or free strokes, the thumb should always "push" the strings.

3. Exit and Relax

The Archer releases the arrow with a light gesture, and agilely repeats the sequence thanks to the flexibility of its movements.

The contact-grip sequence enables a quick release that keeps the fingers close to the strings and facilitates immediate relaxation. The opposite, an *explosive release*, sometimes accompanied by a jumpy hand, tends to be noisy like the plectrum attack, and involves a surplus of force that hampers plucking agility.

The short work/rest cycle, which introduces momentary relaxation, is essential for the free mobility needed for efficient plucking. In this regard, "positive inhibition," a term from the Alexander Technique lexicon signifying a *voluntary* interruption of tension, constitutes an essential element to be added to the practice routine of instrumentalists for the development of the habit of *functional relaxation* (See Appendix I).

Physiological aspects that contribute to relaxation in both hands

1. When the nervous stimulation that causes contraction ceases, the antagonist muscles tend to restore the spontaneous attitude of the fingers by means of the *myotatic reflex*, which maintains the muscle at constant length (See Appendix I) Focusing on this natural response will lead to a permanent economy of effort and fluid mobility. Let us experiment with some exercises to demonstrate this effect, which becomes palpable during rapid changes of tension:

a) The simplest example consists of moving any finger of a fully relaxed hand up or down with the other hand, and then releasing it immediately. The digit will effortlessly return to its previous position.

b) Comfortably rest your right hand with the palm facing up, and execute the following two actions: First, stretch your fingers for a few seconds with moderate strength, as if you were adjusting a glove. Then quickly release all the tension and observe how the hand resumes a natural disposition that is close to roundness. After a short break, forcefully close the hand into a fist, and then, as before, suddenly relax it. The hand will again resume its naturally rounded shape.

c) With the palm of the hand comfortably facing up as before, perform almost imperceptible movements with each finger separately, "letting them return" to their original positions.

2. When playing, the framework for relaxation must go beyond the hands. It must also be experienced from the shoulders, as a projection of the whole body. A basic operation that stimulates relaxation is the frequent review of the sensopostural patterns, which emphasizes the perception of the hands as a "unit."

• Now let us try an elementary exercise for the right hand:

Adopt a rounded hand position, play an open-string chord, and then relax the hand as much as possible, without shifting the forearm support point. Make sure to follow the contact/grip/release-relax sequence and pause between each chord to feel a clear rest. Begin by playing *piano*, and gradually increase the volume, not the plucking frequency.

The starting speed of movements is greater when these are supported by proper muscle tone or *eutony* (See Appendix I). In the following section, we will examine different sensoperceptive exercises that contribute to this state.

•

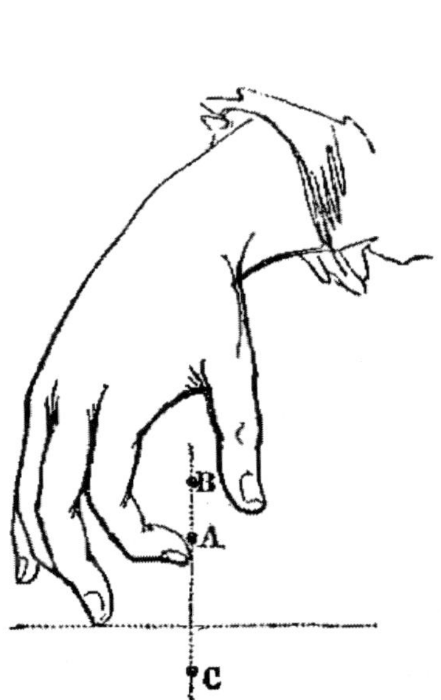

Figure from F. Sor's *Méthode* (1830).

Sensoperceptive Exercises for the Right Hand

You need to develop a plucking action so secure that it allows you to perform even while feeling nervous...

David Russell
Masterclass in Havana, May 1992

In Spanish, the verbs *pulsar* and *tañer* ("to play" or "to pluck" the strings) also mean *to feel with the fingertips*, and it is precisely this direct contact with the strings that turns the guitar into a highly sensory instrument.

With any task that requires a particular skill, the efficiency of our actions grows as we increase and refine our perceptions. In playing a musical instrument, we constantly employ the senses of sight, hearing and touch, but kinetic and tactile sensations are also key elements for the generation of sound.[24]

The following practices are not shortcuts to learning right-hand technical procedures, nor are they meant to replace basic right-hand exercises. They are intended to reinforce the proprioceptive perceptions related to the plucking mechanism, which are essential for effective motor control.

You will get maximum benefit from these exercises through progressive and moderate practice as part of your initial warm-up routine, always with focused attention. At first, play only on open strings with a comfortable "intermediate placement" (See *Hand-Forearm Placements*). Damping the sound by placing a cloth under the strings will contribute to enhanced concentration.

Give yourself a few days to work on these suggestions, always avoiding physical or mental fatigue. "Gather the sensations" and wait for the results.

Stimulating the Perception of Contact

Position the right hand for a four-note chord, establishing a "fleshy" disposition, feeling the strings on your fingertips. Play gently, as if caressing the strings, barely making any sound.

Space out the chords and relax between each repetition. In *i-m/i-a* alternation with rest strokes, keep the distal phalanges flexible. Subsequently, and always in a slow tempo, try to play several passages of your active repertoire with this "soft touch," a practice that also serves as a starting point for the exploration of dynamics when plucking.

It is a good idea to combine this exercise with minimum pressure on the strings in the left hand.

Perception of Grip

The following exercises reinforce the consistency and stability of plucking for greater control of sound.

"Silent Plucking" (Simultaneity with the thumb)

From a four-note chord position, apply a quick "closing" motion to the strings with firm fingers; do not collapse the fingertips. Then relax immediately without plucking, i. e., keeping the fingers on the strings without producing any sound. Pausing between each repetition will allow you to better experience *sensory contrast*.

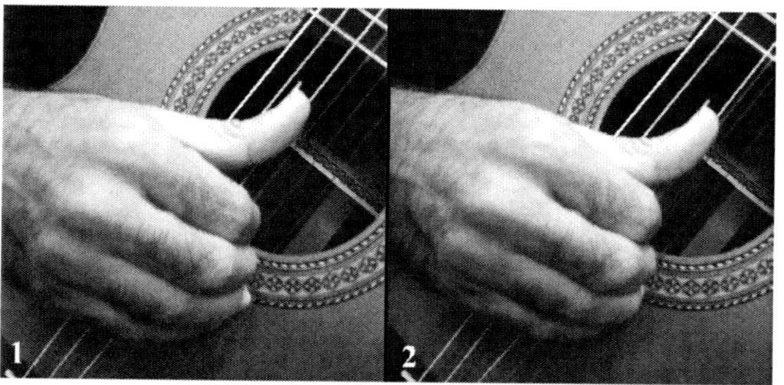

Play different combinations without changing finger location (*i-m-a* on strings 3rd, 2nd and 1st respectively, and thumb on a bass string): *p-i, p-m, p-a, p-ma, p-im, p-i-a*. Using the little finger on 1st the exercise can be extended up to a five-note chord: *p-e, p-ae, p-mae, p-imae*.

Rapid Repositioning

From a close, four-note chord position with fingers on adjacent strings, pluck with each finger and quickly reposition them in their original locations.

Although one of the objectives of this exercise is to develop agility, start slowly with small movements, always releasing the tension between strokes. Then gradually accelerate the tempo along with the plucking intensity.

[24] Blind musicians such as Miguel de Fuenllana (1525?-1579) and Antonio Giménez Manjón (1866-1919) were distinguished virtuosi.

With practice, you will experience a considerable lightening of tension while plucking as a result of using proper muscle tone (eutony) as the basis for movements. The rapid repositioning exercise (staccato mechanism), which reinforces the "habit of proximity" to the strings, can be extended to alternation on a single string to intervals and chords.

"Tick-Tock" (Fingernail Attack)

Alternate *i-m*/*m-a* (fingernail attack), keeping one finger on the string, while the other plucks it, producing a muted, percussive effect similar to a metronome click.

Practice only on the treble strings with a slow tempo. Start on the third string. Later, vary the fingering (*i-a, e-m, e-i, a-m-i*), switch to the second string, and finally to the first. Other combinations including the thumb can be applied to increase the control of *figueta* (*p-i* or *p-m* alternation) and tremolo (*p-a-i-m, p-m-i-a*, etc.).

Release from the Bottom (Fingertip/Nail Attack)

From a fingertip/nail contact, alternate *i-m*, etc. slowly on the treble strings, by first pressing the string down towards the soundboard, and then releasing it with a free stroke. Practice this technique moderately on short scales.

Perception of Thrust (Rest Stroke)

The previous exercises also stimulate the perception of thrust or pushing inherent in rest strokes. In this case, the difference lies in the direction of movement. Perform "silent plucking" with quick and slight pushes of the string towards the bottom, alternating on the same and later on adjacent strings with *i-m, m-a, m-e*, and the thumb.

Another version of the rapid repositioning exercise (with rest-stroke alternation) consists of muting the plucked string with the following finger in the sequence while the first one remains relaxed on the lower string.

The speed of plucking should not be raised before experiencing an increased perception of contact with the strings. After working on the open strings, proceed with short scale passages.

Exploring and Activating Relaxation

If you can stop doing the wrong thing, the right one will happen by itself.

Matthias Alexander. *Aphorisms.*

Feldenkrais declares that *sensitivity decreases when effort increases* (1993:26), therefore *intensifying effort does not improve the result.* These guidelines apply to any activity, and there is no doubt that the performer's perceptive sensibility regarding the instrument is a decisive factor in his or her capacity for artistic re-creation.

The control of tension positively influences the inhibition-excitation processes of the motor cortex that characterize body patterns, which in turn are linked to emotional states.

To actively work on relaxation –verifying its condition and promoting it at different moments during performance– is not only another way to sharpen our perceptions with the instrument; it also indirectly supports the achievement of greater expressive freedom.

From the perspective of mechanism, practice is a gradual construction of automatic responses that must be associated with the qualities that we wish to experience on stage: concentration, fluent mobility, creative enjoyment, etc. It is thus advisable to promote a serene state of mind before beginning a practice session, if necessary, through exercises of progressive relaxation, as proposed in the previous chapter for postural remodeling.

The practice of relaxation in performance should be realized progressively by taking advantage of opportunities (for one or both hands) that appear in plain sight on any score.

In the following excerpt of *Estudio No. 1* by Abel Carlevaro, the longer notes make it possible for the right hand to rest briefly. (Ex. 2.8)

Estudio No. 1, Abel Carlevaro

Ostinato (♩= 88-92)

After attaining a balanced sensopostural platform we can achieve optimal relaxation during the fractions of a second that follow each stroke. However positive we may be in our self-assessment in this regard, we should at times introduce a conscious pause in the execution of thorny passages and attentively experience the resulting sense of increased relaxation. (Position shifts basically accomplish this operation for the left hand.)

Tonicity Patterns (Flexibility of Muscle Tone)

One advanced form of exploration consists of verifying our functional response during the sequence of different technical procedures employed throughout a piece. Supported by logical fingering, this practice will inform our notion of the muscle tone flexibility required for a flowing performance, especially in the most demanding passages.

An exercise which could be described as "attempting the impossible to achieve the possible" consists of selecting a fragment of any piece that demands a continuous right-hand motion, and playing it with minimal exertion, with movements so small and light as if to give the impression of not playing at all. Activating the previously-mentioned sensopostural pattern will contribute to this purpose.

Begin very slowly, hardly producing any sound. Gradually increase the tempo (not dynamics) without the distraction of a metronome, and insert breaks to register the amount of tension. For louder dynamics, return to a slow tempo, and gradually increase both elements at the same time.

Slow, calm study allows clear perception of the muscle tension required for every event, a basic aspect of achieving the muscle tone flexibility necessary for playing.

Arpeggios, tremolo, and repeated chords qualify for this practice, which should be done patiently, without anxiety. (Remember that relaxation comprises both psychic and physical aspects.) (Exs. 2.9)

Estudio XL, Emilio Pujol

Variations Op. 15, Miguel Llobet

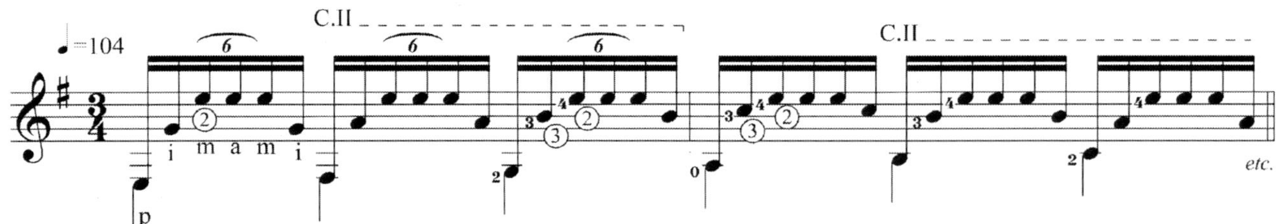

Pieces with a fast tempo or a complex texture always test our management of tension. This approach can be further expanded to the study of pieces that link different technical procedures, such as *Sonata III* by Manuel Ponce. (Ex. 2.10)

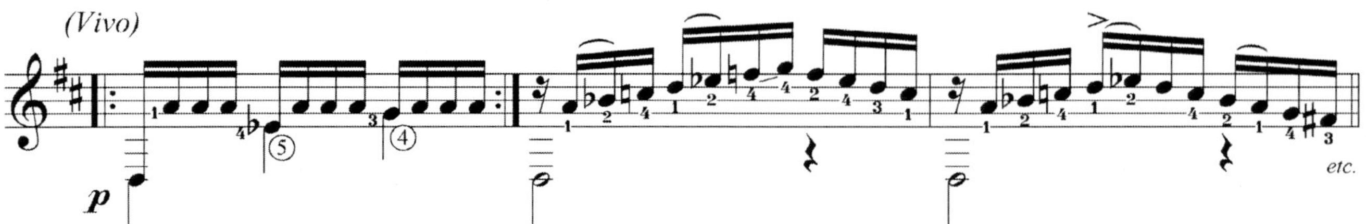

Attempting to imitate the virtuosity of outstanding performers, students without a proper mechanism not only run the risk of injuries, but also the distorting of their musical training. Although to achieve speed in playing you must "try to do it faster," the endeavor will prove worthless without having first experienced the basic perception of free mobility.

It is convenient at this point to reflect on the following suggestions by Feldenkrais:

• *Things can be done with the goal of comfort...*

• *You will find that to do something comfortably, elegant and aesthetically correct, it must be realized with a minimum effort, with a sense of lightness, and the utmost lightness of movement...*

• *We should feel ourselves connected to an easy and light motion...*

• *The quality of motion affects the whole being, and you will notice that consequently, other things you do will also improve...*[25]

Better Perception, Fewer Repetitions

Although repetition is necessary for learning, whether it be a technical procedure or a new score, to do it mechanically –without a defined objective or measure– does more than complicate the process. It also opens the door to both overexertion and a dangerous tendency towards artificiality in expression.

Different muscle groups are activated in performance. This is not the case during repetitive and mechanical practice, which is the source of most injuries. Dominique Royle and Nicola Culf comment on this regard:

> The irony is that striving for perfection through the traditional pattern of intense practicing, highly controlled and rapid finger exercises, and deep concentration for long periods at a time will often not lead to perfection at all! It is more likely to produce fatigue, stress, tension in the body, and a strain on the playing mechanism which ultimately may render it inconsistent and unreliable. An approach to technique and practicing which considers the body as a whole, which respects its needs and limitations, and which regards physical comfort as a priority – has the potential to reach much closer to that elusive dream of perfection.[26]

A positive development of mechanism does not depend essentially on a daily overload of scales and arpeggios; nor is our comprehension of a piece enriched by endless repetitions of passages with an unvarying technical and musical scheme. In agreement with Feldenkrais, we can say that *if muscles are exhausted, musical sensitivity becomes numb.*

We often spend more time and energy repeating the score sections we find difficult than in deciphering their problems in order to overcome them with the appropriate means.

It is important to adopt a working method that takes into consideration the difference between *studying* and *playing*. Essentially, *studying solves performance problems; playing let us reveal what we have learned.*

As we suggested, a general principle that should guide our practice is to seek the best definition of the stimuli to be processed by our nervous system. Objectively, performers must not only comprehend the score (notation, formal structure, expressive contents, etc.), they must also "understand-perceive" the bodily operations implied in performance. Musical discourse cannot flow organically if this component fails.

Feldenkrais' Method shows us that in order to learn, we need time, attention and differentiation; to differentiate, we need to feel. This means that to learn, we must sharpen our faculty of feeling, and if we try to make the most of things by sheer force, we will achieve precisely the opposite of what we need.

The excessive repetition of an exercise or passage is equivalent to imposing a scheme on the body rather than *dialoguing with it, and waiting for its response* (Urshalmi, 2006:17). To enable prompt and effective assimilation, *we should study without demanding of ourselves, but rather by asking ourselves kindly*, as Oscar Ghiglia advises.[27]

•

[25] M. Feldenkrais, San Francisco "Quest" Workshop, 1981.

[26] D. Royle y N. Culf: "The Perfect Technique?," EGTA Guitar Journal no. 6, U.K., 1995.

[27] Alain Riou: "Rencontre avec Oscar Ghiglia," *Les Cahiers de la Guitare*, no. 33, Paris, 1990.

Use of Voluntary Fixation in Plucking

While planting (the first event of the Plucking Cycle) promotes balanced mobility from contact with the strings, rest and free strokes (second event) perform these movements through special muscle work that combines energy and speed.

At times, voluntary fixation in right-hand strokes allows the use of more powerful muscle groups to overcome the string's resistance with less effort, without interfering with fluent mobility. This is an advanced technique that should only be practiced after assimilating the basic technical procedures of both hands.

The following is a basic description of fixation in plucking.

Fixation with i-m-a

1. Prepare a three-note chord position with *i-m-a* on the treble strings with the hand in a relaxed "intermediate position."

2. Imagine that the segment between the fingertips and the elbow is a single unit without joints. Apply a solid grip to the strings and move this segment from the elbow joint (using upper arm and pectoral muscles)[28] with a short movement and minimum hand rotation.

3. Keep the fingers aligned and united. Plucking will be carried out from planting without changing the forearm support point, immediately relaxing after each stroke. (Ex. 2.11)

The first attempts at fixation are often disconcerting to the point of seeming to produce only a useless tension. However, within a few days you will begin to deploy just the required energy, now centered on the *grip* for a markedly improved sound.

[28] Muscles are grouped into muscle chains with different functions (See Appendix I). In general, some produce movement and others guarantee balance. Carlevaro called these chains *muscular aggregates* (1984:30); they do the coordinated work required by fixation in plucking.

Carlevaro points out that fixation does not imply a state of rigidity.

> ... Fixation must not only begin just when necessary, but stop immediately when its need has terminated, with the articulation in question resuming its flexibility and readiness for any mechanical demands (1984:23).

During these exercises you may feel a vague discomfort in the forearm, signaling the need for moderation. It is necessary to progressively assimilate this new form of muscular work whose immediate effect is a greater firmness of plucking. (Trying to achieve this vigorous sound without preparation can lead to an exhausting effort that hinders mobility.)

Fixation with the thumb

1. Place the thumb in playing position, aligned with the other fingers.

2. Firmly, without articulating it (as if it were a plectrum fused to the hand), push the string lightly down and towards the soundboard with a movement from the elbow, and release it without activating the distal phalanx.

3. Begin with rest strokes, always releasing the tension immediately. Then use free strokes, making sure that each one is preceded by contact with the string.

The use of fixation leads to more sound with less effort, and another benefit of this technique resource is better command of the thumb, a digit that can easily surpass the sound produced by *i-m-a.*

Applications

A further step, which should be tackled with flexibility, involves the alternation of thumb fixation with *i-m-a* fixation. The following patterns suggest several uses. (Ex. 2.12)

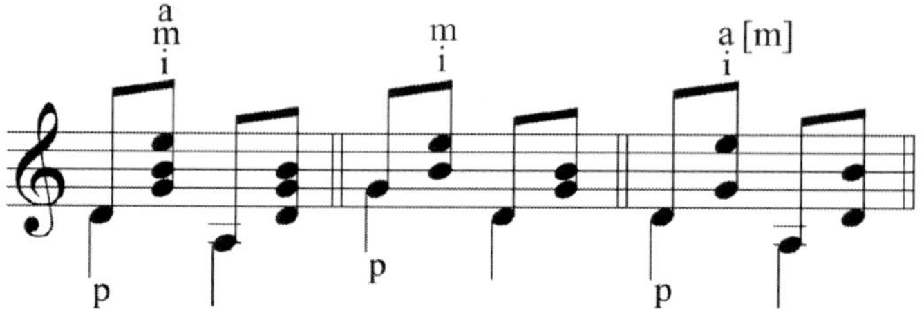

The convenience of this mechanism becomes more evident in passages with repetitive movements, were fixation can be used all the time or by sections. Obviously, it cannot be applied in chords or intervals with the thumb (*Etude Op. 6 No. 9*, F. Sor). (Exs. 2.13)

Sonatina Meridional (Mov. III), Manuel Ponce

¢.II ¢.III ¢.I ¢.III

etc.

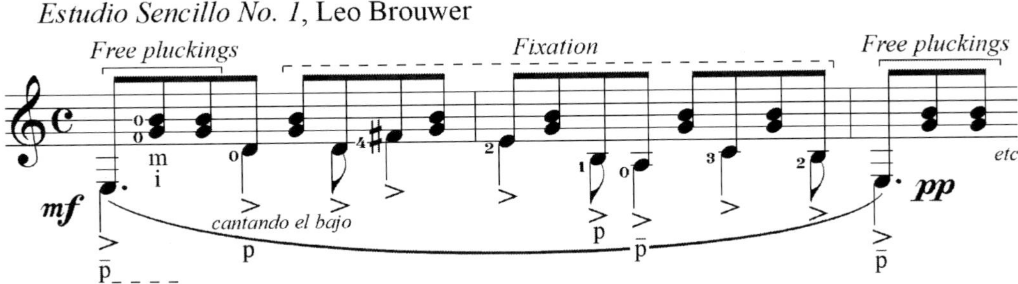

Even a brief use of voluntary fixation (*Sonata Op. 22* by F. Sor) constitutes an effective application of work/rest (tension-release), since the balance between muscle groups is perceived as relaxation in the right hand.

The *Etude Op. 31 No. 12* by Sor presents a repeated rhythmic pattern where fixation (intervals of a third) allows the release of tension before the fast arpeggios that require the use of free strokes. (Exs. 2.14)

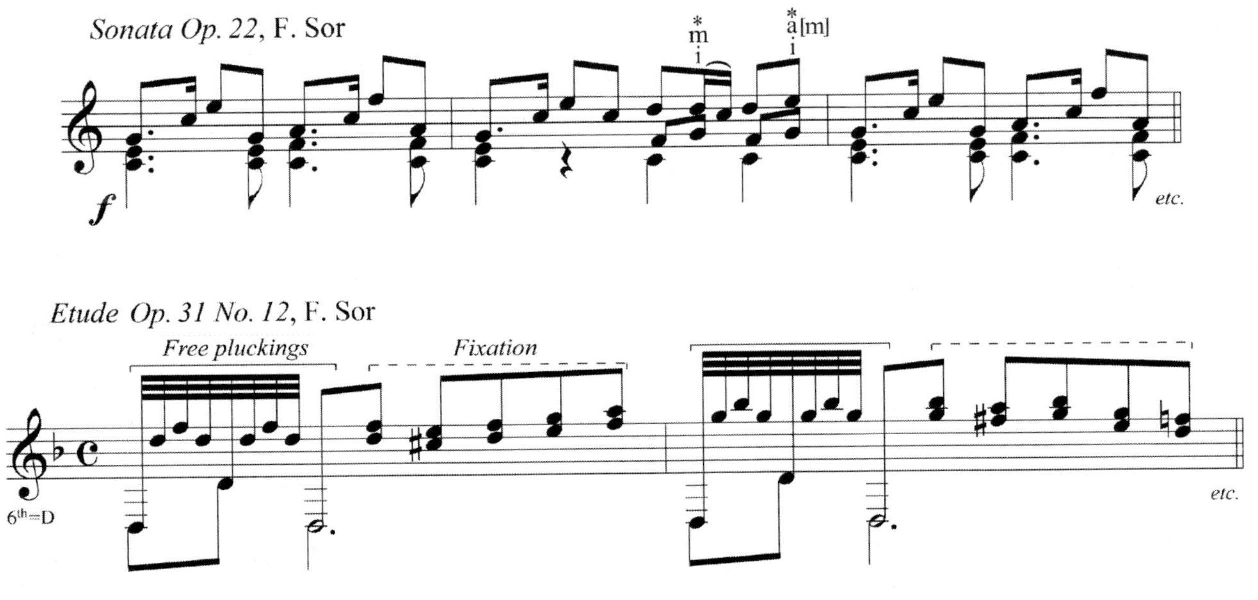

The following passages offer several opportunities for the use of fixation: rest strokes with *i, m, a* or the thumb, broken intervals (See "*Vertical Articulation.*" *Intervals*), and *figueta*. (Exs. 2.15)

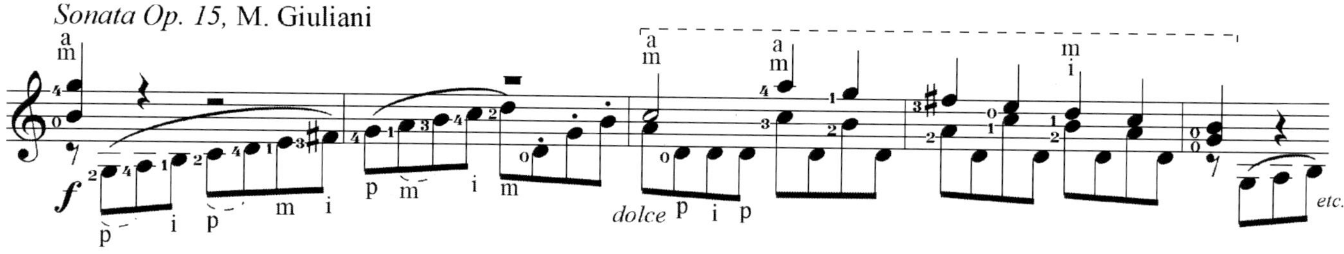

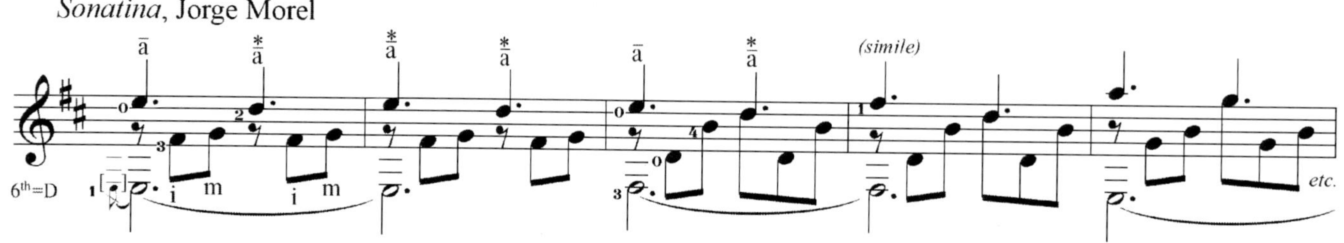

Shortly after beginning the practice of this mechanism, you will begin to experience increased control in standard plucking. This is the natural outcome of greater muscular efficiency, which supports the execution of demanding scores such as Sor's *Etude Op. 6 No. 6.* (Ex. 2.16)

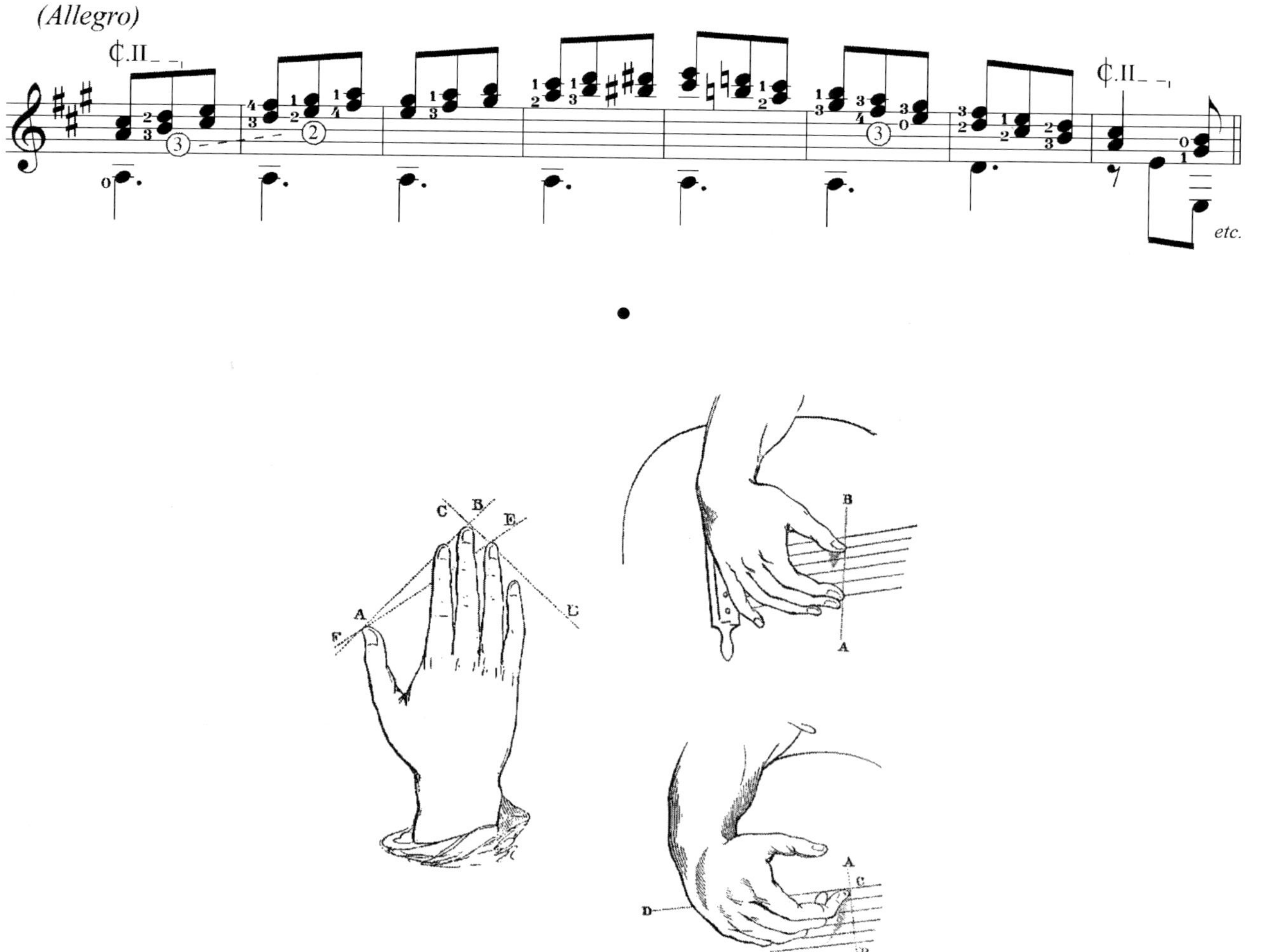

Figures from F. Sor's *Méthode* (1830).

Fingering: Functional Regularities and Options

... Nature should have a procedure answering to what we call fingering on instruments.
Fernando Sor. *Méthode pour la Guitare,* 1830

... It can be affirmed that good technique is incompatible with bad fingering.
Abel Carlevaro. *School of Guitar*, 1984

The analysis of the formal, stylistic, and expressive contents of each score, together with a positive use of our bodily resources, constitute the basis of fingering.

A musical text can have multiple expressive meanings. One definitive aspect in fingering is to consider the possible interpretive options; foregoing this analysis may not preclude the realization of an operative version, but it will greatly inhibit the unfoldment of a richer and more expressive version that uses logical phrasing and exploits the timbric palette of the guitar. Not in vain Fernando Sor considered fingering as *an art* (Sor, 1830:76). Eduardo Fernández affirms that *fingering is already an act of performing* (Fernández, 2002:7).

We will study a group of basic functional regularities, procedures, and available resources for fingering efficiency of both hands, considered separately and together, always keeping in mind the fluidity of the musical discourse.

Alternation of p-i-m-a

Because of its anatomical make-up, the ring finger is a somewhat less gifted finger for plucking. In order to compensate this natural disparity, it is advisable to replace the traditional concept of "working out the finger" with the physiological and sensoperceptive approach of the "hand as a unit," based on the plucking mechanism.[29]

Besides the functional benefit of planting, an elementary action that enables more control over the ring finger is to allow the little finger to "go with it" *as relaxed as possible* with a slight lateral contact.

As we know, alternation with *i-m* or *i-a* is easier than alternation with *m-a*, and clearly, alternation with *a-e* is not effective. In addition, the transit from middle to ring finger on the same string is more difficult than its reverse, hence the basic pattern of tremolo is *p-a-m-i* (or *p-i-a-m-i*, in flamenco style). This drawback is less pronounced in arpeggios and string changes where planting can support balance.

Considering the fast tempo of Villa-Lobos' *Etude No. 1*, alternating *i-m* or *i-a* on the 1st and 2nd strings will always be easier than alternating *m-a*. (Ex. 2.17)

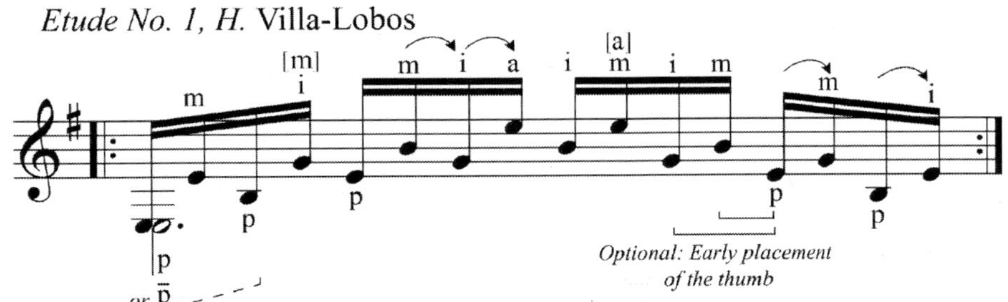

Other possibilities include alternation with *p-i* or *p-m (figueta)* and combinations of three and four fingers, called by Emilio Pujol *ternary* and *quaternary* fingerings: *a-m-i, a-m-i-m, p-a-m-i* (Pujol, 1971:75). Using the little finger we might add *e-m, e-m-i,* and so on.

[29] Dr. Jaume Rosset gives his opinion about the relative "independence" of fingers:
The lack of specific muscles for each finger, and especially the existence of a large number of interconnections between tendons – make this an impossible task from a biomechanical standpoint. Thus, inordinately striving to achieve it is not only useless, but it will surely end up injuring us. ("Independencia de los dedos," 12 Notas, no. 34, Barcelona, 2002-2003)
Charles Postlewate commented that in many of the guitarists he had known with right-hand conditions had the precedent of an excessive work with the ring finger, especially among those who suffer focal dystonia. (See C. Postlewate: "Extending Right-Hand Technique to Include the Little Finger," *GFA Soundboard*, USA, summer 2002)

Renaissance lutenists and vihuelists used *figueta* technique, which was also widely practiced during the Classic-Romantic period and mentioned by Sor in his *Méthode*. With its agile mobility, *p-i* alternation generates a clear articulation similar to the *staccato* effect that can be considered both a "stylistic option" and a current technique. (Ex. 2.18)

Fantasía Op. 19, Luigi Legnani

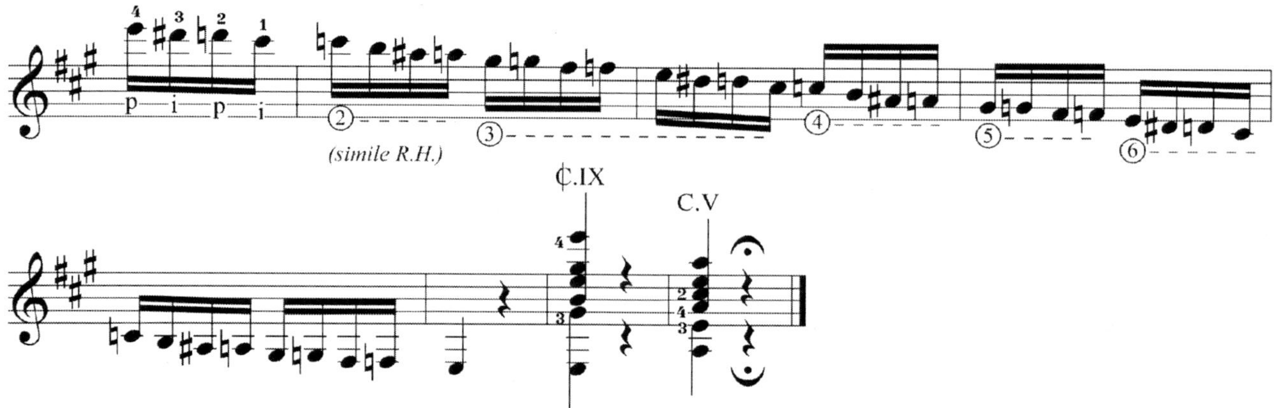

Executing the figueta with a slight fixation is very effective in repeated notes. (Exs. 2.19)

En los trigales, Joaquín Rodrigo

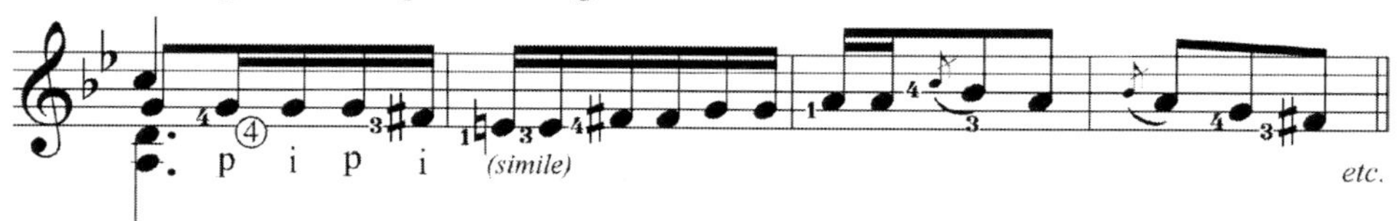

Etude No. 5, Francis Kleynjans

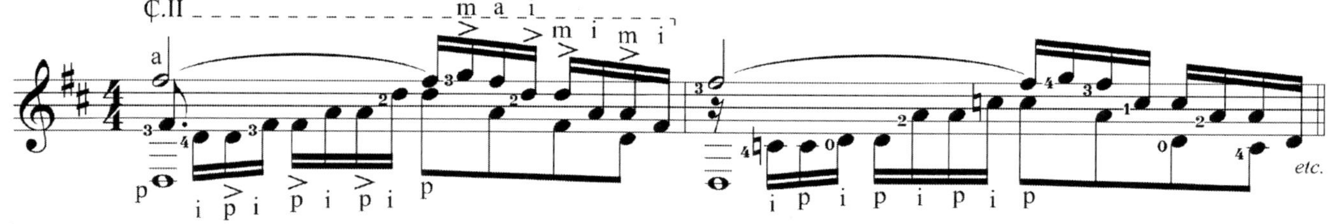

Tango No. 3, Astor Piazzolla (vers. L. Brouwer)

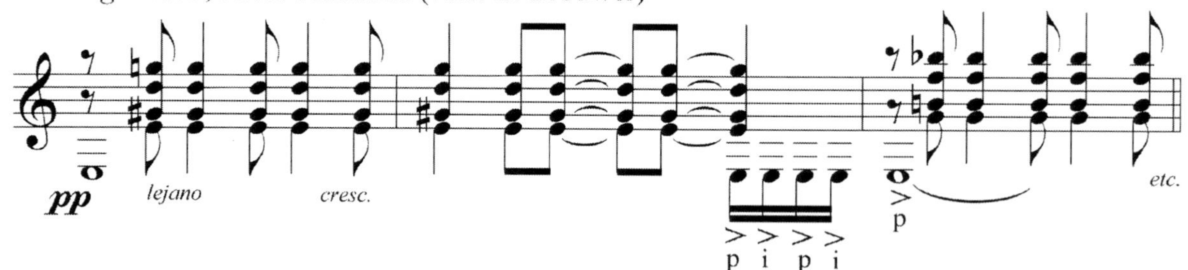

Even the brief use of *p-i* alternation in arpeggios and scales offers a convenient stability that helps to preserve the roundness of the hand and the alignment of the fingers, conditions that foster relaxation. (Exs. 2.20)

Prelude BWV 1006a, J. S. Bach

Usher Waltz, Op. 29, Nikita Koshkin

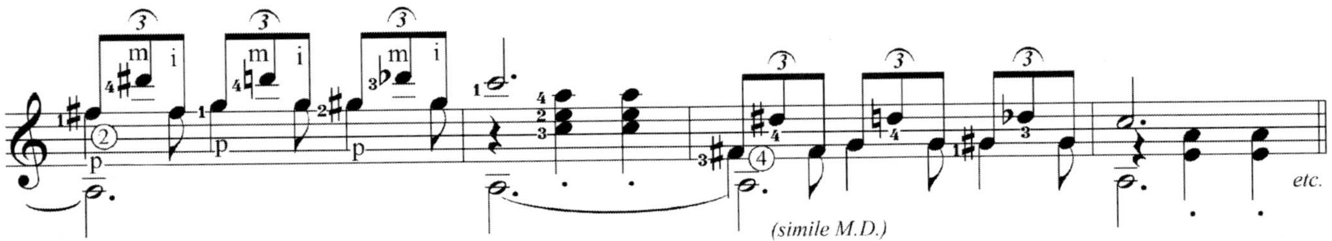

Ternary and quaternary fingerings are particularly effective in fast passages. (Exs. 2.21)

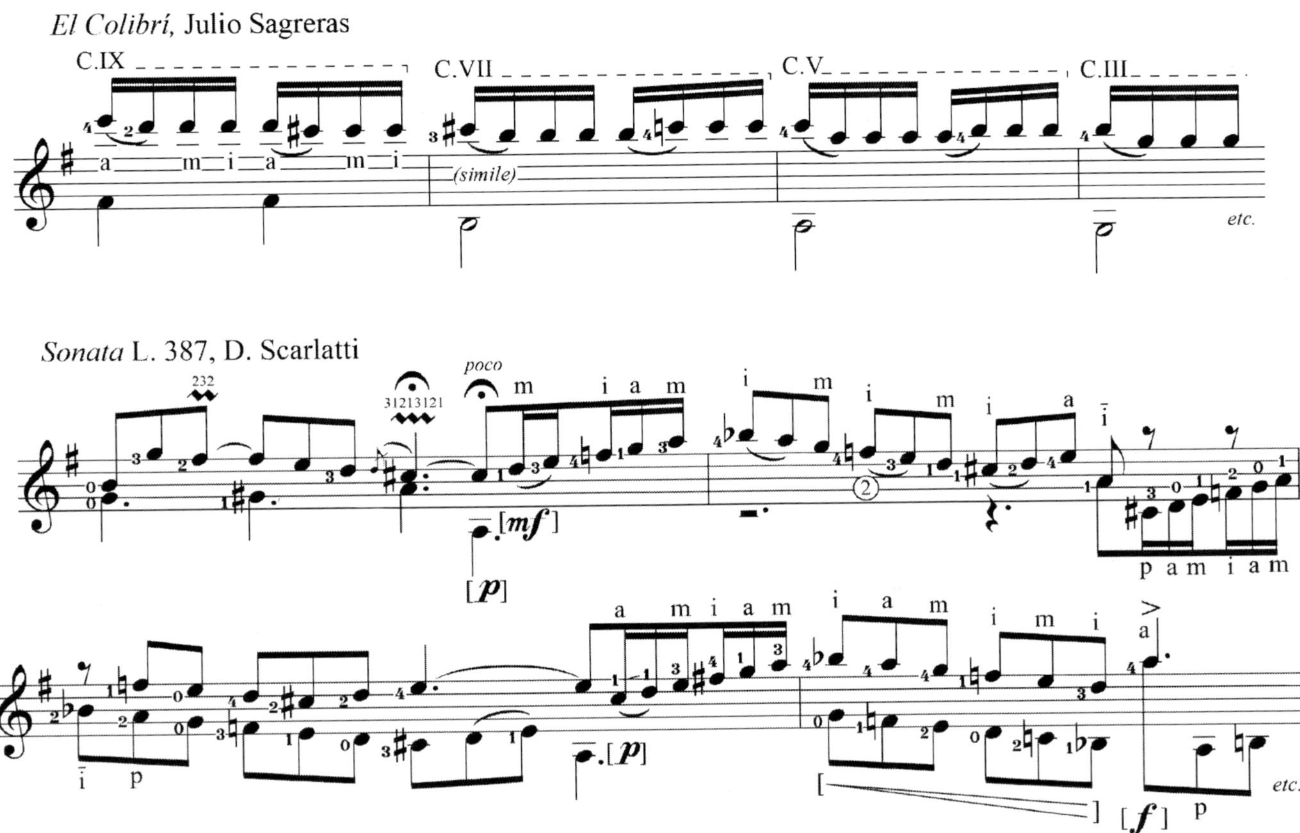

Finger Crossing

During performance we usually focus our visual attention on the left hand, given the wide range of its movements, while relying on the tactile-auditory perception to control the right hand. Since this skill is present mostly in its formative stage in beginners, it is usual for them to neglect alternation stability in scales.

Finger crossing occurs when plucking from one string to the next with the finger most distant from the target string. This action is problematic, mainly when repeated successively or even in isolated fast passages. For example, in the first of the following fragments, there are two instances of finger crossing with the index from 3rd to 2nd, and from 2nd to 1st strings *(a)*, when a greater balance would result by using the middle or ring fingers *(b)*. In *Etude No. 7* by Villa-Lobos, playing the second E of the scale on the open 1st string introduces an otherwise avoidable crossed fingering *(c)*. (Exs. 2.22)

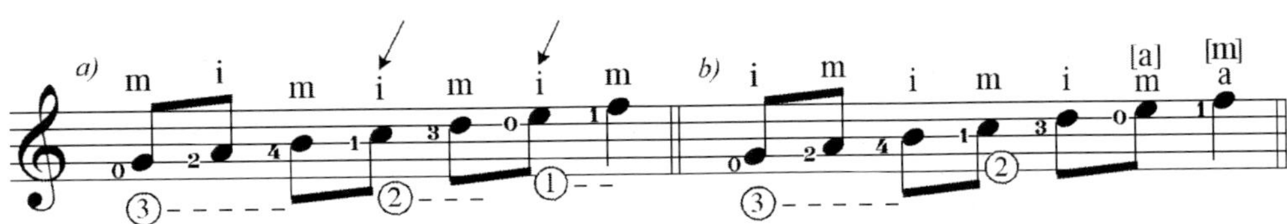

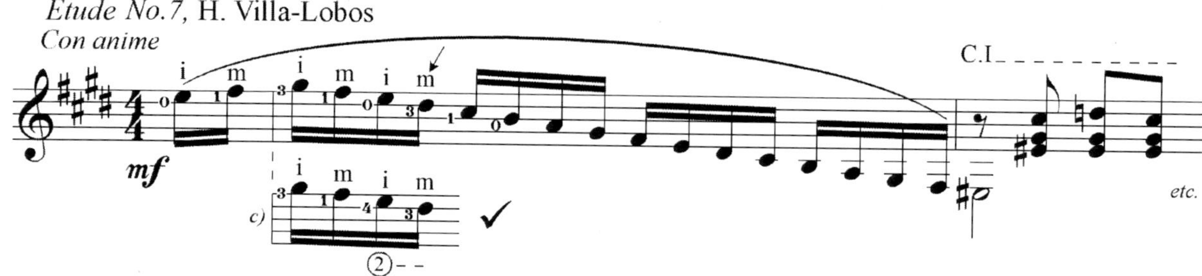

Inserting the ring finger or the thumb is often enough to maintain a fluent alternation. (Exs. 2.23)

In the next example, using the ring finger prevents crossing repetitions as well as a continuous gap between *i* and *m*. (Ex. 2.24)

In descending scale passages, repeating the index –preferably after a slur with rest stroke– is another way to avoid awkward string crossings. This "sweep" is commonly used in *picado* (rapid flamenco scales passages), with *m* or *a* as well (Ex. 2.25)

Although we generally experience more control over the index, the balance of the alternation sequence will depend on the characteristics of each segment.

Let's examine two fingering options before the chord in the second measure of this fragment of *Fandanguillo* by Turina. In the first one, the index must jump from the 2nd string (G) to the 4th (G♯), also forcing a longer trajectory of thumb towards the 6th string (E). (Ex. 2.26)

Fandanguillo Op.36, Joaquín Turina

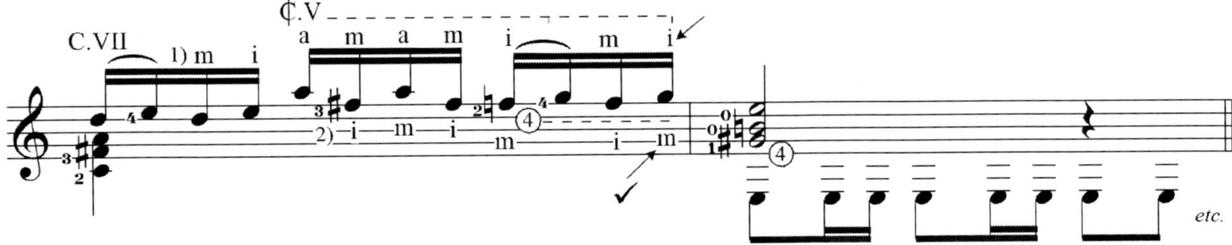

In the second option, the middle finger remains on the same string that it will pluck for the chord. Considering the speed of the passage, these differences can be decisive.

We will later examine other alternatives when studying the alternation of free and rest strokes.

The Little Finger

According to the precursor methods of Federico Moretti, Fernando Ferandiere, and Antonio Abreu, published in Spain in the late eighteenth century, the ring finger was used so rarely that it was not included in the first fingering symbologies, which appeared at the time. Sor declared that he only used this finger in chords and for certain arpeggios where it is absolutely necessary (Sor, 1830:10). Meanwhile, Aguado declared that *all the fingers of the hand will be useful for plucking, though rarely the little one* (*Escuela de Guitarra*, 1825), and reaffirmed it in the Appendix of his *Nuevo Método para Guitarra* (1849):

> It also serves to the position and suitable firmness of these fingers [index and middle] when using the ring finger, and even the little finger.

Aguado adds in a footnote that he has verified with his students that it is possible to overcome the difficulty of using both fingers.

In 1929 Domingo Prat published *La nueva técnica de la guitarra... para la práctica de los cinco dedos de la mano derecha (The New Guitar Technique... for the Practice of the Five Fingers of the Right-Hand)*, which was the first serious attempt at incorporating the use of the little finger to the technique of the instrument.

Guitarists still limit the use of this finger to strumming although there are no compelling physiological reasons for such restriction. On the contrary, its anatomy is a crucial component for the optimal functioning of the hand.

With the passage of time, the use of the ring finger turned into a basic element of technique, and implementing the little finger became the latest challenge, *the final frontier of the possibilities of the right hand*, in the words of Charles Postlewate, who widely demonstrated the functional benefit of this finger for the plucking mechanism.[30]

Ricardo Iznaola affirms that:

> Regular training of *e* should be undertaken to improve the freedom and dexterity of the articulation of *a,* as well as for the general strengthening of the outer part of the hand. Without this work on *e*, the outer part of the hand might atrophy, therefore weakening it as a whole." (Iznaola, 1997:126)

Applications

Once integrated into our perception of hand unity in plucking, the little finger can be used in different ways on any score traditionally conceived for four fingers.

Artificial Harmonics

Playing artificial harmonics with the little finger allows a clearer sound since the plucking contact point is further from the *node* (contact point of the index finger with the string) creating a larger vibration profile. With the little finger, it is possible to accompany the harmonic with three standard notes. (Ex. 2.27)

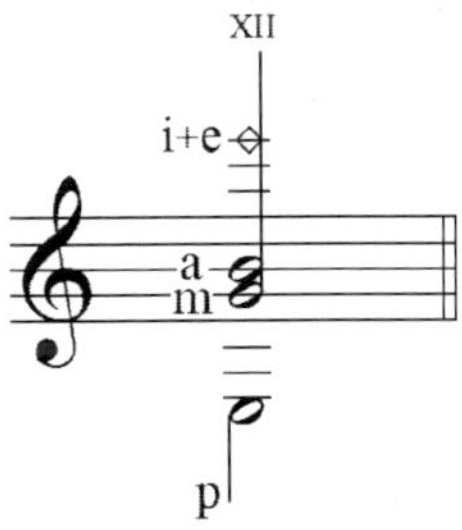

[30] Stephen Rekas: "An Interview with Charles Postlewate," *GFA Soundboard*, USA, 2003.
The guitarist who uses this book [Right-Hand Studies for Five Fingers, Mel Bay Publications, Inc., Pacific MO., USA, 2001] *will find that, in addition to gaining the use of the little-finger, the other fingers of the right hand will gain increasing strength, independence and dexterity* (C. Postlewate).

Five-Note Chords

In *Etude No. 4* by Villa-Lobos, five-note chords can be performed without displacements of the thumb. A perfect guitar connoisseur, this composer regularly used the little finger in playing his works. (See Santos, 1985:17). (Exs. 2.28)

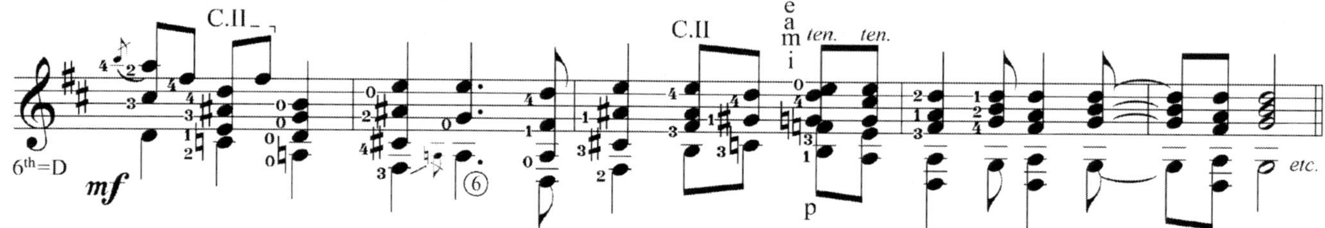

Arpeggios

The little finger can produce a good sound when applied with a more lateral attack on the 1st string. (Ex. 2.29)

Planting alternatives increase when using *e*. Notice the possibility of an early placement in the following study. (Ex. 2.30)

The use of the little finger also expands the options for compositions and transcriptions for the instrument.

More About the Thumb

Timbre

The thumb offers a wide range of possibilities, combining functionality with improved sound quality. Its fingertip/nail attack provides a convenient brilliance in melodic passages on basses (*Prelude No. 1* by Villa-Lobos); while the fingertip attack (flesh) can soften the sound and equalize the low register in chords and pedal tones. (Exs. 2.31)

Prelude No. 1, H. Villa-Lobos

Sonata Eroica Op. 150, M. Giuliani

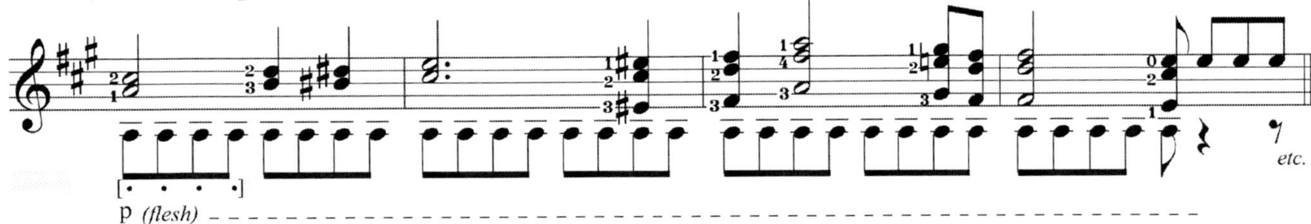

La Serenor, (Col.lectici Íntim), Vicent Asencio

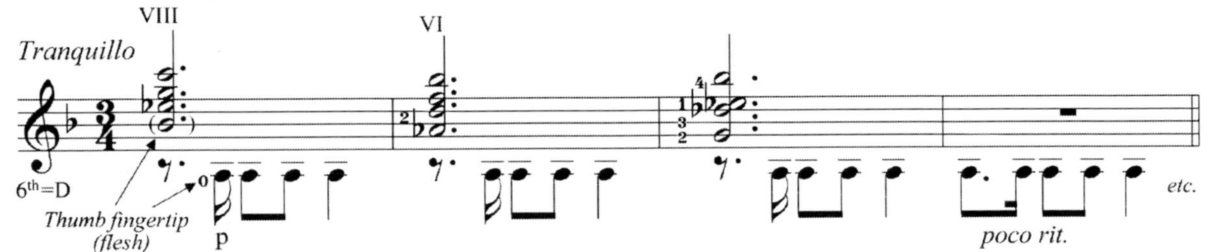

In tremolo pieces, better contrast of the voices can be achieved by playing pedal basses with rest strokes using the flesh of the thumb. (Ex. 2.32) See Ex. 2.6, *Recuerdos de la Alhambra*, by Tárrega, p. 31.

Un sueño en la floresta, A. Barrios Mangoré

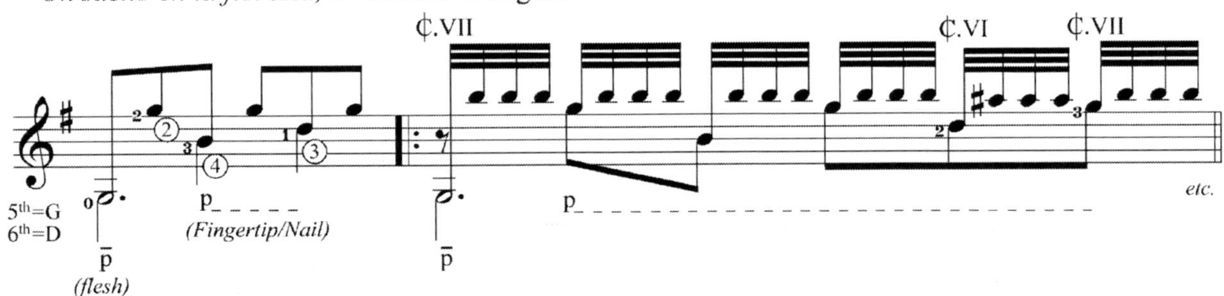

Fingering fluency and color management are linked in this segment of the following *Prelude* by Santiago de Murcia. Alternating *p-i,* instead of using only the thumb in the lower voice contributes to the clarity of the articulation. Moreover, thumb repetition is less functional in rapid changes toward the 6th string. (Ex. 2.33)

Preludio, Santiago de Murcia (17th century)

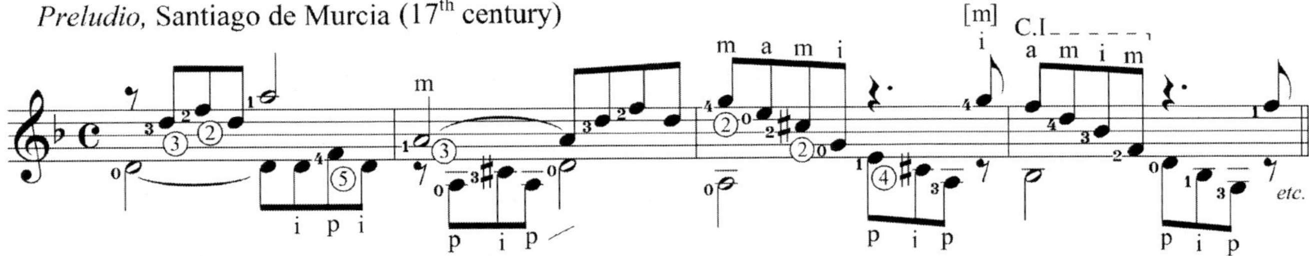

In another context, the sequence of simultaneity between *i-m* and the thumb generates an enriching contrast. (Ex. 2.34)

Fandanguillo (Suite Castellana), F. Moreno Torroba

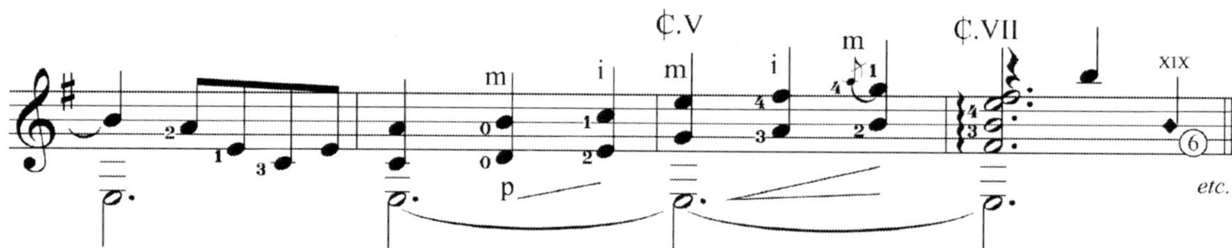

Twin-Stroke

Twin-stroke technique links timbre and accentuation (See Carlevaro, 1984:31). In this case, plucking of two or more consecutive strings begins with the fingertip and ends with the nail, emphasizing the last note. In the example below, the twin-stroke underscores the final note of the phrase, which in turn sets off the beginning of the next section. (Ex. 2.35)

Chaconne BWV 1004, J. S. Bach

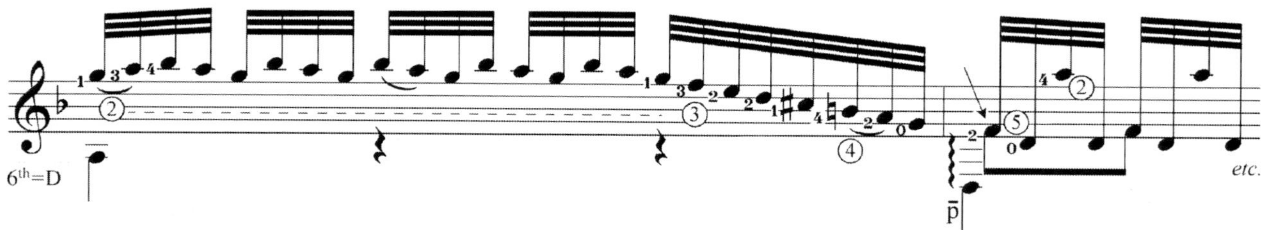

A typical use of this procedure can be found in *Confesión* by Barrios Mangoré, whose melody unfolds on the 3rd and 4th strings. (Ex. 2.36)

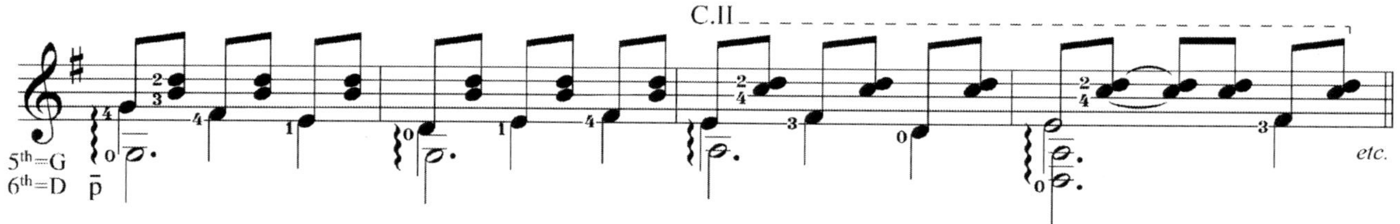

Support-Planting

The use of the thumb in support-planting consists of lightly resting it on the string, generally after a rest stroke or anticipating the next note to be played, in some cases lightly supporting the hand.

As a point of reference for the positioning of *i-m-a*, this technique contributes both to relaxation and stability in the movement of the fingers, especially when the thumb is placed on the string closest to the index (See Ex. 3.81, *Etude No. 1* by H. Villa-Lobos, p. 102). This reinforcement of balance can be experienced by contrasting it with its opposite sensation: the tension and instability felt by playing an *i-m-a* arpeggio on the treble strings while the thumb is unsupported or in the air.

In the mazurca *Sueño* by Tárrega, thumb support on the 4th string helps to stabilize the interval and chord plucking. In this case, it is easier to play rest strokes with the thumb on the downbeats by arpeggiating the chords. (Ex. 2.37)

Sueño (Mazurca), F. Tárrega

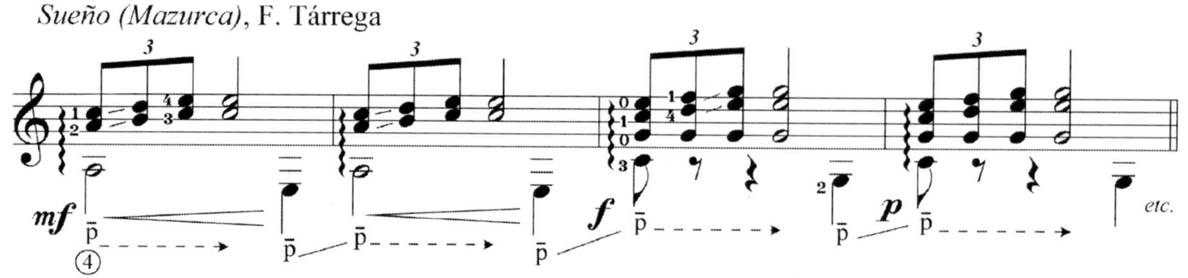

In the following example the thumb supports the glissando balance of the index in *Sonatina Meridional* (Ponce) (Ex. 2.38).

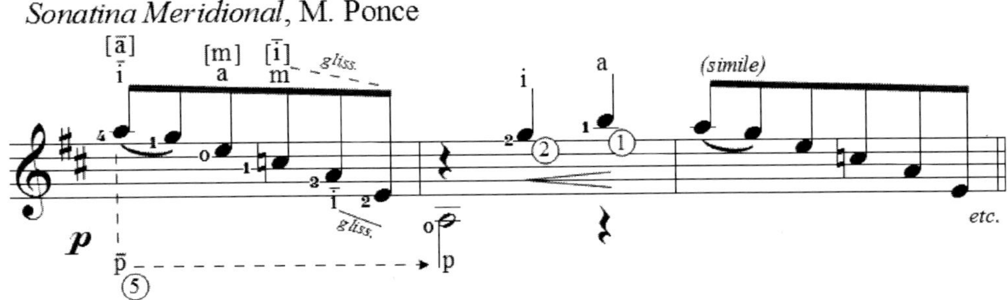

Maestro Alirio Díaz used support-planting freely and to great effect in Lauro's *Venezuelan Waltz No. 3 (Natalia),* where indeed, his thumb rarely ceased to be in contact with the strings. (Ex. 2.39)

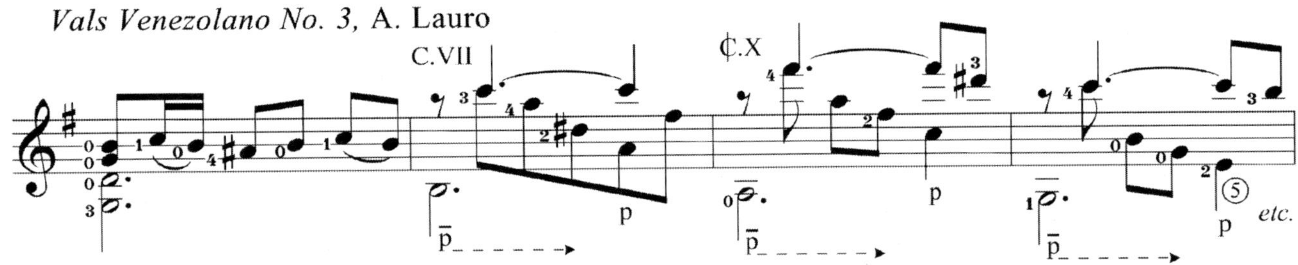

Thumb support increases stability in the execution of fast scales and certain types of strumming, and forms an integral part of flamenco technique.

Displacements

While six-note block chords are executed with a vigorous slide of the thumb simultaneously with *i-m-a (-e)* free strokes (Exs. 2.40), thumb rest strokes in arpeggiated chords or left-hand arpeggios (as in examples 2.41) produce a smooth and connected sound known as *legato articulation.*

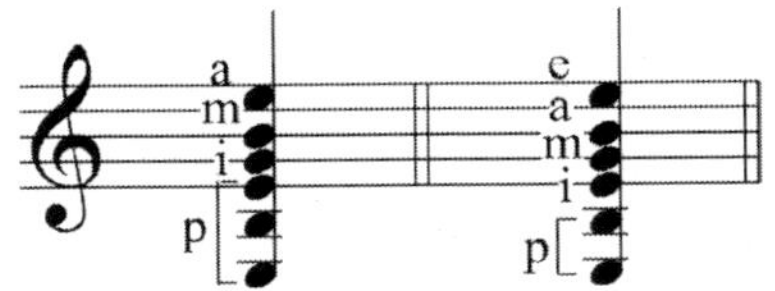

In slow to moderate tempi it is easy for the thumb to play consecutive rest strokes on the bass strings, but achieving the same control in fast movements is a complex task, even after planting.

At the beginning of *Scherzo* by Tomás Damas, the slur favors the thumb rest stroke *(a)*, while in bar 23, three consecutive strokes are made: two rest strokes on the 6th and 5th strings, and one free stroke on the 4th string *(b)*. In this case, another possibility is to limit the thumb to two strings (rest stroke only on the 6th string), and then cross the middle finger over the ring *(c)*. Observe the thumb being used as support-planting. (Exs. 2.41)

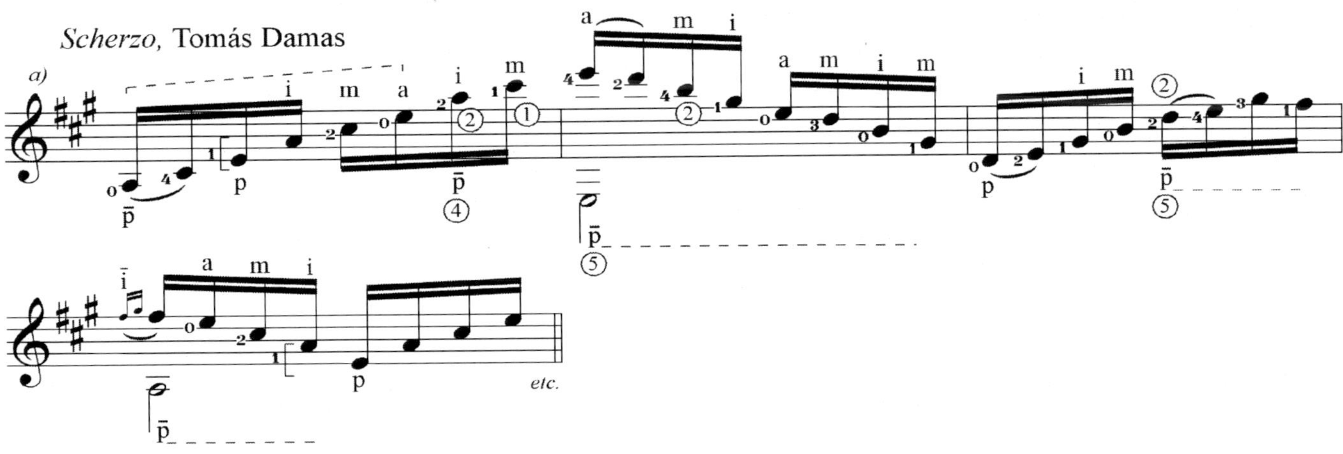

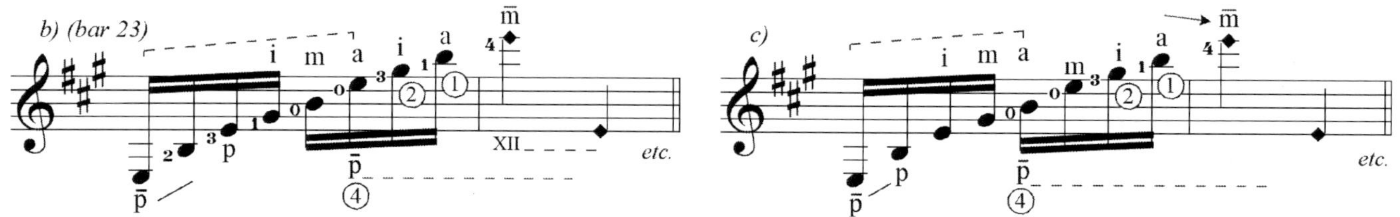

Sliding the thumb for support (rest strokes) is linked to consecutive planting in the following passage. (Ex. 2.42) See Ex. 2.17, *Etude No. 1* by H. Villa-Lobos, p. 41.

Decamerón Negro, L. Brouwer

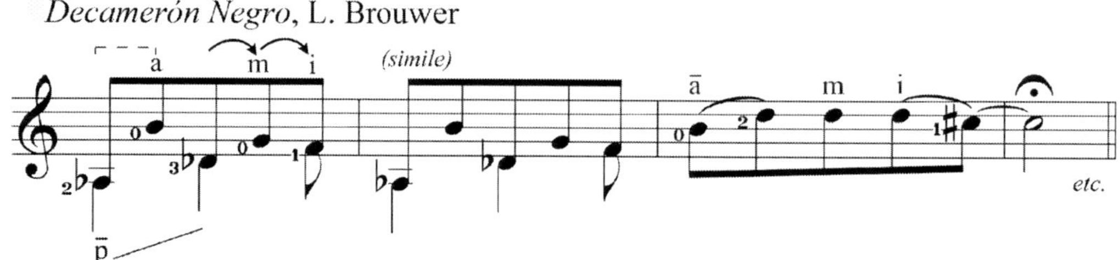

In this passage the thumb marks the displacements of the hand besides favoring balance, and the successive use of the index, which preserves the alignment of the fingers. (Ex. 2.43)

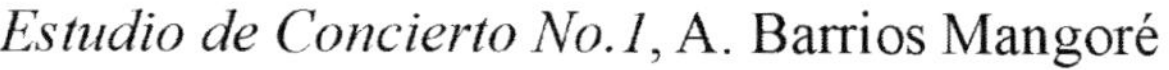

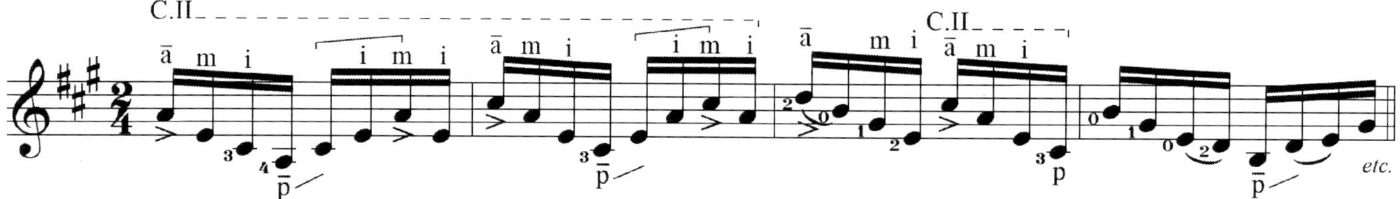

Control of Resonance by Damping

Damping the vibrations of one or more strings with the thumb contributes to phrasing clarity not only by specifying durations, but also by avoiding added notes that can appear as a result of sympathetic resonance, an effect that is especially noticeable on fine-tuned open strings. Based on the "Principle of Resonance," the sympathetic harmonics appear continuously in performance and reinforce legato, mainly in the most common tonalities of the instrument. These harmonics can also be used to "extend" a particular note (See *Direct Use of Sympathetic Resonance*).

Damping a vibrating string is accomplished by repositioning or placing the side of the thumb on the string, preferably as planting for the next stroke. (Exs. 2.44)

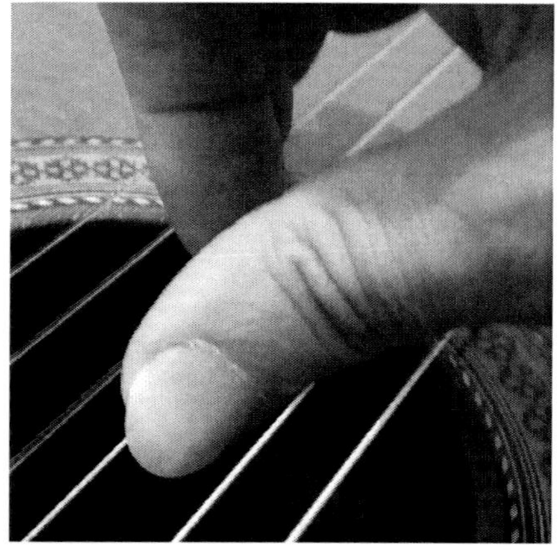

Melancholy Galliard, J. Dowland (17th century)

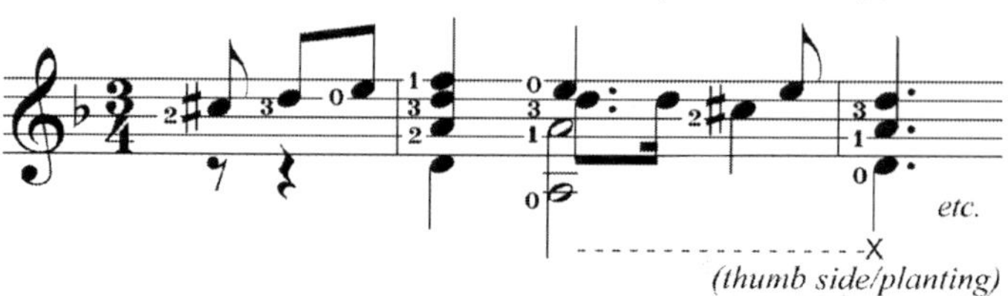

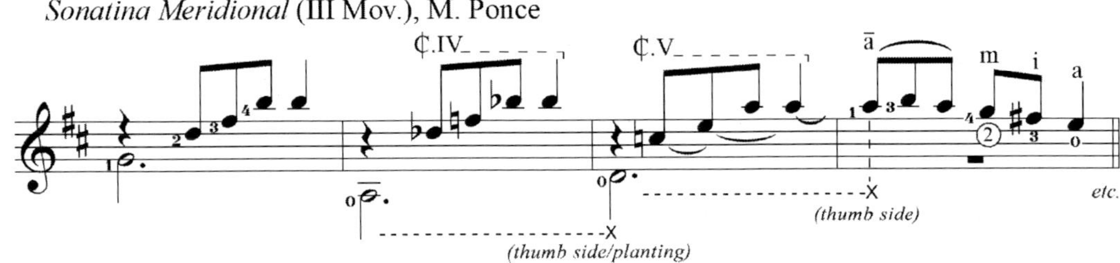

Implicit in the score, the rhythmic sense of *Elogio de la Danza* by Brouwer demands muting of the open 6th string (E). (Ex. 2.45)

In *Fandanguillo* (Turina), damping the 6th and 5th strings by placing the edge of the thumb over them, prevents sympathetic harmonics from interfering with the second-string melody. (Ex. 2.46)

Sonatina Meridional (Mov. II) by M. Ponce: After removing finger 2 from E (6th), the open string is prone to vibrate. To prevent this, and to facilitate a smooth release of finger 2, the thumb damps the 6th string prior to the C-A portamento on the 2nd. (Ex. 2.47)

•

Right-Hand Articulation Techniques

Articulation, dynamics, and timbre are inseparable components of the structure of a phrase and characterize its expressive essence.

Legato and Staccato

Guitar performance is conditioned by a relatively fast decay or extinction of sonority. Therefore, our legato possibilities lie both in handling the real resonance of the instrument, and in a set of technical-interpretive resources that may include timbric and dynamic distinctions of the notes, to achieve a "suggestion of continuity."

Depending on the score, the importance of certain notes, although brief, can be emphasized by an expressive intention –which embraces agogic accents– emphasizing its importance in the melodic discourse. This subjective extension is particularly useful on the guitar, since it is not always possible to realize the full duration of the notes on the staff.

The importance of analyzing each piece to adapt different articulations towards expressive meanings is obvious. As a basic connection of notes, *legato* depends on the combined action of both hands. In the right hand, it is favored by a regular (not accentuated), smooth, and slanted attack (fingertip/nail) towards the Zone of Resonance. (Exs. 2.48)

Fantasy, S. L. Weiss

Tema variado y Final, M. Ponce

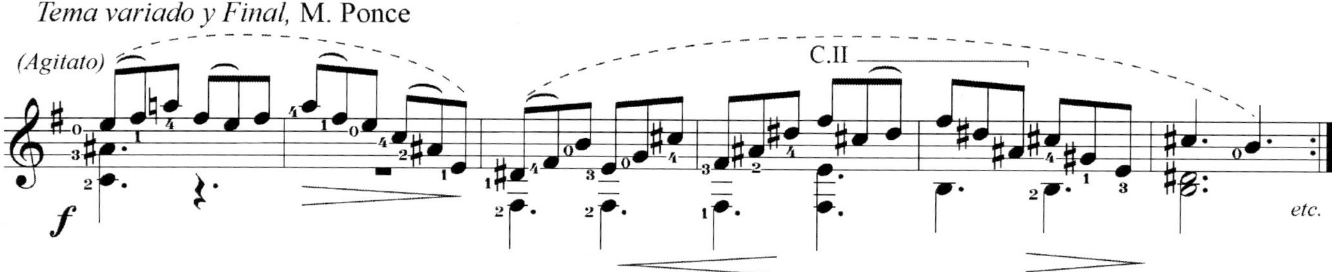

A slight separation between notes (*non legato*) brings clarity, while the staccato is a plain shortening of value in relative degrees: *mezzo-staccato*, *staccato,* and *staccatissimo*.

Often performed by muting the strings with both hands at the same time, staccato articulation can introduce a diversity of contrasts. In *Etude Op. 29 No. 17* by Sor, staccato emphasizes the character of a military march, and in the last bars of *Le Tombeau de Debussy* by Falla, it suggests an orchestral effect. (Exs. 2.49)

Regardless of the sound image desired – even in sometimes sign-saturated contemporary scores– every performer should exercise a criterion of articulation, first of all, to guarantee the clarity of phrasing. Let's look at an example from the Classical-Romantic repertoire. The fourth of the *Variations Op. 107* by Mauro Giuliani presents a schematic layout of alternated silences between voices whose literal execution would be of little interest. (Ex. 2.50)

A more attractive result can be obtained with a discreet change of durations. (Ex. 2.51)

The insertion of staccati in the following fragments aids the contrasting of slurs, glissandi, and repeated notes. (Exs. 2.52)

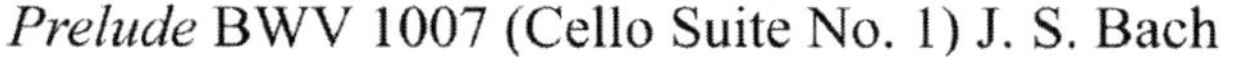

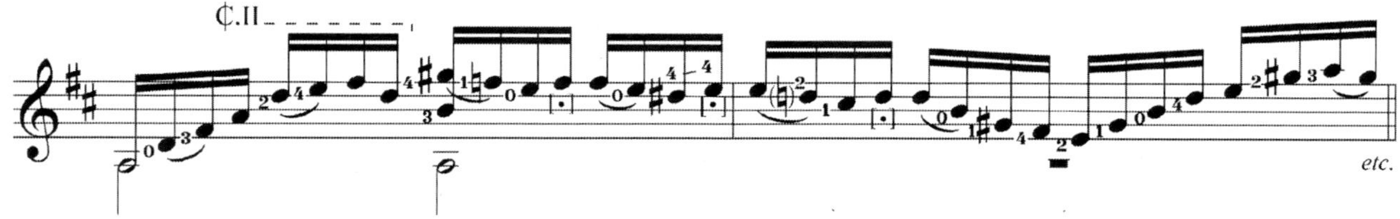

Nuevo Estudio Sencillo No.7 (Omaggio a Piazzolla), L. Brouwer

Rest/Free Stroke Alternation

Ideally, fingering should merge mechanical ease with expressive resources. The use of rest/free stroke alternation (on one or two strings) depends on the particularities of each passage, determining both mobility and phrasing character.

Let us consider that:

• The slight timbric differentiation between strokes operates as a subtle form of articulation.

An essential element of the idiomatic features of the guitar lies in its special "sonorous diction." Fingering encompasses both a conscious handling of tonal registry, and of various effects, along with the natural contrast existing between thumb and *i-m-a* strokes, ascending and descending slurs, and between slurred and plucked notes. These differences can be emphasized or attenuated depending on interpretation.

• If necessary, free strokes can generate a sound quality very similar to the rest stroke, but without the economy of effort that the latter implies.

• From a comfortable postural disposition of the hand, each rest stroke in the rest/free alternation can contribute to mobility balance.

It is a common practice to emphasize the melodic line with rest strokes. (Ex. 2.53)

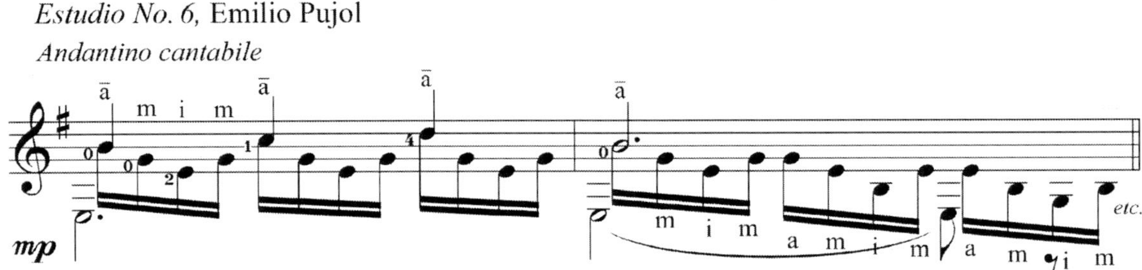

However, rest strokes can interrupt resonance in ascending passages. In the following example they are only applied optionally on the climax notes of each motif. (Ex. 2.54)

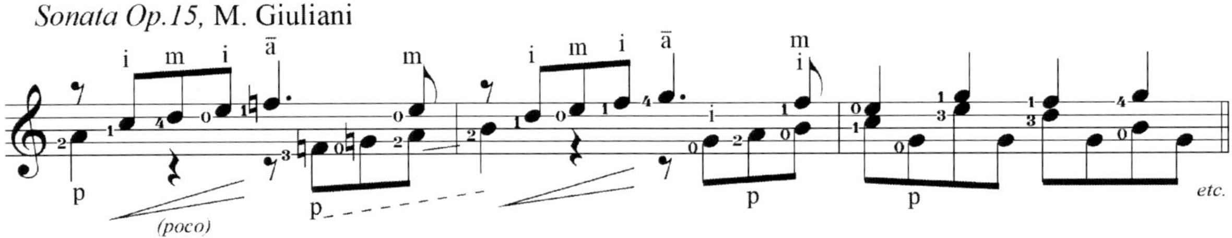

In slurs, non-accented rest strokes enhance stability, since the light contact with the adjacent string may practically extend until the next plucking. (Ex. 2.55)

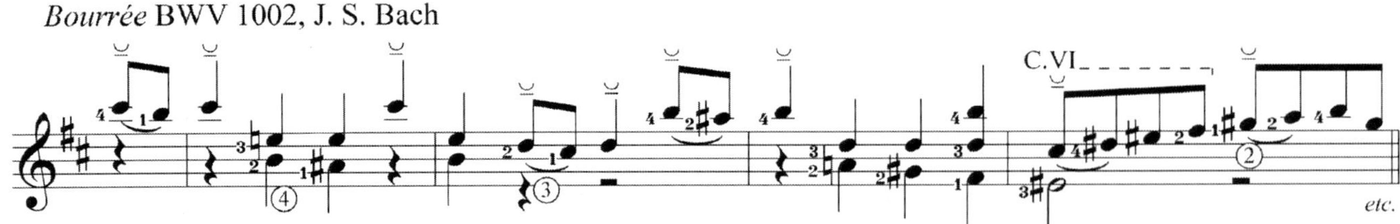

On the other hand, the vibrational energy of rest strokes reinforces the effect of fast glissandi and the expressive intensity of portamenti and vibrato. (Exs. 2.56)

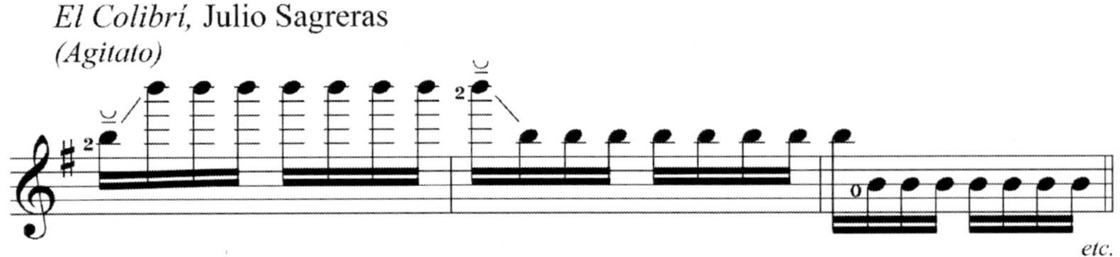

Sevilla (Suite Iberia, Op. 47), Isaac Albéniz

In extended linear passages that are played with only one type of stroke –either free or rest– accentuating notes is relatively easy at slow tempi, but becomes more challenging as the tempo increases. This can be solved by alternating rest and free strokes, especially if the scale progresses toward the 6th string, in the same direction as the finger strokes.

In this excerpt from *Vals Op. 8 No. 4* by Barrios Mangoré, playing the slurs with rest strokes contributes to the lightness of movement. (Ex. 2.57)

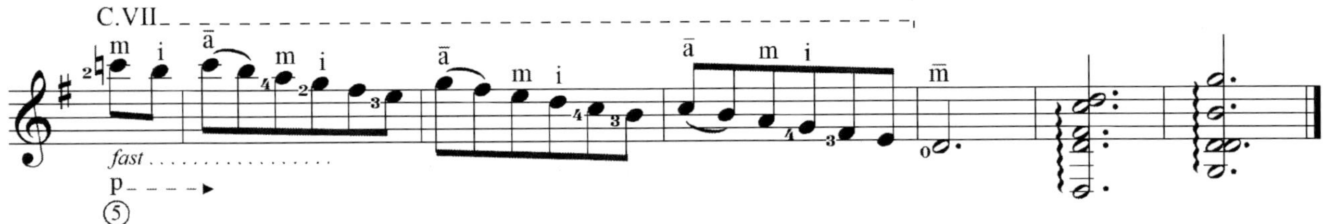

The following stroke-alternation patterns omit the less functional transition of *m* to *a* (which obviously does not invalidate its use). (Ex. 2.58)

Stroke-alternation is also performed within arpeggio movements, maintaining the finger alignment to prevent crossed fingers. This mechanism emphasizes articulation in the following passage from Brouwer's *Estudio Sencillo No. 11*. (Ex. 2.59)

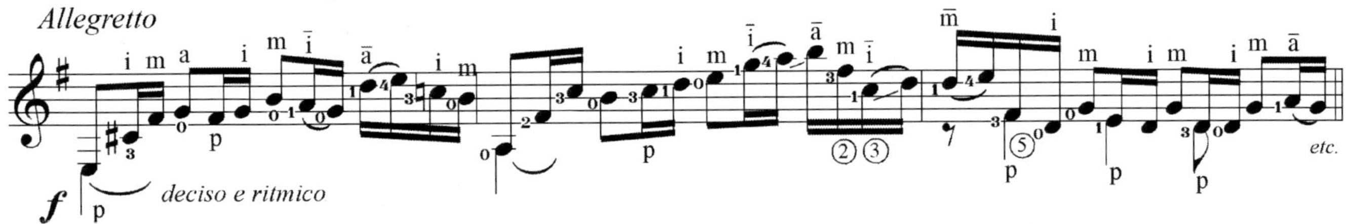

In *Prelude* BWV 996 by J. S. Bach, the optional combination of strokes enhances the suggested linear polyphony. (Ex. 2.60)

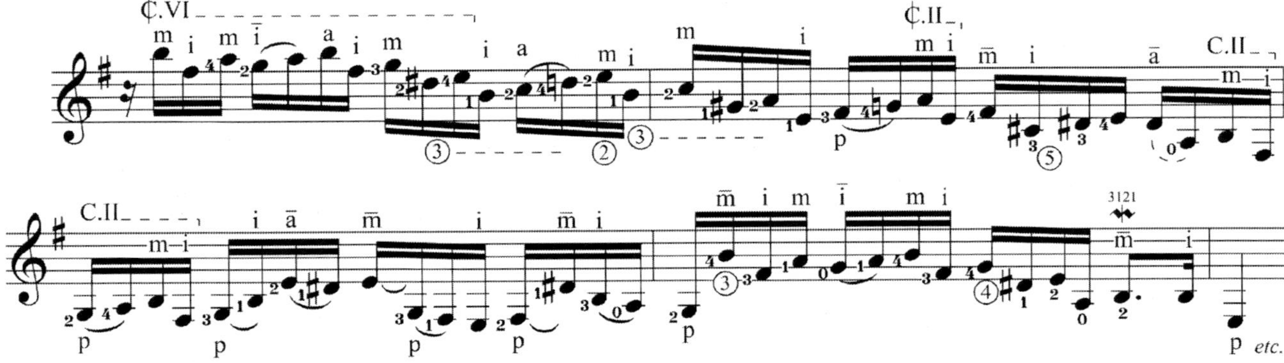

"Vertical Articulation"

Intervals

When plucking two adjacent strings simultaneously it is only possible to use free strokes, but more options exist when plucking non-adjacent strings, i. e.: free stroke with all digits, rest stroke with thumb and free stroke with *i-m-a* (and its opposite), and, although rare – rest stroke with the thumb and another finger simultaneously.

Executing a perfectly simultaneous rest stroke with the thumb in an interval is complex and does not always clarify the musical texture. To overcome this difficulty, the interval is slightly broken with the lowest note usually played first. Broken intervals allow for a selective highlighting in any melodic line. Although effective, especially in polyphonies, it is advisable to avoid the excessive use of this option. (Exs. 2.61)

Granada (Suite Iberia, Op.47), Isaac Albéniz

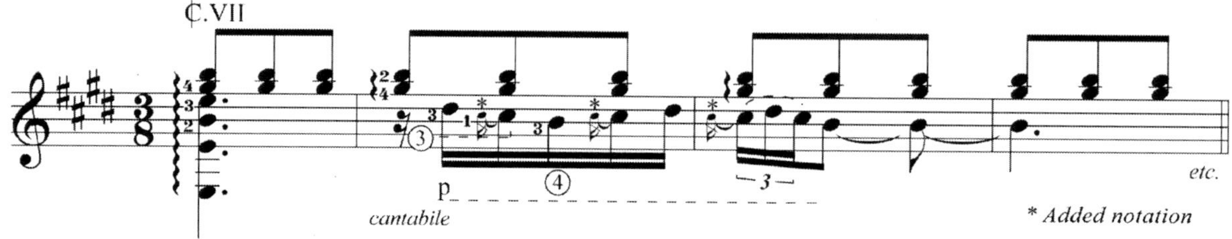

Etude No. 7, H. Villa-Lobos

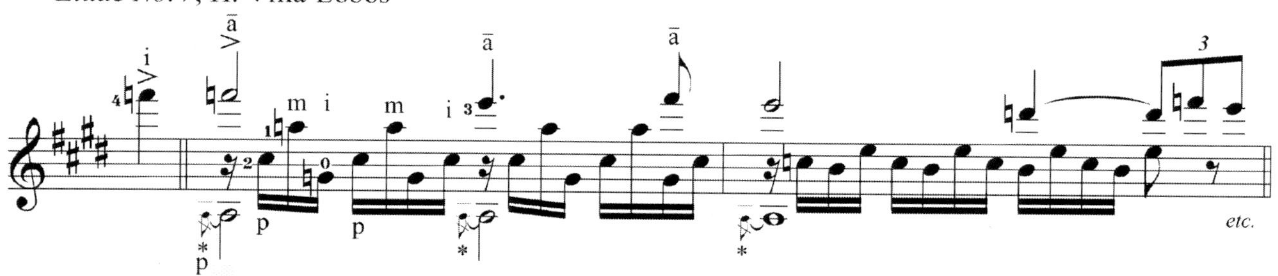

Arpeggiated Chords

Arpeggiated or rolled chords –a rapid succession of chord tones symbolized by a wavy line– are usually executed from the lowest note. Besides providing its own expressive effect, the arpeggiated chord brings out the melody (*Passacaglia* by J. Rodrigo) and supports rhythmic enhancement (*Danza Negra* by A. Lauro). (Exs. 2.62)

Passacaglia (Tres piezas españolas), J. Rodrigo

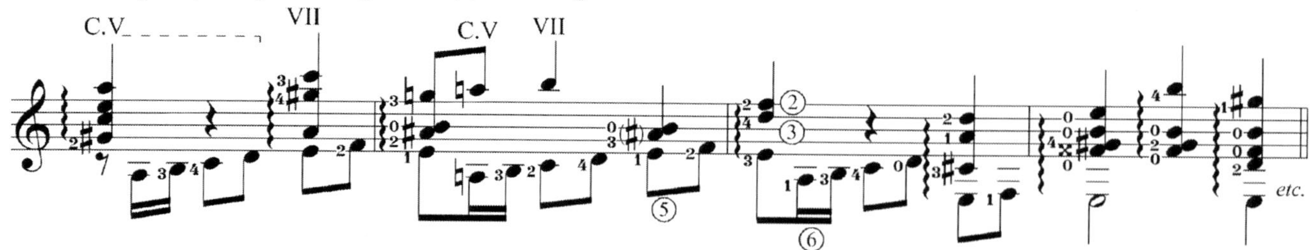

Danza Negra (Suite Venezolana), A. Lauro

The expanding sound of rolled chords can emphasize expressiveness in moderate to slow passages (*Sonatina* by F. M. Torroba, and *Sonata Op. 47* by A. Ginastera), enhance phrase endings (*Minuet Op. 11 No. 5* by F. Sor), and break the monotony of reiteration (*Etude No. 6* by Villa-Lobos). (Exs. 2.63)

Sonatina (II Mov.), F. Moreno Torroba

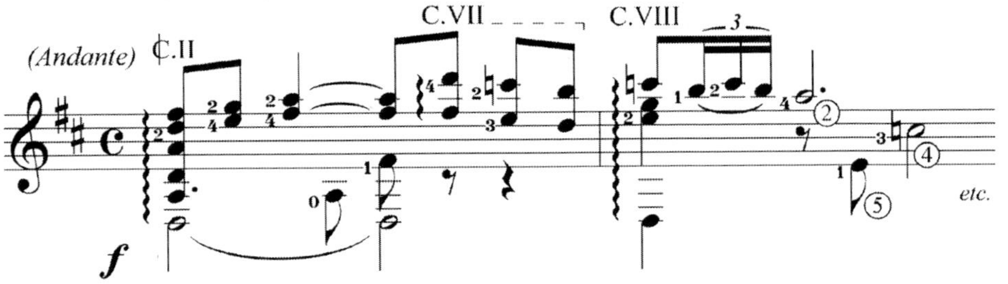

(Andante) ¢.II C.VII C.VIII *f* *etc.*

Sonata Op. 47 (I. Esordio), Alberto Ginastera

Solenne ♩= 64 *arpeggiato lento* *fff* *sim.* *sempre tutta forza* *vibr.* *etc.*

Minué Op. 11 No. 5, Fernando Sor

¢.II *f* *ff*

Etude No. 6, H. Villa-Lobos

Poco Allegro

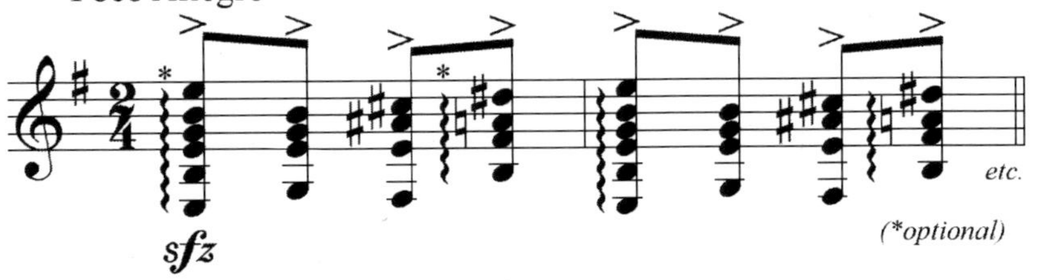

sfz *etc.* (*optional)

Similar to the technique for emulating the harp described by Aguado, a maximum arpeggio-legato is achieved by brushing the fleshy part of the thumb across the lower strings followed by a more perpendicular attack of *i-m-a* (fingertip/nail) with a slight rotation of the aligned hand. The harp-like effect is enhanced by plucking near or towards the fretboard. (Ex. 2.64)

*Prelude No. 24 (Chant populaire espagnol)**, Manuel Ponce

Moderato espressivo

No. 6 in Schott-Eschig Edition

It is also possible to combine staccati with arpeggiated chords. In this case, the fast plucking needs a firm grip and the use of fixation. (Ex. 2.65)

Sonata Mexicana, Manuel Ponce
Allegro moderato

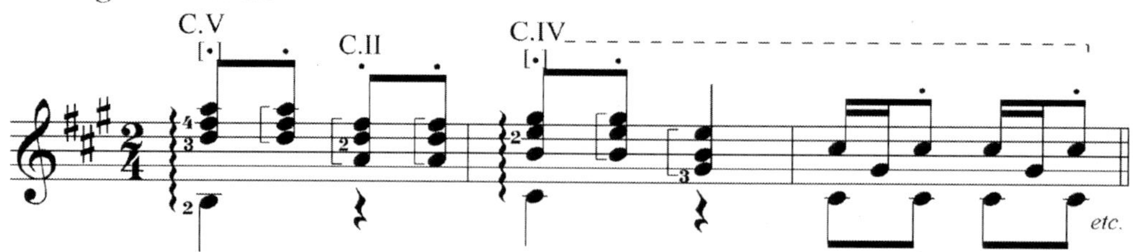

Care should be taken with the plucking speed of arpeggiated chords. Executed too slowly –relative to the tempo of the piece– it can alter the rhythmic pulse or meaning of the music. In the following example it would delay the final note of the phrase. (Ex. 2.66)

Sonata Clásica (III Mov.), Manuel Ponce

From an interpretative viewpoint one must consider that, regardless of style or period, continuous rolling of chords can affect the clarity of musical discourse. Due to the marked effect of this technique, the interpreter must define its application and frequency within the phrase. (Ex. 2.67)

Pavana VI, Luis Milán (1536)

In *Estudio Sencillo No. 15* by Brouwer, arpeggiated chords can be used to emphasize *a)* metric accent or *b)* dance character (Sarabande), among other options. (Ex. 2.68)

Estudio Sencillo No. 15, L. Brouwer
Sarabande

Arpeggiated chords help to clarify the motif of *Fugue* BWV 998 by J. S. Bach. (Ex. 2.69)

Dynamic Enhancement (Highlighting Notes)

Dynamic change is not only the most evident of all expressive intentions; it is linked to metric accents, articulation and the differentiation between melodic and harmonic planes– all definitive aspects of decoding musical content. With such overriding importance as an interpretive element, the handling of dynamics goes far beyond a simple fluctuation between *pianissimo* and *fortissimo* poles.

Several exercises can be done to enhance the control of sound volume in performance, but obviously, the definitive handling of dynamics is established within the context of each piece.

While linear dynamics (nuances, *crescendo-decrescendo*) offer different possibilities, emphasizing isolated notes in arpeggios, intervals or chords has a specific complexity.

In the following examples the framed notes demand additional energy. (Exs. 2.70)

Practice in highlighting notes through dynamic change can be initiated with simple linear or arpeggio passages. Given the limited dynamic range of the instrument, these exercises may require not only applying more energy to a given string, but also reducing it on others. (Ex. 2.71)

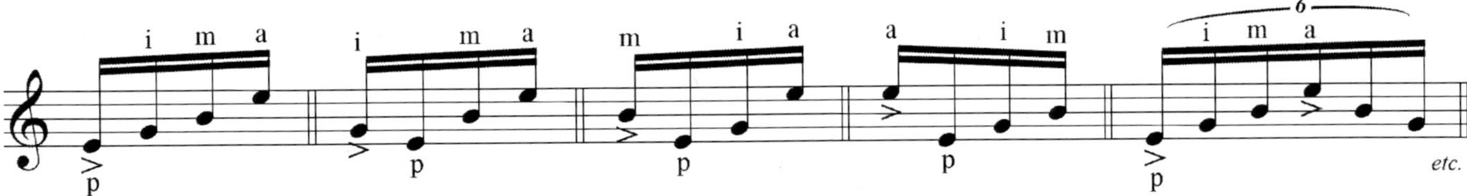

Some sections of J. S. Bach's *Chaconne* demand the ability to highlight notes within an arpeggio. (Ex. 2.72)

Broken intervals or arpeggiated chords can help to emphasize isolated notes, but achieving the same result in block chords or intervals requires training. Here are some suggestions:

1. Select a sequence of three-note chords *(p-i-m)*, preferably with a choral structure like *Estudio Sencillo No. 2* by Brouwer. (Ex. 2.73)

2. Identify the melodic line "sung" by each finger, and then begin by accenting the bass line with the thumb.
3. Play each chord several times to emphasize the tactile-auditory contrast of the emphasized notes.
4. Once a consistent result is achieved, proceed to work on the middle finger, leaving the index for last, since it may prove the most difficult to control due to its location.

After several days of patient study, take a break before extending the work to four-note chords, adding the ring finger. *Exercise No. 82* by Emilio Pujol (1952:86) is ideal for this practice. (Ex. 2.74)

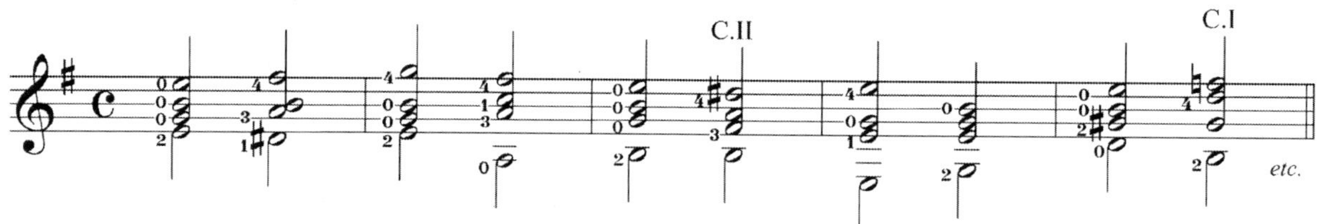

The following graph summarizes the standard plucking sequence and its basic aspects.

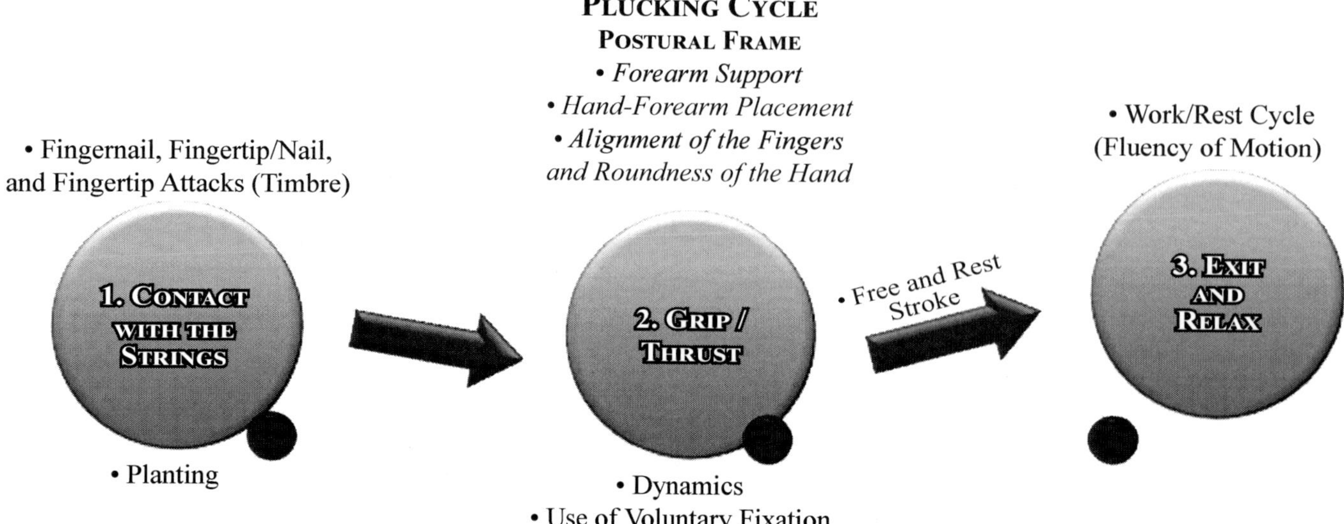

Strumming (*Rasgueado*)

With a strong rhythmic character and a varied typology, spanning from flamenco to Latin American traditional dances, *rasgueado* testifies to the rich folk heritage of the guitar. This technique went hand in hand with the resurgence of the "plucked guitar" during the Baroque period. (Exs. 2.75)

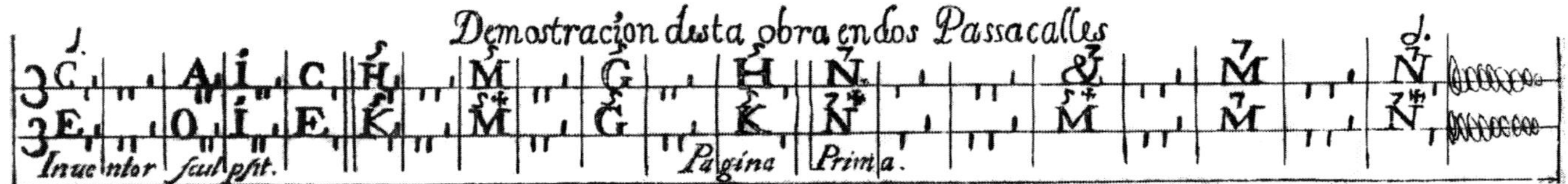

Baroque Guitar Tablature (Italian Alphabet). Engraving (detail) of *Instrucción de música sobre la guitarra española...* by Gaspar Sanz (Zaragoza, 1674). The letters indicate chords, while up and down marks on the line show the strum direction in a triple meter.

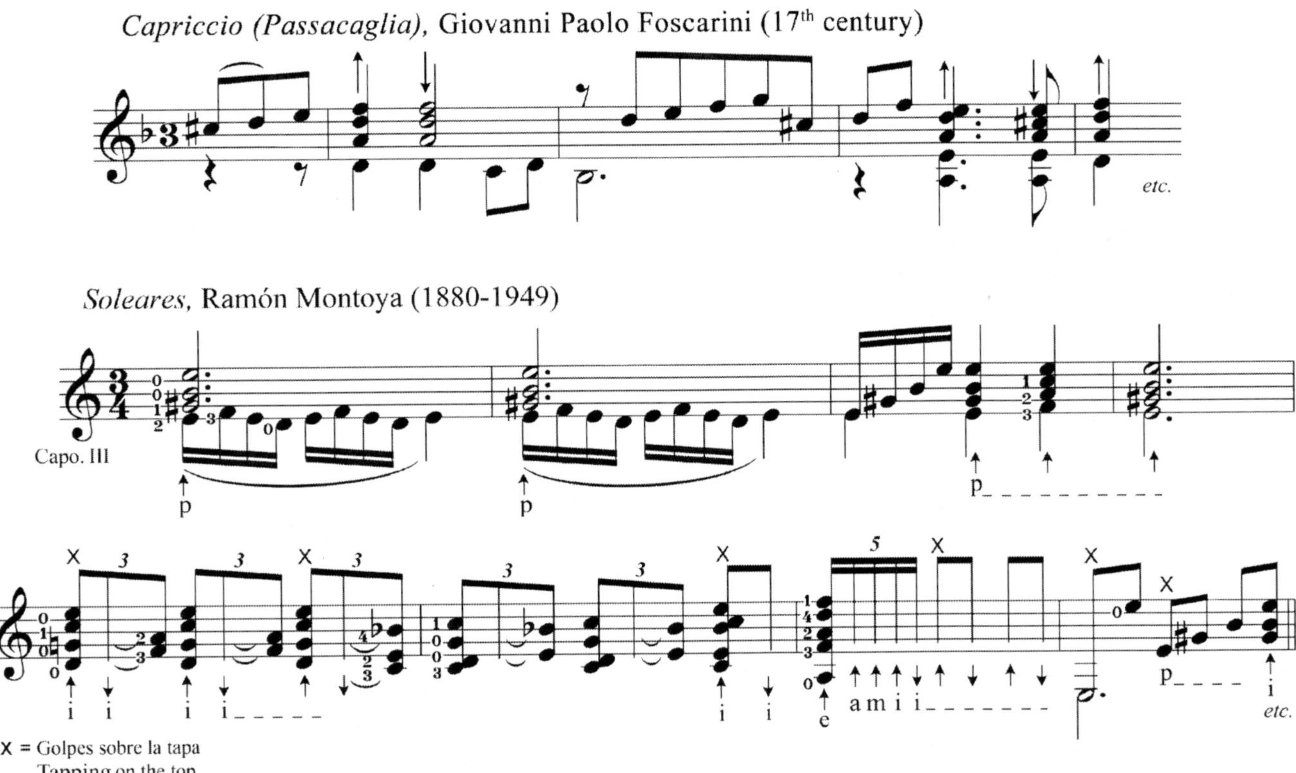

We will only discuss essential elements of rasgueado, taking for granted the wide range of forms and nuances that strumming assumes.

Emilio Pujol classifies strumming as normal or common, *rayado* or dry, *graneado* (grainy), and *double* or continuous. Except for the thumb, normal strumming consists of striking the strings with the backs of the nails. Dry rasgueado (or *rayado*) is produced by a sharp blow of the fingers or thumb on the strings, with its resulting sounds almost always heard simultaneously (See Pujol, 1971:138).

Rayado is symbolized by straight arrows that indicate its direction, and can be performed with one or with more fingers at once if a faster attack is desired. The thumb strikes with the hand rotation, followed by the index or *a-m-i* moving in the opposite direction. (Ex. 2.76)

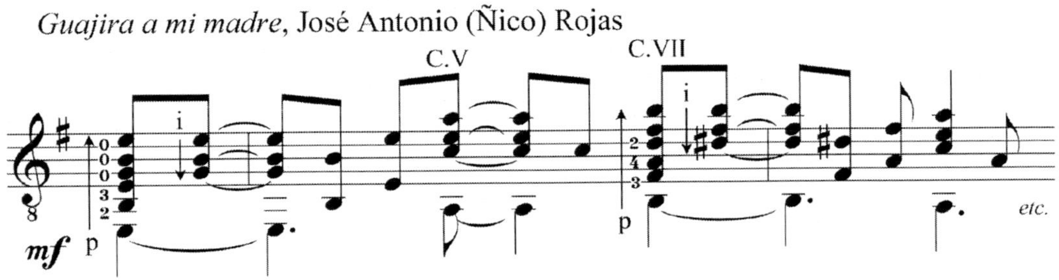

The use of dry strumming with the thumb heightens the Hispanic sonority in several passages of Fernando Sor's compositions. (Exs. 2.77)

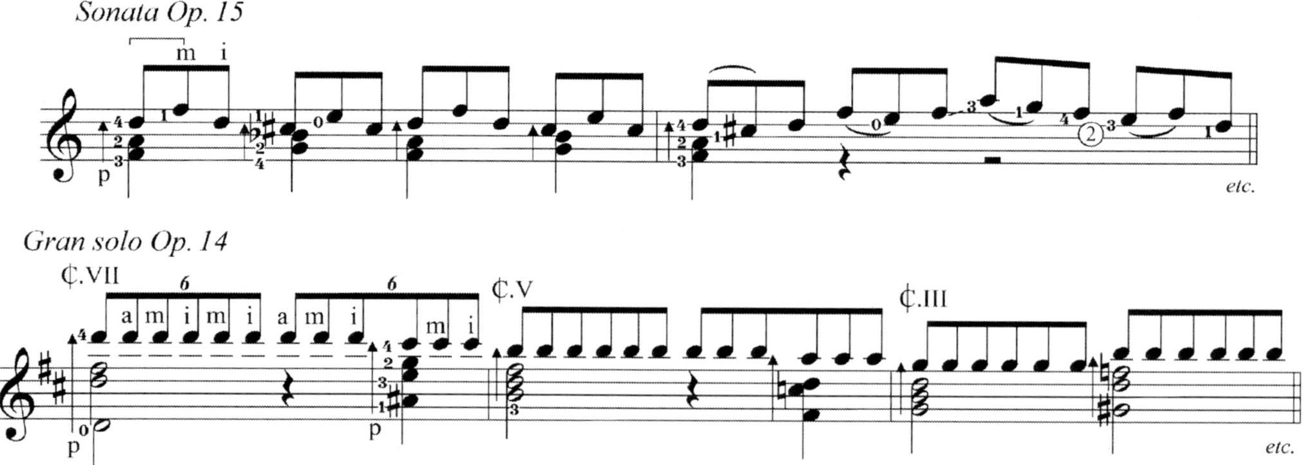

Let's examine some traditional Latin American basic rhythm schemes where *rayado* alternates with percussive taps on the fretboard. (Exs. 2.78)

Graneado strumming differs from *rayado* in the consecutive deployment of the fingers. Simple strum patterns from the ring finger or the pinky are also executed with a progressive rotation of the hand toward the thumb, which can be previously planted, supporting the stability of *i-m-a-e*. The fingers strike the strings from their closest point, ensuring the resonance of all chord notes. (Exs. 2.79)

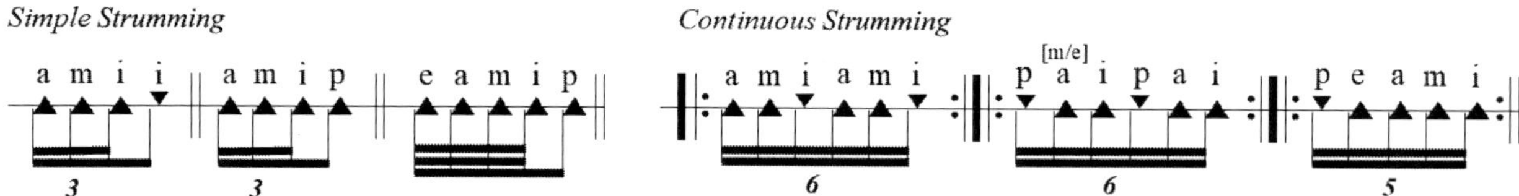

At the ending of *Sonata Op. 61* by Joaquin Turina, *continuous* (or *round*) and simple strumming can be applied, for which the use of fingernails is favorable due to their light touch on the strings. (Ex. 2.80)

Usually, strumming notation is rhythmically accurate but only approximate in terms of actual execution. Thus, it is up to the performer to determine the means of execution within the style and character of each piece.

Observe the difference between the original notation and its possible execution in *Sonata a la Española* by Joaquin Rodrigo. (Ex. 2.81)

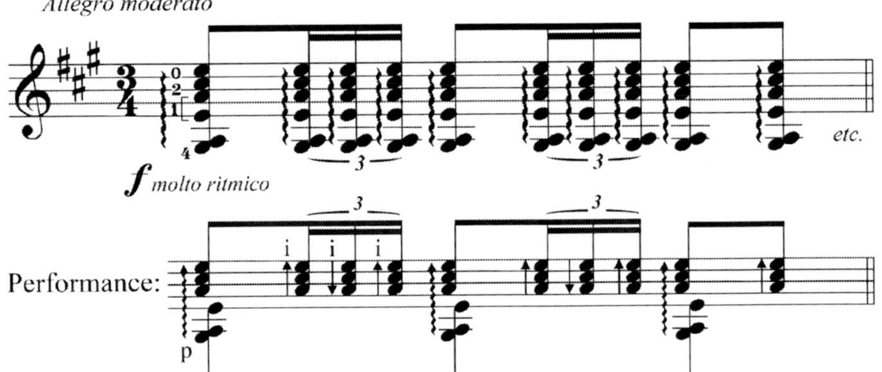

Preparatory Exercises

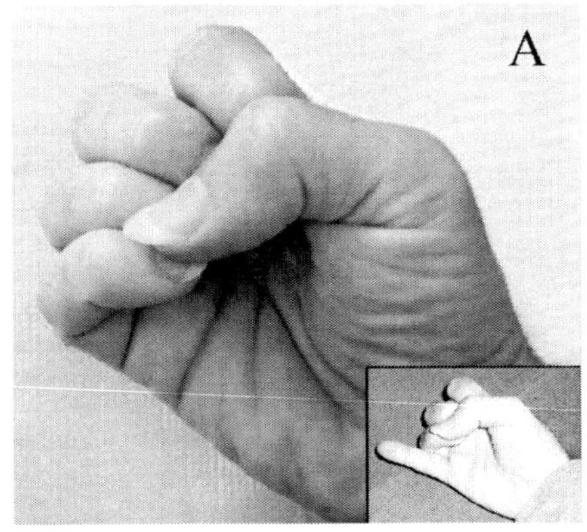

Unlike standard plucking, which mainly employs the flexor muscles, in strumming, the muscles involved with rasgueado are the extensors. A preparatory exercise for rasgueado consists of curling *i-m-a-e* and bracing them against the thumb to later flick them out evenly from the little finger to index with moderate force (Photo A).

Without actually playing the guitar, practice a number of repetitions with precise rhythm, and increase the speed gradually. Avoid fatigue with brief pauses. The aim of this exercise is to develop coordination and to progressively tone up musculature. (Ex. 2.82)

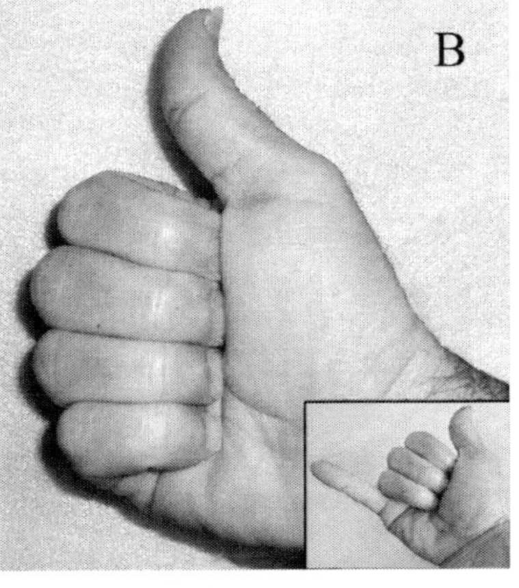

After a few days of practice, repeat the above sequence, now bracing the fingers against the *thenar eminence* in the palm (Photo B) (See Appendix I).

The next step is to practice the finger releases striking the strings, strumming slowly at first, one finger at a time and later increasing the pace, strumming fast with a slight rotation of the hand.

Continuous strumming –distinctive of flamenco style– can be performed with different finger combinations covering a greater or smaller number of strings: *p-e-i, p-a-i, p-m-i, p-a-m-i, p-e-a-m-i*, etc.

Control of the upward "turnaround" strokes with the thumb (*p-e, p-a*, or *p-m*) requires flexible hand rotation with minimal forearm displacement. (Exs. 2.83)

Functional Relaxation in Strumming

The flexibility of muscle tone is an indispensable component in strumming, whose rapid and sustained mobility involves complex muscle function.

Just as the extensor muscles help in reestablishing the round and relaxed position of the fingers after plucking, in the case of rasgueado, the balancing task is performed by powerful flexors.

Basic elements of standard plucking, including short rests between strums (work/rest cycle) and metric accentuation, are essential for precision, effort management and free mobility in the execution of strumming.

Let's examine the original rasgueado notation in three of Joaquin Rodrigo's scores, along with suggestions for their actual execution. (Exs. 2.84)

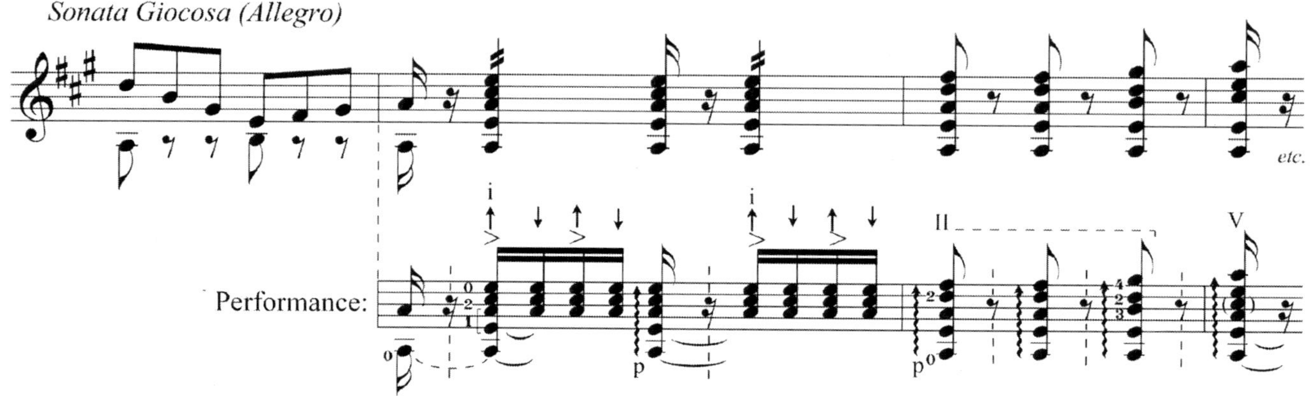

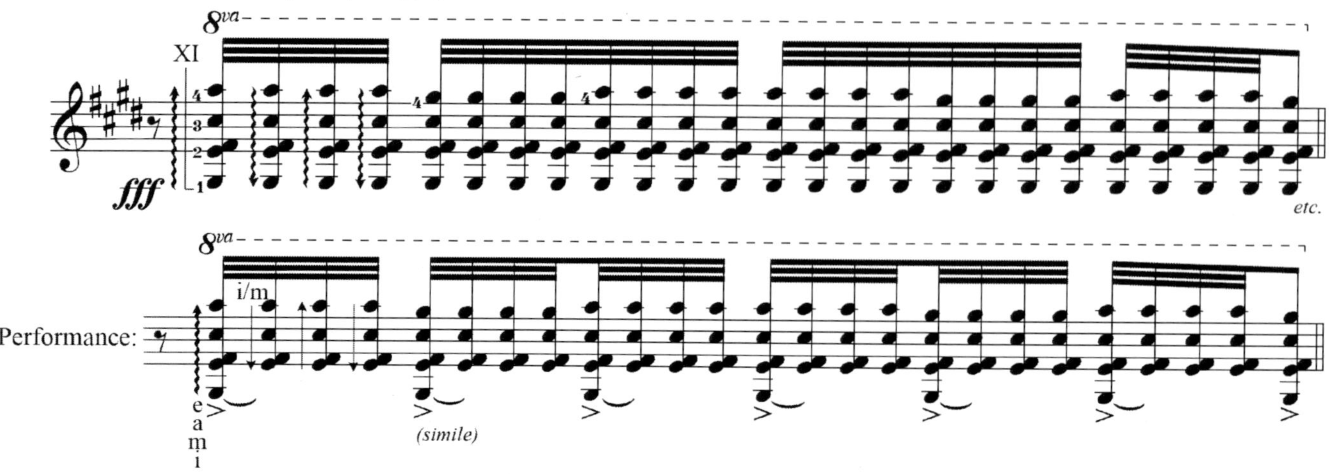

III. THE LEFT HAND

This instrument will be played with both hands,
the left one placed loose and free to run up to the last fret...
FERNANDO FERANDIERE
Arte de tocar la guitarra española por música... Madrid, 1799

Require more skill than strength [to play the guitar] ...
FERNANDO SOR
Méthode pour la Guitare. Paris, 1830

To achievement of positive functional balance in playing the guitar demands permanent application of resources to economize effort. This is particularly true in the use of the left hand.

As in the previous chapter, we will begin with the analysis of the postural framework and the most natural attitudes in exercising mobility.

THE POSTURAL FRAME

Maximum efficiency in the left hand can be obtained by considering three biomechanical aspects of the limb: *Roundness of the Hand, Hand-Forearm Alignment/Control of the Arm Angles, and Hand Rotation/Control of Supination.*

HAND ROUNDNESS

The most efficient way of holding any object is achieved by curving the fingers towards the palm.

The rounded hand, being an expression of spontaneous relaxation, is also a model for work on the fretboard. This approach results in economy of effort and stability while pressing the strings (*pisado*) and consequently, greater operational independence for playing both linear segments and chord positions.

Let us consider a simple example when fretting a D minor chord, where using finger 4 instead of 3 prevents unnecessary tension and helps to preserve the roundness of the relaxed hand. Similar cases could be made for the A7 and G major chords in first position.[31] (Ex. 3.1)

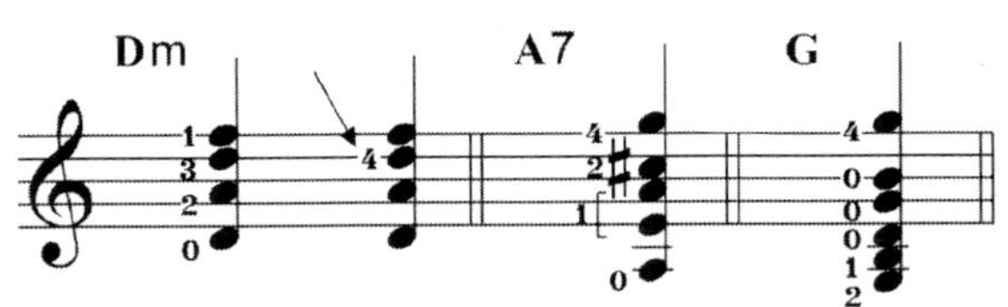

•

The use of fingering that "closes towards 1" brings stability and lightness in the following passages. (Exs. 3.2)

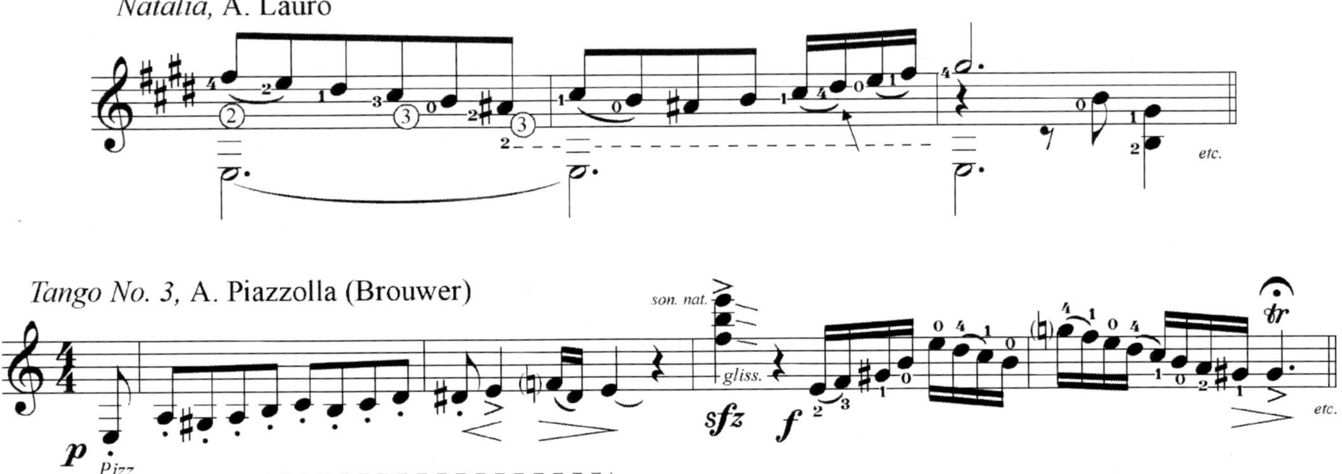

[31] *Position* or *quadruple*: Area of the four left-hand fingers placed on consecutive frets. The position is determined by the fret played by finger 1. Therefore, finger 4 placed on F (thirteenth fret on the first string) defines the tenth position.

Hand-Forearm Alignment/Control of the Arm Angles

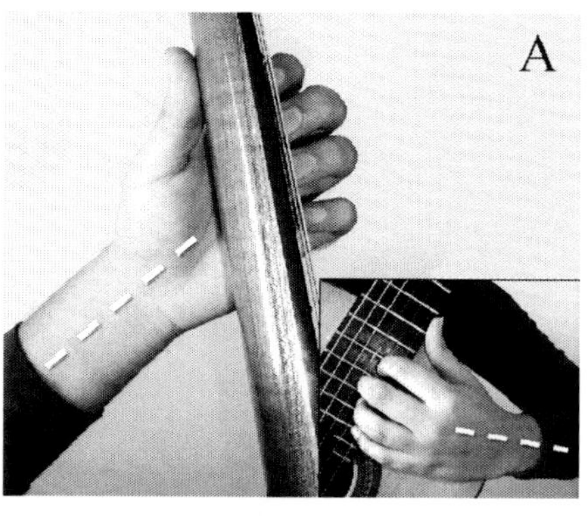

From the imaginary forearm-palm-middle finger axis, maintaining a flexible hand alignment in different positions is crucial for optimal functional capacity along the fretboard (Photo A).

Reinforced by an inadequate placement of the instrument, the habit of curving the wrist hampers mobility, and may injure this joint (Photo B). The carpal ganglion cyst frequently suffered by guitarists is a consequence of this negative practice.

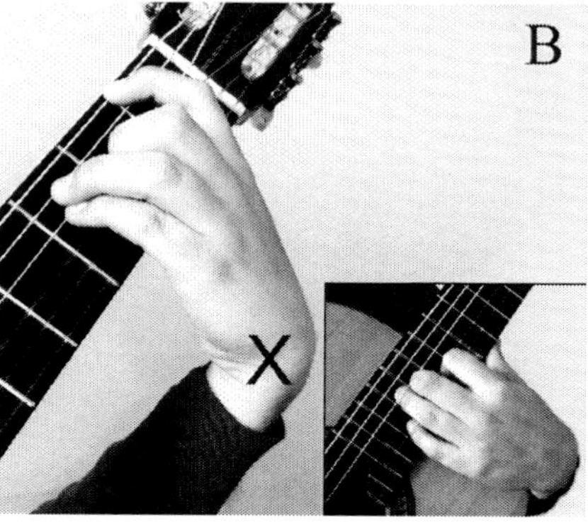

Preserving the hand-forearm alignment during performance requires dynamic control of the arm angles. The following series of actions (without the guitar in-hand) explains this process:

- With your right hand hold the left one closed into a fist on your chest.
- Next, move the hand a few inches forward and slightly to the left, *without moving other parts of the arm or torso.*

If you were holding the instrument, the hand would now be close to the fretboard middle-zone, with the wrist flexed.

- Note that to retrieve the hand-forearm alignment without altering this location; it will be necessary to lean the torso forward and to the left, simultaneously separating the elbow from the torso.

Likewise, as we move the hand toward the treble strings (transverse displacement), maintaining alignment requires moving the elbow backwards and out, gradually away from the torso. In addition, this procedure should include a hand rotation, which we will analyze next.

The following outline summarizes the biomechanical interaction of the three articular arm angles related to hand alignment during performance.

Angle:	Is modified by:
A (Wrist)	Altering B and C
B (Arm curvature)	Leaning the torso (left and forward)
C (Armpit)	Leaning the torso or moving the elbow

Once the benefits of the hand-forearm alignment have been experienced, our perception of comfort will dictate the necessary left-hand adjustments during performance. Here are some examples:

In this passage of *Prelude No. 1* by Tárrega it is favorable to readjust the elbow in two instances following the C major chord on beat 1 of the second measure.[32] (Ex. 3.3)

[32] From this point on we will use a more precise barré symbology. The superscripted number indicates the strings covered (I^5, II^3). Zero (I^0) means that pressing is done only with the first finger phalange (See *Barré in Advance*). Letter *h* designates a "hinge" barré.

In passages such as this from *Microestudio No. 12* by Abel Carlevaro, maintaining hand-forearm alignment requires a progressive leaning of the torso; this leaning tendency can be reduced by temporarily raising the guitar (especially from ninth position onwards) by lifting the heel. (Ex. 3.4)

The hand-forearm alignment does not necessitate wrist fixation, but it favors its eventual use. As we will see, during position shifts (mostly towards the first position), the alignment is interrupted to promote relaxation and fluent mobility.

Hand Rotation/Control of Supination

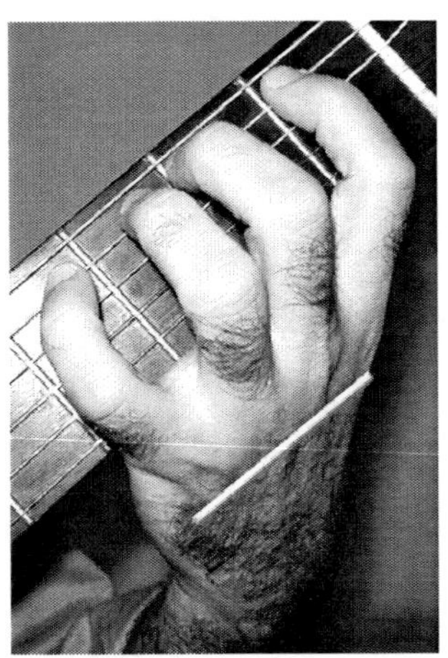

Unlike pianists, who comfortably pronate both hands to play, we guitarists are forced to supinate our left hand to fret the instrument (See Appendix I).

A common "geometric approach" to guitar teaching holds that we should always keep the palm parallel to the edge of the fretboard. While the objective is to keep the fingers near the strings, this permanent frontal disposition generates a significant amount of tension in the forearm, interferes with the natural roundness of the hand, and restricts mobility in position shifts.

As the guitar neck is raised, supination is reduced, but there is still another possibility for the hand: to "let it turn" until the area of the palm near the metacarpal joint of finger 1 contacts the edge of the fretboard; this can be achieved by simply relaxing the forearm.

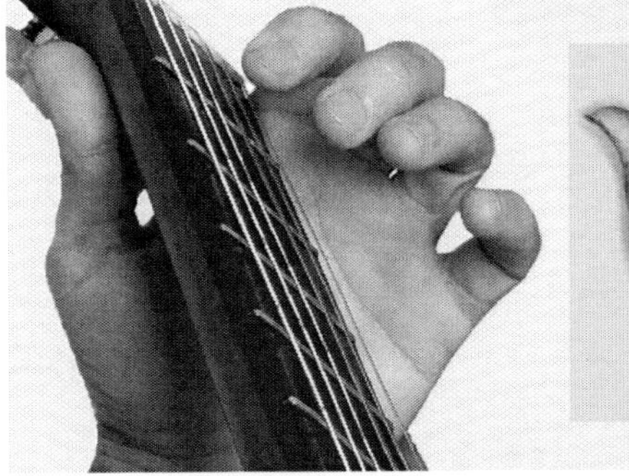

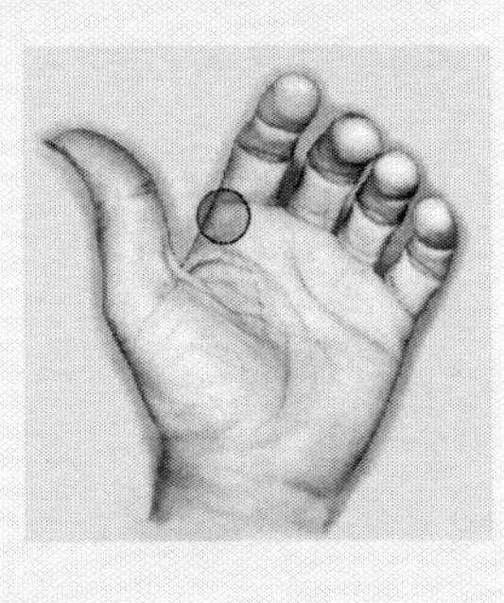

We have mentioned the importance of identifying each postural disposition, not only formally but perceptively. Control of supination does not consist of imitating the "violinist's hand." This would be a justified taboo if we were unaware of how to optimize energy during performance.

In addition to pronosupination, another way to rotate the hand is produced indirectly by approaching or separating the elbow from the torso with the hand and forearm aligned. Naturally linked, both maneuvers are associated with relaxation, and support ease and control of displacements due to their important functional gains (See *Movement Transmission in Longitudinal Shifts*).

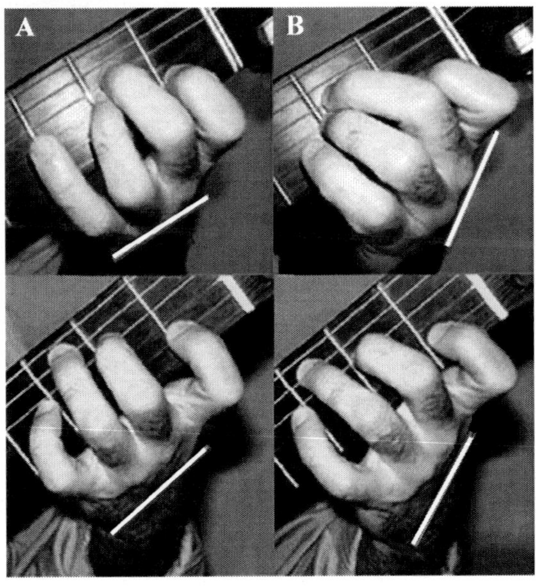

Observe the slight rotation in two chord positions (Photo B). The gentle lean of the hand favors relaxation, flexible opening of the fingers, and lighter fretting.

Besides the above-mentioned "parallel-to-the-strings disposition," there is the tendency to avoid contact with the edge of the fretboard. This avoidance normally happens when fretting the first three strings, but becomes uncomfortable as we progress lower from the fourth string (sometimes from the third string) since the fingers are forced to flatten, breaking of roundness and often bending the wrist, which increases the fretting effort.

Reducing supination allows easy access to the treble strings from the tenth position on. Otherwise it would be necessary to abruptly move the arm forward in front of the soundboard. (Exs. 3.5)

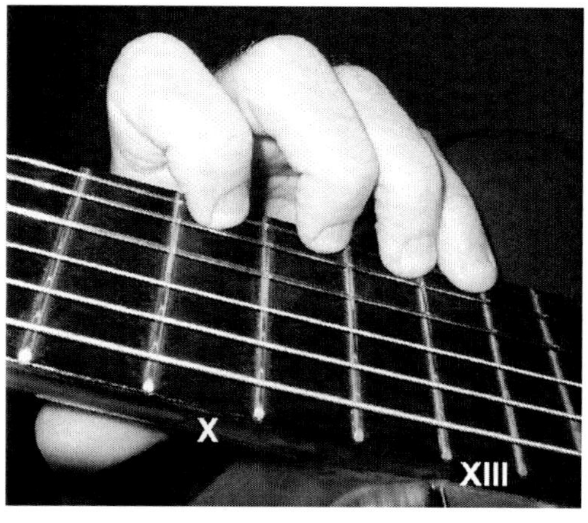

Minué Op.11 No.6, F. Sor

Progressive rotation of the hand sets up comfortable transverse mobility. (Ex. 3.6)

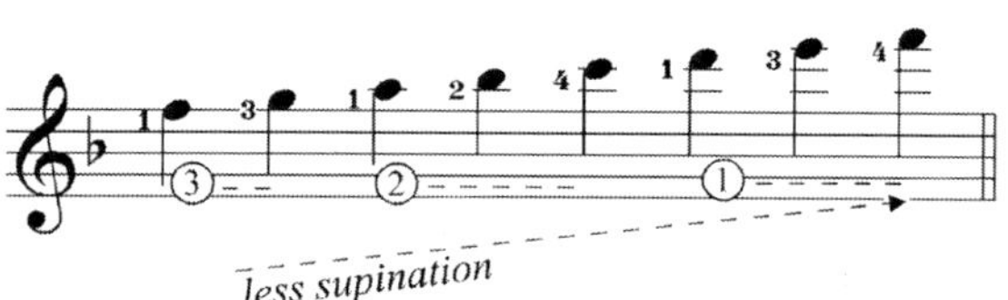

The habit of relaxing the hand whenever possible, resuming the rounded shape with minimum supination, favors a permanent economy of effort. Following this indispensable "body logic" can make the difference between enjoying the performance or experiencing a current discomfort, when, despite our continued efforts, our results are not directly correlated with the energy and time devoted to practice.

Left-Hand Sensopostural Pattern

The following sequence of actions integrates the above-mentioned biomechanical aspects with two basic perceptions in performance: *weight* and *flotation*.

• With the guitar comfortably held, drop the left arm for a few minutes to experience its weight through relaxation.[33] Relax your shoulders and lean your head forward. Hold the instrument with your right arm resting on the upper side.

• Then slowly raise your relaxed left hand (aligned with the forearm and with supination reduced) until it is level with the guitar neck, and hold it there for a few seconds focusing your attention on that apparent weightless of the arm known as *flotation*, which results from a sustained balance between various muscle groups.[34]

• Next, while maintaining relaxation, move the thumb slightly away, just enough to clear a space for the neck and fretboard to "enter" the hand (without altering the fingers) until the hand makes contact with the edge of the neck at the point near the first joint of the index, as previously described.

• The last action will be to place the fingers on the strings without pressing them. This will be the moment to define the necessary energy for an effective *pisado* (pressure on the string).

Remember that activating the sensopostural patterns *at the beginning and during study* helps to establish the advantages of our physiology as permanent guidelines in performance.

•

[33] Experiencing weight is a way to regulate the state of tension, and also contributes to psychic relaxation. Our motor function unfolds under conditions imposed by gravity and its effect, weight, whose perception is linked to the handling of balance. We will study the use of this "passive energy" as a means to reduce the fretting effort.

[34] This sensation is the result of a slight contraction of the arm abductors working together with the scapular muscles, mainly the trapezius and the rhomboid. (See Iznaola, 2000:48).

The Placement-Release Cycle

We will next study a three-step sequence of left-hand mobility on the fretboard that links different technical procedures and resources:

1. Contact with the strings: Balanced positioning. Planting on linear passages.
2. Pressing (*Pisado*): Minimum pressure. Flotation. Use of weight.
3. Relax and Release: The position shift begins by relaxing the hand.

1. Contact with the Strings

During performance, for a gentle encounter with the strings before pressing, it is necessary to first cushion the inertia of position changes on the fretboard. This is made possible by the use of semicircular movements of the hand, and by the application of different resources for economy of effort and precision that we will discuss below.

Contact and string-pressing should occur immediately behind the fret (as long as an extension is not required). This way, the sound is clearly defined by exerting minimal pressure.

Balance of Positioning

Preserving the roundness of the hand while playing allows the best use of the "curvilinear force" of the fingers by means of a vertical pisado on the string. In turn, a control of fretting and shifts demands a defined balance in which the placement of the thumb plays a decisive role.

Thumb Placement

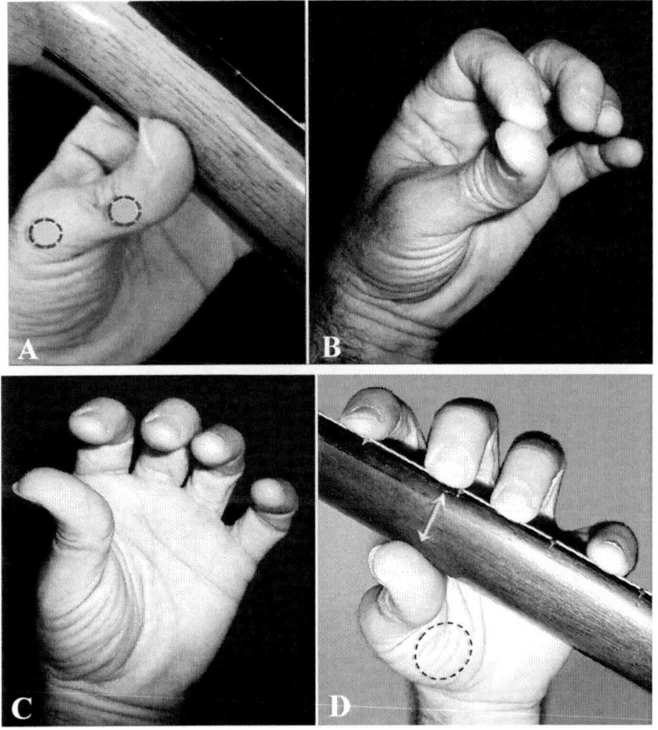

In its regular position, the thumb contacts the neck towards its inner side, thereby partially fixing its middle and distal joints, which flex in a different direction to the one induced by this contact (Photo A).

The thumb contact point with the neck is near its natural encounter with the tip of index (Photo B).

Palm View

By placing the thumb ahead of finger 1 (or between 1 and 2), balanced control of pressure can be achieved (Photo C).

By contrast, placing the thumb directly opposite finger 2 (or between 2 and 3 toward the middle of the palm) generates tension throughout the hand, an effect that is especially noticeable on the thenar eminence zone (Photo D). Generally, extensions force this dislocation, and flatten the thumb, which requires additional work to immobilize its joints.[35]

[35] Urshalmi reminds us that thumb placement is often neglected by teachers, who cannot observe because they are always seated in front of their students. (Urshalmi, 2006:86)

Side View

The rectangle in figure A suggests an estimated area of balance between the thumb and finger 1 from a relaxed position of the hand. Hand roundness and position balance are disrupted by a static positioning of the thumb in transverse shifts (Fig. B), or when the thumb is displaced from the center in barré positions (Fig. C), which we are forced to do when playing from the ninth position.

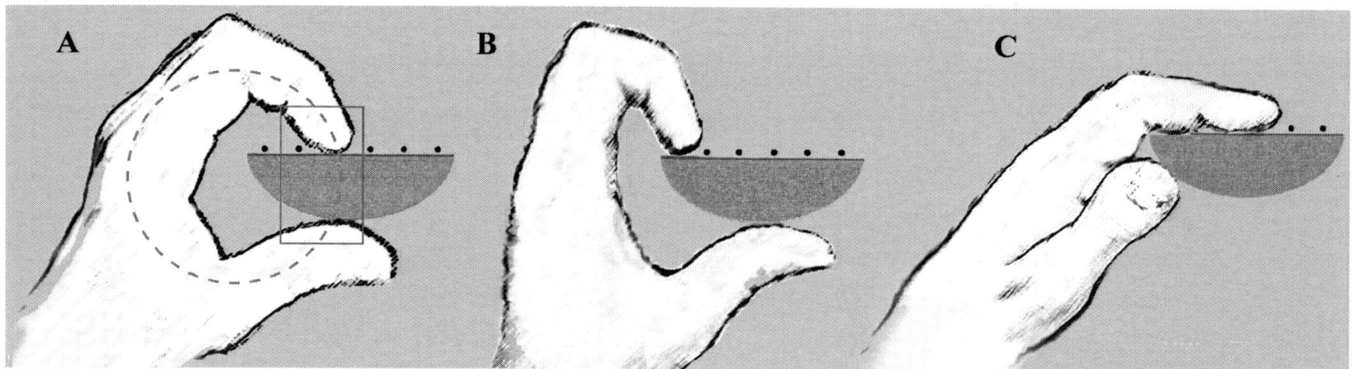

The roundness of the hand is also disrupted by the pronounced concavity of the metacarpal joints, which is associated with a fixed "frontal disposition" that hinders the fluidity of fingering.

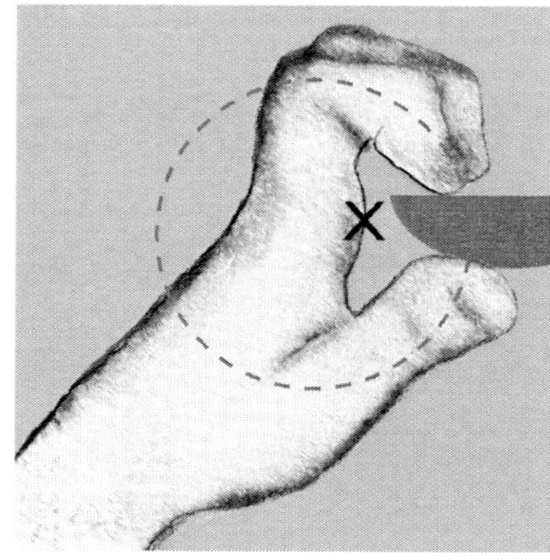

Thumb Position Readjustments

The work of the left hand requires constant readjustments, even while in the same fretboard position. As mentioned earlier, once the postural aspects that favor balance and economy of effort have been assimilated, habitual perception of these factors will dictate the best use of each resource.

In addition to providing relaxation, any release of string pressure facilitates a readjustment of the thumb (*Etude Op. 6 No. 9* by Sor). This maneuver contributes to guaranteeing the necessary stability for slurs (*Etude Op. 38 No. 18* by Coste). (Exs. 3.7)

Etude Op. 6 No. 9, Fernando Sor

Etude Op. 38 No. 18, Napoleón Coste

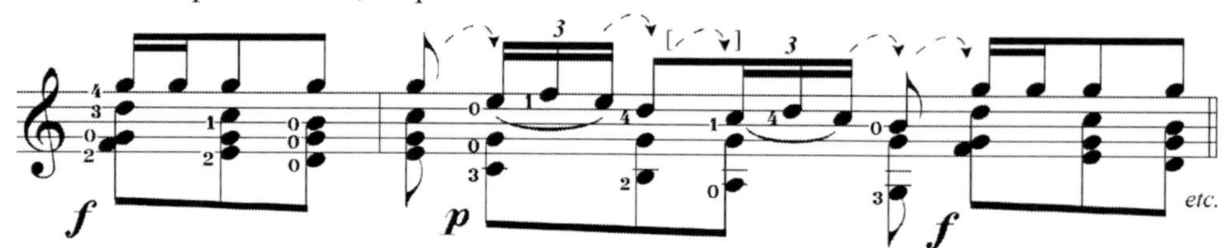

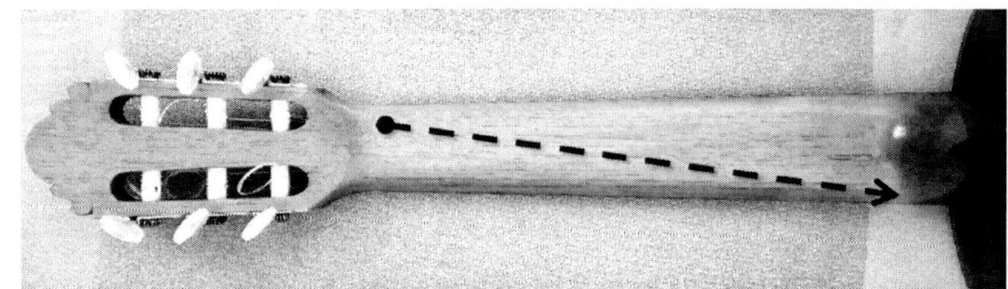

In ascending scale passages played toward the soundbox, the thumb glides diagonally across the back of the neck towards the side of the fingerboard.

From the thirteenth position, the thumb can be placed along the joint of the neck with the soundbox, so the palm contact with the side of the upper bout preserves the roundness and alignment of the hand for balanced vertical finger pressure.

In large position shifts that leap toward the soundbox, the thumb can be lifted from the neck or slide smoothly along it, but in the opposite direction it is more favorable to lift it. Only in playing glissandi and portamenti is a slight contact advisable in both directions.

The thumb can also function as an axis of movement in short partial shifts. A typical example is the fast alternation of two chords in *Prelude No. 1* by H. Villa-Lobos. (Ex. 3.8)

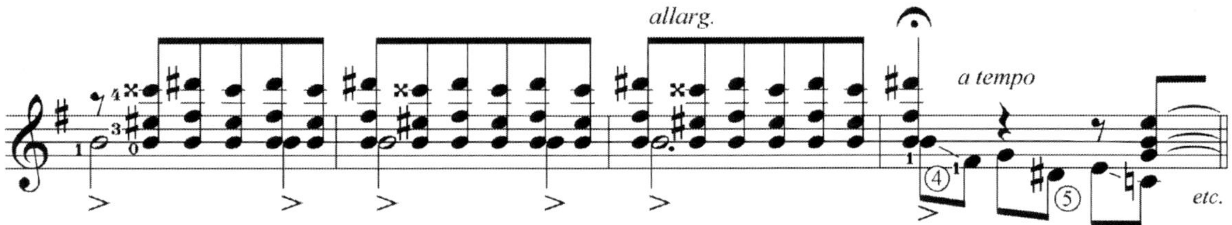

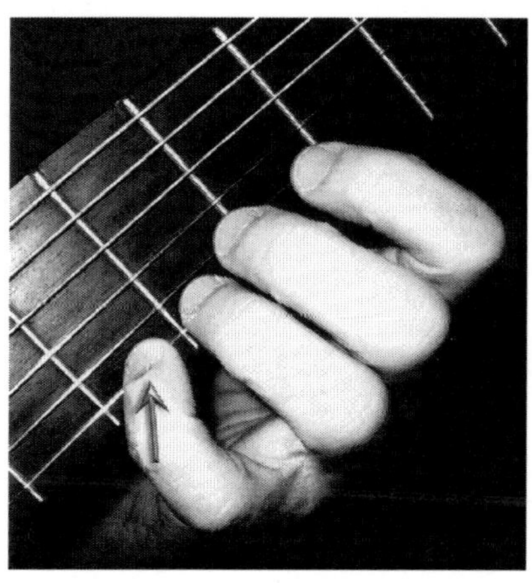

Placement of Finger 4

Frequently, young beginners have weak fingers, in particular the little finger.

As in thumb placement, finger 4 may be slightly inclined to firm up the middle and distal joints, both in chord positions and in melodic lines. This small inclination is also recommended for finger 1. The curving of both fingers is spontaneously required when we hold a spherical object, such as a baseball.

Planting in linear passages

As in the right hand, the effective mobility of the fingers comprises an elementary coordination. In the left hand, planting on linear passages does more than consolidate balance and economize movement. It bears witness to a clear functional regularity: *It is easier to move the fingers together rather than separately.* For these reasons, planting should be practiced from the very beginning of learning to play the instrument.

Let's analyze a simple planting example in the C major scale in first position. When ascending, finger 2 (E) remains in position when 3 is placed and is only released, together with 3, when plucking G (3rd open string). When descending, both fingers are placed at the same time on the 4th string (F-E). (Ex. 3.9)

During string changes, keeping the fingers in position as much as possible supports both stability and legato (sustain of resonance).

The continuous line in the following examples indicates effective fretting. The dashed line represents surface contact or sliding over the strings. (Ex. 3.10)

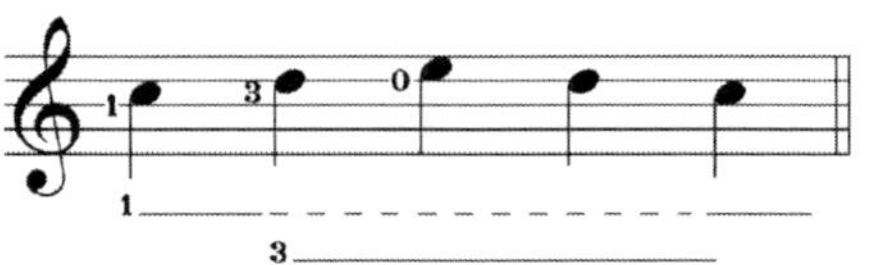

Given its proximity to the thumb, the index finger (1) is crucial for hand function, and especially for balance in fingering, as a safety factor.

Divergent vectors of force determine the unstable balance that occurs when finger 1 ceases to press in thumb-index opposition. The resulting imbalance needs to be compensated by more muscular work. Although it is not an exceptional case, the example below shows the value of planting, whose regularity has a significant importance in performance. (Ex. 3.11)

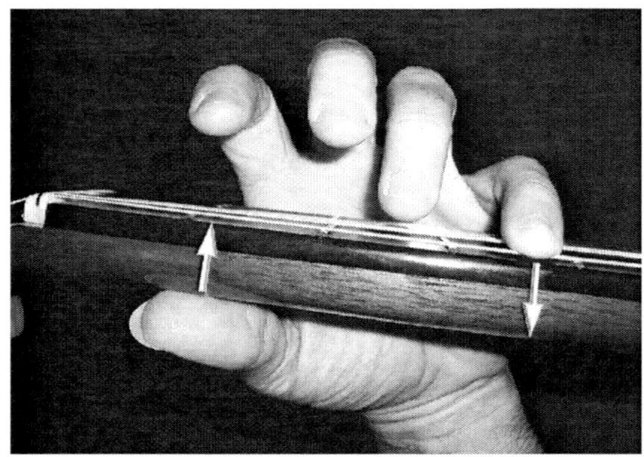

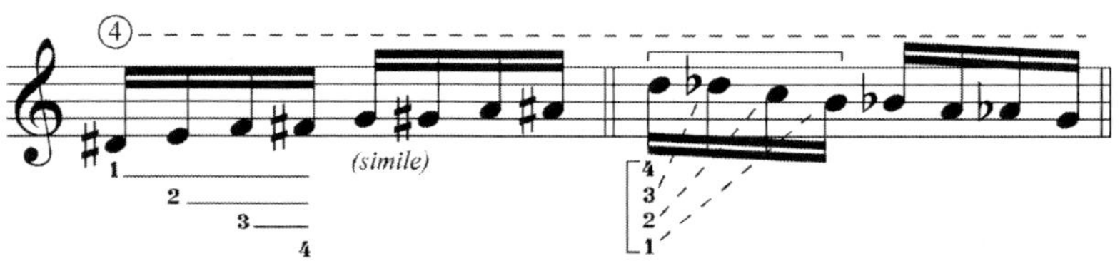

Let's examine the handling of planting from the perspective of finger 1, which may include sliding over the string's surface (as in glissandi), preserving the finger's location within the quadruple (span of four frets). (Exs 3.12)

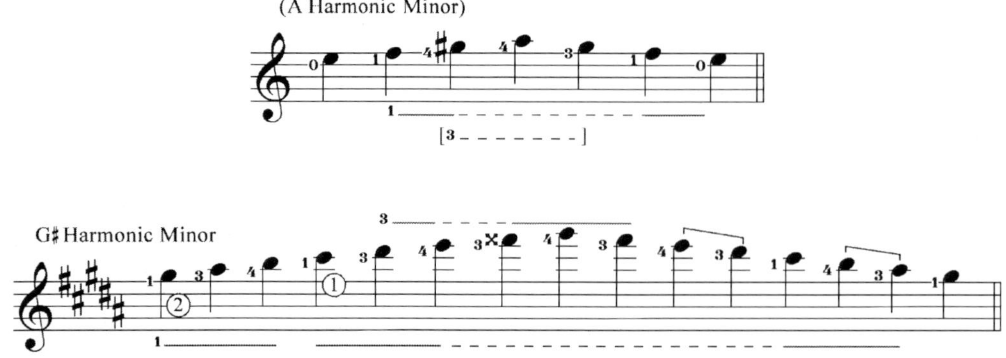

In the next E minor scale, after playing B on the 1st string when ascending, finger 1 keeps its position until the transition from G to F♯ on the 2nd string. Notice that it also remains briefly placed in transverse shifts toward the basses. (Ex. 3.13)

In the vigorous endings of both *Soleares* (*Homenaje a Tárrega,* Op. 69) by Turina, and *Arpa del Guerrero* (from *Decameron Negro* by Leo Brouwer), planting guarantees a balanced mobility along with an effective *legato*. (Exs. 3.14)

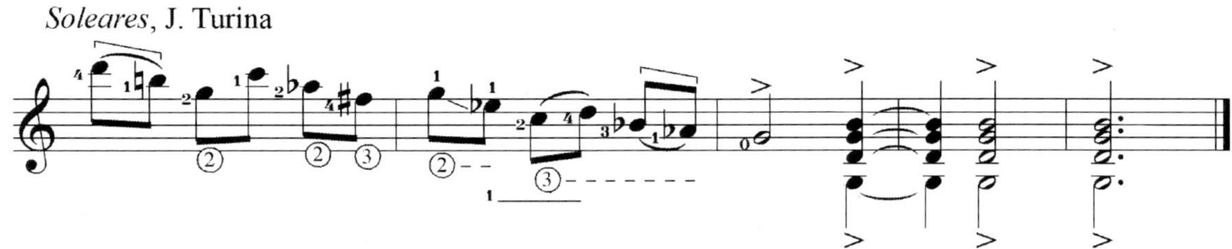

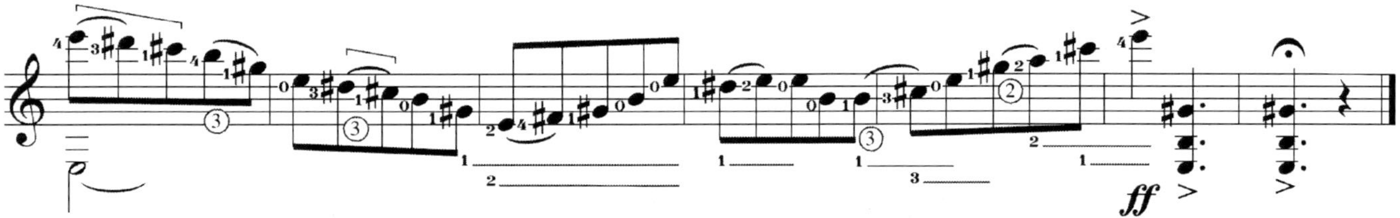

2. Finger Pressure *(Pisado)*

The transit from contact with the strings to pressing on them should follow an ancient Oriental precept: *Smoothness precedes force*. We would only specify in this case …*necessary effort instead of force.*

Aguado thus describes his perception of a light *pisado*:

> When this fine degree of pressure has been found it feels like tickling at the fingertips... (Aguado, 1849:13)

The innate grasp reflex develops from birth until we acquire the habit of using only the necessary energy to hold an object. Similarly, while fretting the strings we must try to apply only the necessary pressure for a clear and defined sound. Excessive pressing obstructs mobility, and is harmful in the short term.

With the habit of optimal finger pressure, favored by the already mentioned flotation awareness, the fingertips show a polished and even surface, while a profuse callosity is associated with a continuous surplus of exertion.

Identifying the minimum pressure required to achieve a clear sound is easy. Simply place a finger vertically just behind the fret, and gradually increase the pressure on the string while plucking it repeatedly, until the note begins to sound clearly. The double nature of this simple exercise –mechanical and sensoperceptive– can notably favor our development on the fingerboard.

Frequently, improper positioning of the instrument, of the hand, or of the entire arm forces us to overfret in order to produce a clear sound.

Exertion of pisado may vary depending on the complexity of passages, but we usually tend to increase it when plucking harder. Urshalmi suggests the practice of intentionally causing notes to buzz by applying minimal pressure, promoting economy of effort through active relaxation (Urshalmi, 2006:75).

Weight and Flotation

It is clear that flotation is a basic component of the left-hand technique. In addition, the weight of the arm compensates pressure as an aid in fretting and favors mobility.

Characteristic of an advanced mechanism, this resource is particularly effective in fixed chord positions –especially with the barré– and shifts toward the soundbox.

> We almost always use our muscles to counteract their own weight due to the effects of gravity. However, the guitar offers us an outcome, a force opposite to weightiness that can help the body without appealing to useless contractions ... For example, in the left arm the elbow naturally pulls down the hand by the action of its weight. ... With a proper use of this resource the effort can be lessened to avoid tension...
>
> The guitar is the ground, and the movement of the arms, the earthly attraction. The result is a force that we feel innately, but not in an intellectual manner. Playing the guitar will no longer be the work of the hands but of the whole body.
>
> Oscar Ghiglia[36]

The use of weight is conditioned by the height of the position, the placement of the hand on the fretboard, and the tempo or frequency of shifts. Use of weight also requires a flexible placement of the thumb. It is not possible to synchronize this resource with extensions or with the traditional placement of the instrument where the left arm is pulled back and outside of its most comfortable and efficient area, which is forward.

The slight bending of the wrist shown in the photo below seems to contradict the recommended alignment principle (valid for flotation), but as we will see, this momentary fixation of the hand does not hinder its mobility during execution if we follow the three steps of the Placement-Release Cycle.

The use of weight is ideal in *Etudes No. 1* and *4* by Villa-Lobos given the profusion of fixed chord positions. (Obviously, for position shifts it will be necessary to resume flotation briefly.)

In the descending diminished-chords passage of *Etude No. 1,* weight can easily be applied from the seventh or sixth position. (Ex. 3.15)

Etude No.1, H. Villa-Lobos

With the use of weight we alleviate the effort of the left-hand thumb. The weight vectors resolve mainly on the thigh, without affecting the instrument. This mechanism should not be confused with a forced pulling back of the neck, which turns this segment into a lever whose thrust against the right forearm support point creates an uncomfortable instability.

Linked to the control of relaxation in performing, the use of weight becomes another expression of the work/rest cycle, which together with other resources for economy of effort must be pre-established during the study of every score.

---

[36] Alain Riou: "Rencontre avec Oscar Ghiglia," *Les Cahiers de la Guitare*, no. 33.

3. Release (Relax) and Exit

In melodic passages, relaxation is carried out by transferring the pressure towards the finger on the "active note," while the other fingers are relaxed without separating then from the strings.

Except for glissandi, position shifts begin by releasing pressure until it is completely gone. A way to support this process is feeling how the strings "return to us" the energy previously applied.

Once the pressure is released, the vertical exit of the fingers favors the execution of curvilinear (or ballistic) movement on longitudinal shifts, a more economical and functional motion than the straight line. The benefit of curvilinear mobility –especially in shifts toward the first position– is that the main work is performed at the beginning of the movement, which then continues due to inertia. In addition, the vertical exit of the fingers prevents friction on the wound basses and its noisy effect.

Beyond the basic work with fingering, studying at a slow tempo is really useful when we also anticipate as much as possible what must ultimately happen –in mechanical terms– during performance, that is, with the proper tempo and musical character. This complex task is simplified as the most efficient sensopostural and mobility patterns are assumed.

The following illustration provides a summary of the left-hand Placement-Release Cycle which also frames the wider displacements or position shifts.

Placement-Release Cycle

Postural Frame

• *Hand Roundness*
• *Hand-Forearm Alignment/Control of the Arm Angles*
• *Hand Rotation/Control of Supination*

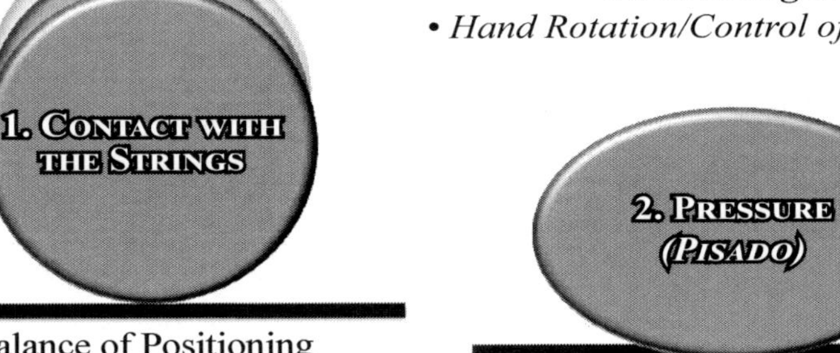

• Balance of Positioning
• Planting on Linear Passages

• Minimum Pressure
• Flotation
• Use of Weight

• The position shift begins by relaxing the hand

•

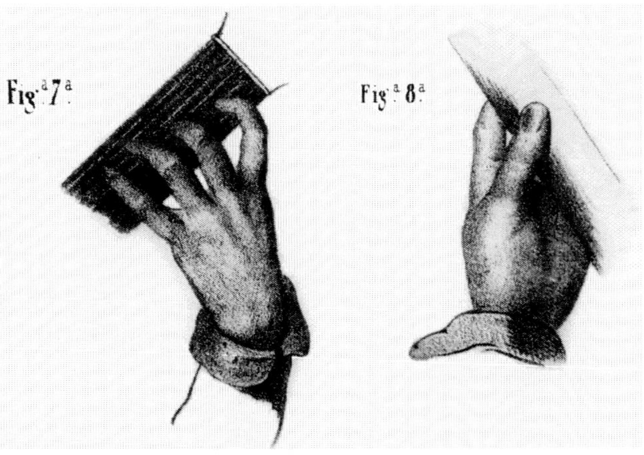

Engravings from Dionisio Aguado's Method (1849).

Position Shifts

During performance, as in everyday tasks, all actions that occur within physiological limits should give us intrinsically pleasant sensations.

Efficient mobility with the instrument favors both musical realization and our stage presence. While a tiring performance can only reflect agitation and distress, a fluent one will always support artistic communication. This leads us to the theme of gesture, which can be seen not only as the result of a free deployment in execution and a resource of "body memory," but as an expression of a creative connection with the instrument.[37]

As in dance, where all the steps are related, each shift of the left hand implies a harmonious linking of actions. It is necessary to consider the mechanism of displacements, its mobility as an integral part of fingering that, though being logical, can be hampered or fail if the shifts are not fluent enough.

Let's look at some factors in relation to this analysis:[38]

• Movement can be divided into three stages: *beginning*, *development*, and *end*. Although the highest importance is commonly given to development, for the instrumentalist, all phases are decisive.

• The weight-resistance (to gravity) relationship is a basic principle of movement, because a degree of muscular tension is required to overcome weight.

• When the applied energy exceeds the gravitational attraction, it can be said that muscle tension is resisting weight. If the energy is sufficient, the result will be a firm movement. If the required effort is minimal, the movement is perceived as loose and light.

• Shifts performed with mastery invariably have an easy deployment, without errors or interruptions cause by lack of coordination. The fluency of a movement is established by the characteristics of its spatial, dynamic and temporal development.

• Optimal dynamic execution presents progressive degrees of applied effort. Sudden start and abrupt changes between minimum and maximum muscle tension during movement are signs of poor fluency which may cause rhythmic disturbances as well.

• Fluid movements are not executed with sudden changes of speed, but with a gradual transition. Abrupt changes are evidence of lack of control and usually result in a poor performance.

• Ergonomic studies related to speed, precision, and economy of effort conclude that hand movements with a curvilinear trajectory are performed faster, more efficiently, and more coordinated than those with a straight line. In guitar performance, this principle is valid for longitudinal shifts, which occasionally must be executed with straight movements in glissandi and portamenti.

Types of Position Shifts

Carlevaro classifies position shifts as *total* and *partial* (1984:94).

A total position shift is performed with the arm-hand-fingers mechanism and the help of the back and shoulder muscles. Partial shifts involve only some of these components, i.e., thumb-fixing for a repeated oscillation between two intervals or chords. See Ex. 3.8, *Prelude No. 1* by H. Villa-Lobos, p. 71.

Position shifts may be performed in different ways: (Carlevaro, 1969:VII)

• By Substitution: When a finger (or fingers) replaces another at the same fret. This is typical in shifts to near positions.

• By Displacement: When the same finger (or fingers) establishes the new position after shifting.

• By Leap: The shift is performed without a slide or substitution, with no common element that serves as a guide for the shift.

[37] See Elena Esteban Muñoz: "When Gesture Sounds: Bodily Significance in Musical Performance," http://www.performancescience.org/ISPS2007/Proceedings/Rows/10EstebanMunoz.pdf.

[38] See Meinel, 1977:153-157.

Movement Transmission in Longitudinal Shifts

We can easily prove that moving the hands (arms) towards the body requires less effort than moving them away, and also that mobility on inclined planes is more complex than on horizontal or vertical ones. Thus, diagonal shifts towards the first position imply a difficulty that is only diminished by a suitable mobility of the arm.

A relaxed attitude in shifting positions brings into play the entire arm segments in a synergy that contributes to a spontaneous flexibility of movements. Position shifts must be made with smooth, undulating and weightless gestures, unlike moving the whole limb as a block, which happens when the displacement is initiated by the hand, involving a superfluous load.

While downward shifts have in their favor the weight and its associated relaxation, shifts towards the first positions require coordinated movement. This chain begins with a slight moving anticipation of the elbow that begins from the "launching" hand position, without affecting the duration of the note(s) (Photo 1). Preceded by this subtle "preparation for change," and once in the air with the relaxed wrist (2), the hand begins a curvilinear trajectory towards the new position (3), where it resumes its alignment with the forearm when the elbow height is readjusted (4).

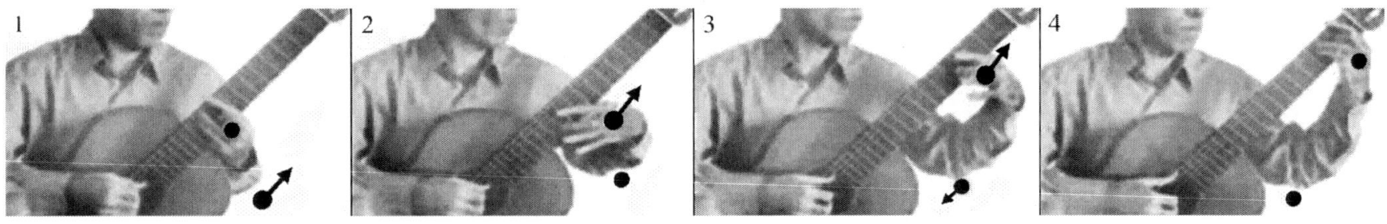

Shift toward the first position executed with curvilinear motion.

As previously mentioned, contrary to the concept of a fixed left-hand "frontal position," its easy rotation is part of a free linkage mobility that facilitates both work/rest alternation and ideal functional relaxation.[39]

The combined effect of longitudinal movement (semicircular) with hand rotation in shifts to both high and low positions produces an ease that is the result of seemingly shortened distances, like walking on an escalator. (Exs. 3.16)

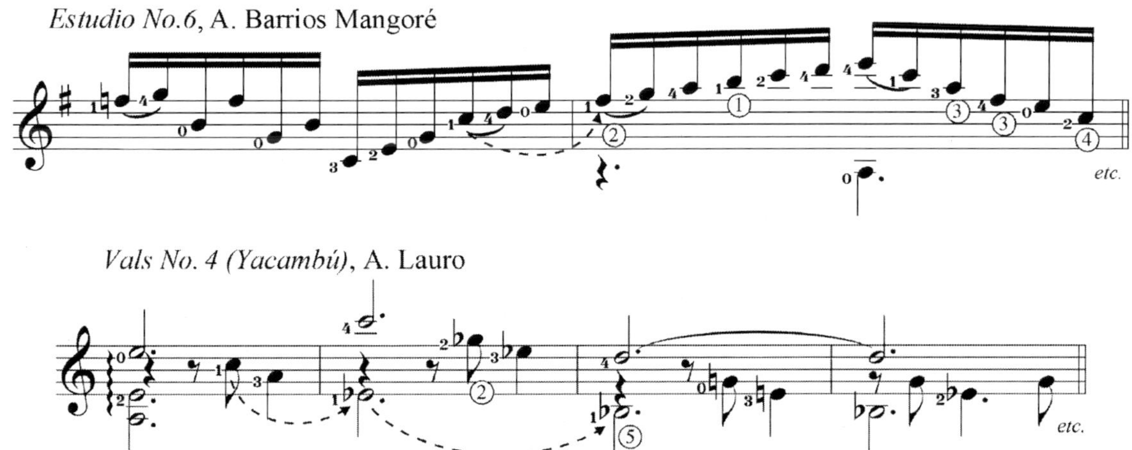

[39] Other ergonomic data reveals that rotational movements are faster than direct or straight ones (Zinchenko, 1985:293-295).

When moving to nearby positions, small turns of the hand reflect the relaxed disposition of the whole limb. In addition, superficial contact with the edge of the fretboard can serve as a guide, especially in larger shifts. (Ex. 3.17)

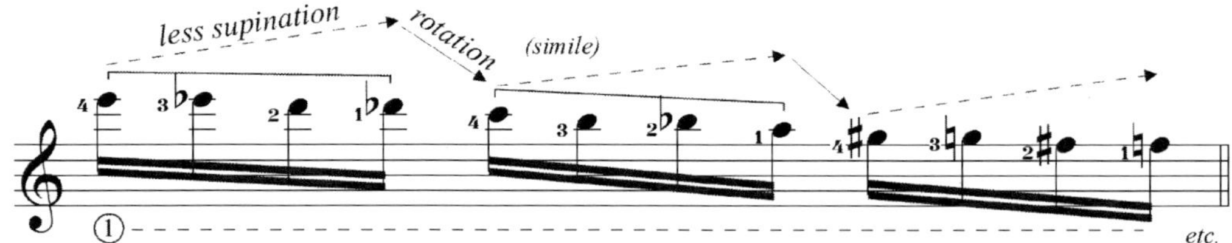

Students often keep the left hand rigid while shifting between intervals or chords of similar shape –especially barré chords– when it is more effective to briefly resume a relaxed disposition, which together with the concatenated movement of the arm, favors the new position.

Hand Presentation on the Fretboard and Transverse Shifts

Left-hand presentations (placement of the fingers in relation to the fretboard) are related to the specific elbow/arm positions needed to ensure alignment and the handling of supination in shifts.

Carlevaro describes three forms of presentation: *longitudinal, transverse*, and *mixed* (1984:63).

- Longitudinal: Fingers are aligned on the same string (low elbow, near the torso).
- Transverse: Pressing two or more strings at the same fret with elbow held back and away from torso.
- Mixed: Resulting from the assimilation and adjustment of previous presentations in a free form that is dependent on the particular demands of each score.

According to the following mixed presentations we can deduce the arm displacements (symbolized by the elbow location) for a relaxed positioning of the fingers.

a) Finger 4 on the 4th string: low elbow, near the torso.

b) Finger 1 on the 4th string: elbow back and away from the torso. (Exs. 3.18)

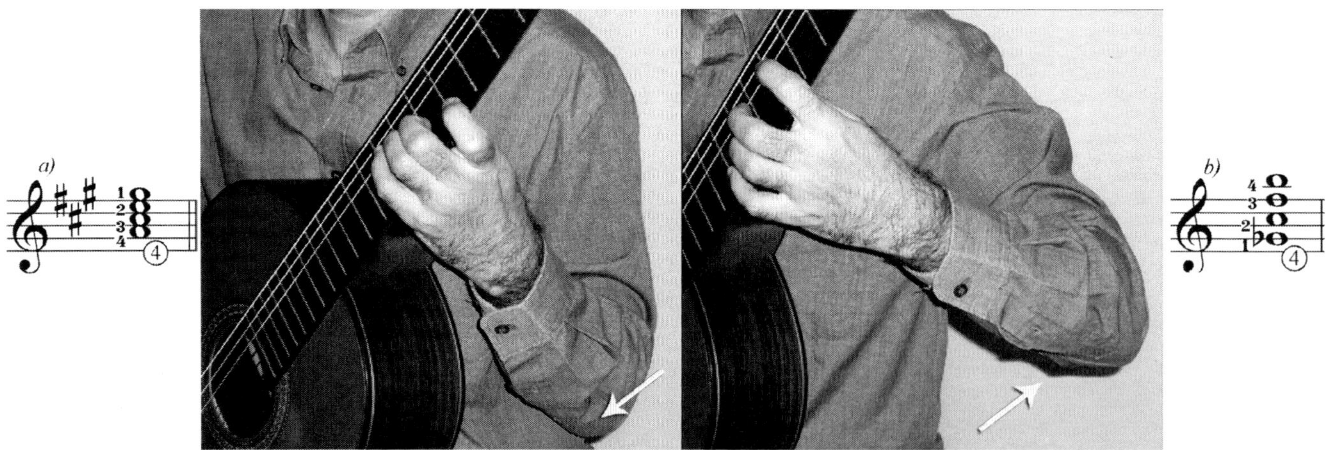

Mixed presentations.

The loose transit of the elbow (backward or forward) facilitates transverse shifts, and its simultaneous separation or approach to the torso –maintaining the arm-forearm alignment– also favors hand rotation. In linear passages with string changes, these adjustments are performed gradually.

In a short scale from 3rd to 1st string, the thumb works as an axis *(a)*, but in longer segments it will be necessary to slide it transversely *(b)*. (Exs. 3.19)

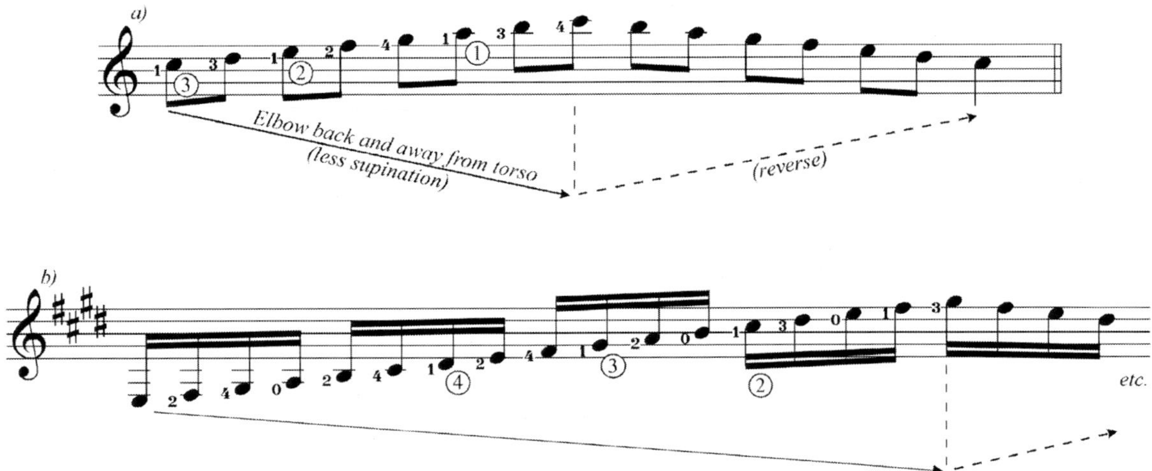

Studying these actions makes the habit of natural mobility possible, favoring the use of numerous resources to enrich the expressive discourse in every score.

> Art itself arises at the moment that this uninterrupted line is established, whether it be sound, voice, drawing or movement. As long as there are only sounds, note emissions and separate exclamations instead of music, or separate lines instead of coordinated movement, we will not be able to talk about music, singing, drawing or painting, dancing, architecture, sculpture or, ultimately, dramatic art.
>
> K. Stanislavski (1986:73)

Perceptual Guidelines for Mobility in Shiftings

Since confidence is a prerequisite of freedom [in performing], *it is confidence that one should stubbornly strive for, first of all.*
(Neuhaus,1973:88)

From the perspective of mobility, achieving a safe excution requires the use of various strategies during study. The following set of perceptive guidelines is suggested to stimulate precision and economy of movement in shifting positions.

Perception of Effort

• Beginning of movement: Pressure release (hand relaxation) and vertical exit. Nimbleness in resuming relaxation is related to placement balance.

• Displacements toward the soundbox: Effort release. Perception of weight or falling. Once tension is released, the arm weight can be used to assist movement.

• Displacements toward the lower (first) positions: Slight elbow movement in advance. "The arm leads the hand" with a concatenated transmission of semicircular movements and a relaxed wrist.

• End of movement: Soft contact with the strings followed by minimum pressure. Optional use of weight. Placement balance is supported by *planting* in linear passages.

Visual Orientation

Obviously important to the instrumentalist, visual-motor coordination is linked to the kinesthetic sense, which allows us to manage space through the perception of the surrounding area or edges of objects, information which is mainly provided by visual stimuli.

Frequent inaccuracy in shifting during practice reinforces the possibilities of "negative learning," in addition to other possible insecurity factors that are usually attributed to a lack of concentration.

Memory, the basis of all musical activity, is supported by the synthesis of different associated forms of observation: *auditory memory*, *motor* (also called *tactile, muscular* or *kinesthetic*), *visual* and *analytical* (or conceptual) *memory*.[40]

For effective location in displacements it is

[40] See P. Scholes, 1973:758-759. In a certain way it can be affirmed that we memorize with the whole body. Theiler and Lippman ("Effects of Mental Practice and Modeling on Guitar and Vocal Performance," in *Journal of General Psychology*, 1995) argue that for guitarists, kinesthetic codifying –balance perception– and images are particularly important for memorizing.

advisable to establish two aspects in advance:

- Reference points on the fretboard
- Visualization strategies

Reference Points on the Fretboard

Observing the fretboard from the perspective of the space between frets is functional for positioning purposes.

While frets are obviously the metallic bars that divide the fretboard, we usually give the same name to the area *between* them. In eighteenth-century Spain –when frets were still made of gut strings– they were called *casillas* (lockers), a custom that still persists in some South American countries.

A small mark on the edge of the fretboard at the seventh fret makes an effective reference point to easily locate the fifth and ninth positions.[41] For the fourth and tenth positions the references can be the nut and the juncture of the neck with the soundbox (twelfth fret) respectively. Another option would be to mark the seventeenth space, which delimit the fourteenth position.

Visualization Strategies

In larger shifts we usually look in advance for the "destination point" to establish a quick energy-efficient response that also guarantees tempo accuracy. Combining several orientation procedures promotes fast automatic shifts which, once established, will be controlled mainly through peripheral vision, whose fundamental function within optical physiology is movement detection.

In this segment of Villa-Lobos' *Etude No. 2*, finger 1 replaces 4 (reference point) at the same fret. Letters represent the reference points before shifts (by substitution), an action that can be associated with planting. (Ex. 3.20)

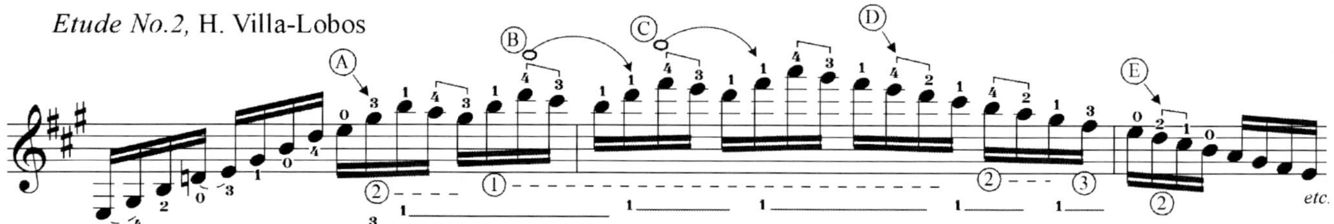

Quadruple range: Visualizing the space of the four-fret span of each position is an additional resource related to chord positions. (Ex. 3.21)

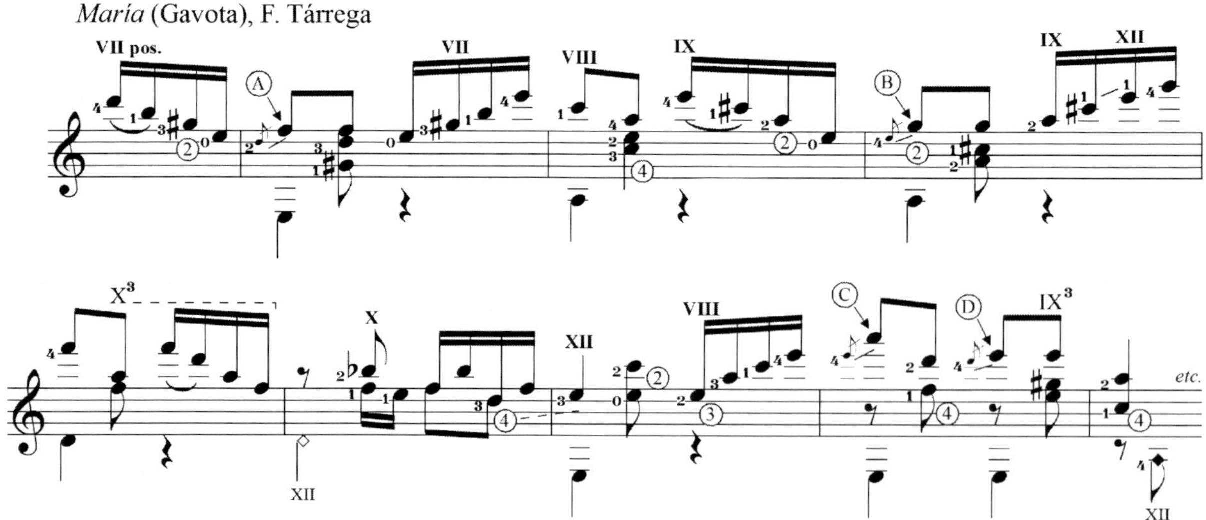

Along with mental visualization (or vivid mental images), an excellent way to memorize scores,[42] it is useful to try playing without looking at the fretboard or the left hand. This practice allows us to corroborate the precision of shifts within the set of perceptions inherent to each passage.

---

[41] While the sixth fret marks the middle of the fretboard, it is less useful than the seventh in score reading because, unlike the seventh, the notes encompassed are mostly unrelated to the principal guitar keys: E, A, D, etc.

[42] See Iznaola, 2001:16, and Urshalmi, 2006:87

Observing the right hand may be a priority at times, as in this fragment of *Tonadilla (La Maja de Goya)* by Enrique Granados, in which both hands must move simultaneously for the execution of the harmonics. (Ex. 3.22)

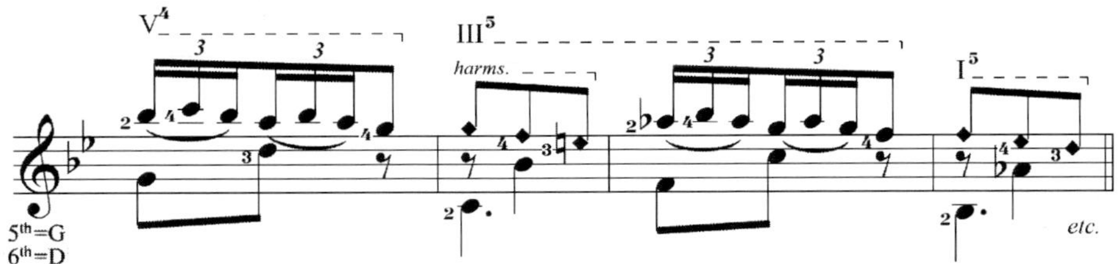

Studying visual orientation from the beginning of work with a score makes it unnecessary to continually monitor of shifts with an exhausting zeal that does not guarantee safety in performance.

Practice of Shifts by Leap

Although according to geometry, the shortest distance between two points is a straight line, with the guitar we can move on a fretboard with greater economy of effort, speed, and precision through curvilinear (or semicircular) trajectories.

It is advisable to rehearse these loose and undulating movements "in the air" first, before applying them to exercises on one string, and later on diatonic scales with transverse shifts.

Since shifts take place in fractions of a second, in order to maintain metric precision it is necessary to slightly shorten the launching notes. In the next exercise, the notes will be shortened with a staccato performed with an agile release of pressure (relaxation of the whole hand). Different forms of articulation can conceal these *cuts*, to the point of not being able to perceive an interruption of the music (See *Left-Hand Articulation Techniques*). (Ex. 3.23)

Chord shifts follow the same pattern of curvilinear mobility.[43] (Ex. 3.24)

[43] See Abel Carlevaros's *Serie Didáctica, Cuaderno no.3, Left-Hand Technique.*

In addition to their greater fluency, curvilinear movements make it possible to eliminate both friction on the metal-wound bass strings, and the noise derived from those brief but frequent "brakes."

Reducing Noise in Shifting

The intense recreation of the expressive content of each score demands that we raise our technical skills to the level of a superior aesthetic.

The acoustic characteristics of the guitar enhance both its rich timbric range and the risk of added noises while playing, most of them avoidable, but including percussive sounds, clicking of the strings on the frets, hissing nails, and friction on the winding of the bass strings –all effects that should be addressed in a qualitative criterion of sound in performance.

> Technique in art is a means to reveal poetry. It is not reduced to perfect physical mastery. It is a category of maximum amplitude that must embrace the three levels of personality: physical-somatic, psychic–mental or emotional, and spiritual. All technique must be highly spiritualized.
>
> José Suárez Tajonera[44]

The polished surface of the treble strings favors the execution of portamenti, while the noisy chirping of the basses –always noticeable between strokes– continuously tarnishes the sound. Avoiding this friction with a vertical release invariably contributes to the transparency of phrasing. Let's examine two brief examples in *Lágrima (Prelude)* by Tárrega. In the first bar, the vertical release of fingers 1 and 3 from the 4th string enables a clearer audition of the *legato* provided by portamenti. (Ex. 3.25)

Lágrima (Prelude), F. Tárrega

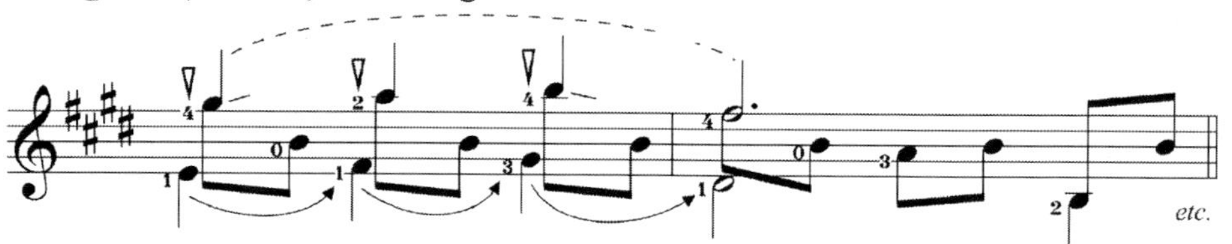

In the second excerpt, finger 1 slides over the 3rd string, while 3 and 2 *shift from above* the fretboard, staying close to the strings after lifting away from them. Far from being a difficult task, this procedure adds an additional lightness to shifts. (Ex. 3.26)

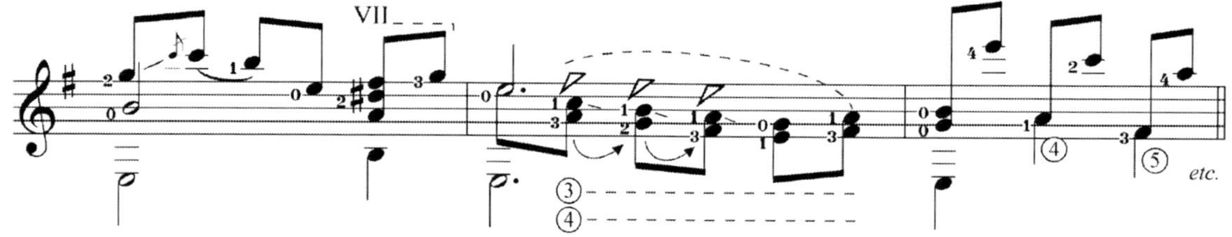

Shifts *from above* using finger 1 enhance fluency in this fast chromatic passage. (Ex. 3.27)

Introduction et Caprice Op.23, Giulio Regondi

The typical fixed-chord displacements in Heitor Villa-Lobos' guitar works imply a strong friction that affects mobility. In *Prelude No. 2,* this is avoided with shifts from above of 1, 3 and 4, sliding only with finger 2 on the 3rd string. (Ex. 3.28)

Prelude No.2, H. Villa-Lobos

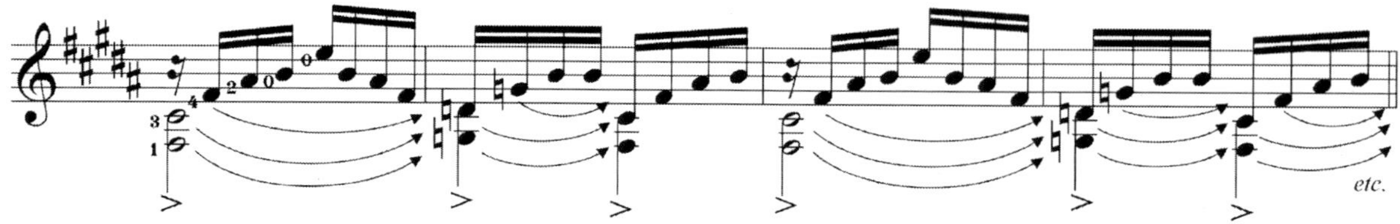

[44] From an interview, newspaper *Juventud Rebelde*, Havana, January 4th, 2008.

Once integrated in our mechanism, these apparently complex operations become a flexible tool in performance. The following are some patterns that can help in training: (Ex. 3.29)

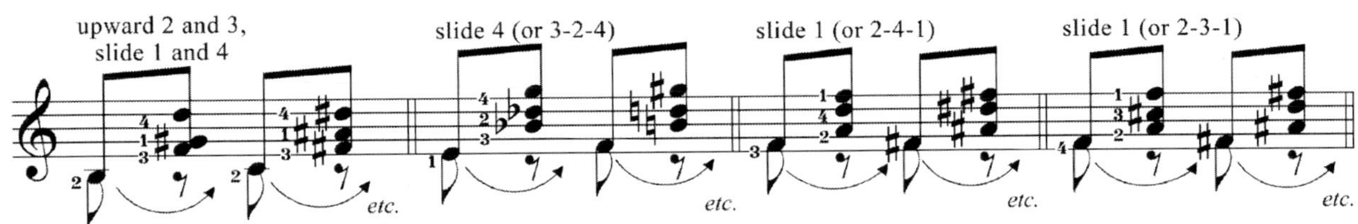

Noise in glissandi and portamenti on the bass strings can be diminished with a slight flattening of the fingers, exerting more pressure during movement. Using weight, the effort is reduced in the ascending portamenti of *Prelude No. 1* by Tárrega, whereas the descending glissandi in *Etude No. 8* by Villa-Lobos can be executed with a movement of the arm with a fixed wrist. (Exs. 3.30)

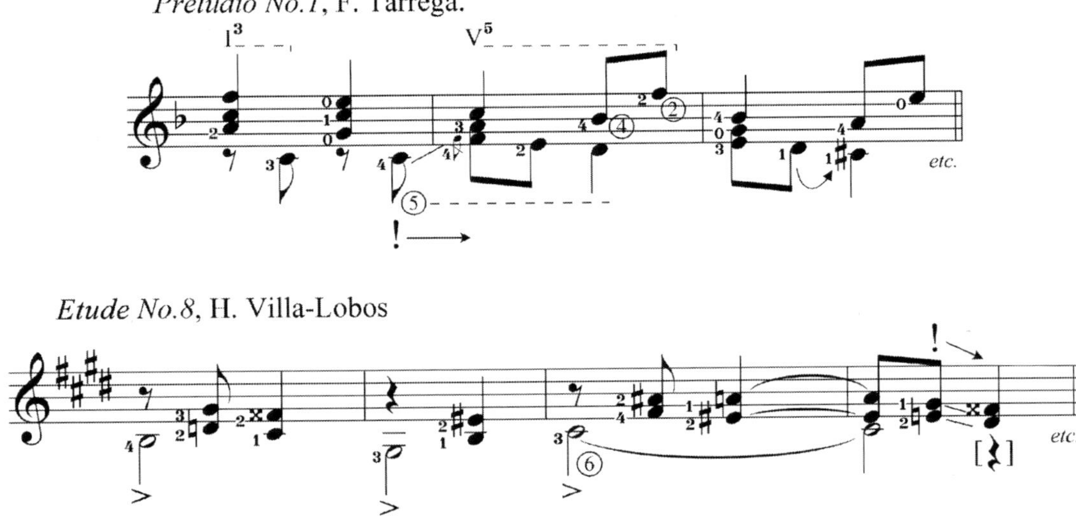

Other means for Precision and Economy of Effort in Shifting

Mechanics of the Support Point

Carlevaro describes this resource as *a means by which one or more fingers on the fingerboard serving as a leaning point or fulcrum enable the arm to function as a lever of the first type to extend or join the other fingers in favor of greater mechanical ease* (1984:128).

In examples 3.25-26 *(Lágrima)*, the *shifts from above* are executed using fingers 4 and 2 as support points in the first case, and finger 1 in the second.

Pivot Finger

A variant of this mechanism is the *pivot finger*, defined as the fretting finger that allows the hand to rotate to arrive at a new position, while sustaining –if necessary– the sound of the fretted note. In the following fragments the use of the pivot finger markedly enhances mobility balance. (Exs. 3.31)

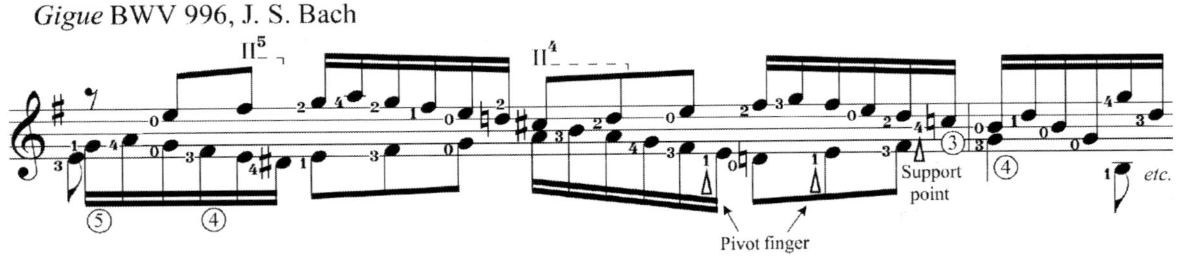

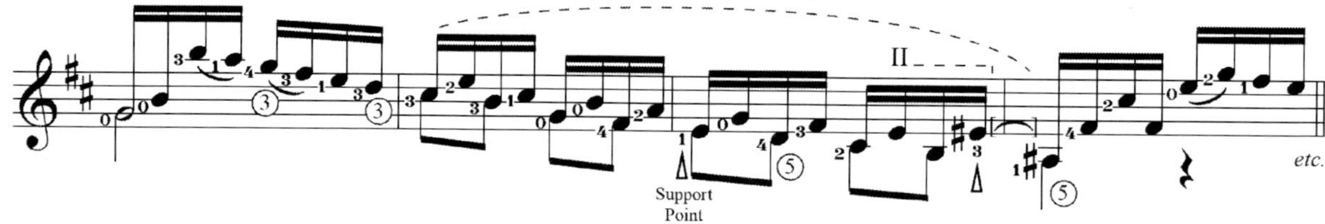

Avoiding Successive Shifts in Opposite Directions

Generally, successive shifts in opposite directions can be avoided with alternatives favorable to phrasing intention. (Exs. 3.32)

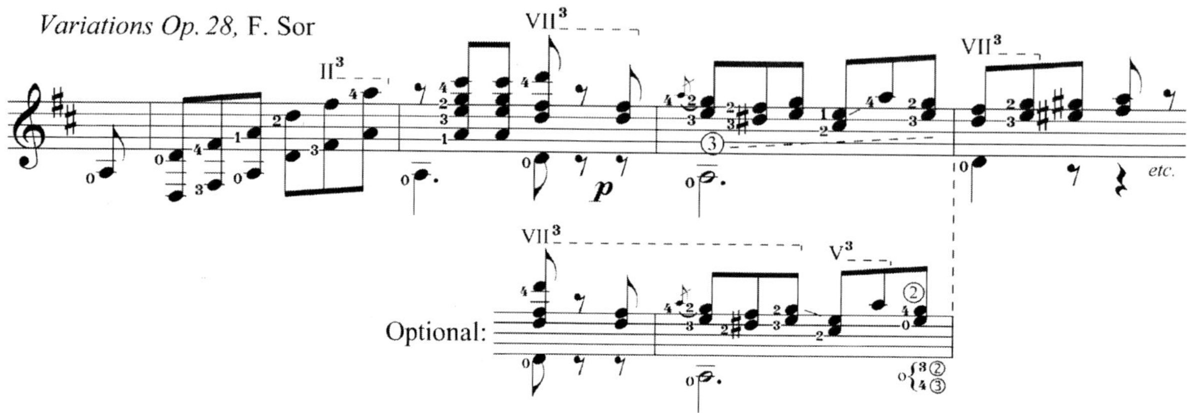

In all cases, and especially if it is not viable to simplify shifts, a precise visual orientation and concatenated mobility of the arm will work best. (Ex. 3.33)

Using Less Supination in Linear Passages

In melodic passages –especially descending passages– fingerings that increase supination must be prevented as far as possible. In the first of the following examples, displacement begins with finger 3, when greater fluency and relaxation can be achieved using 1, which facilitates a small rotation of the hand as well *(b)*. (Exs. 3.34)

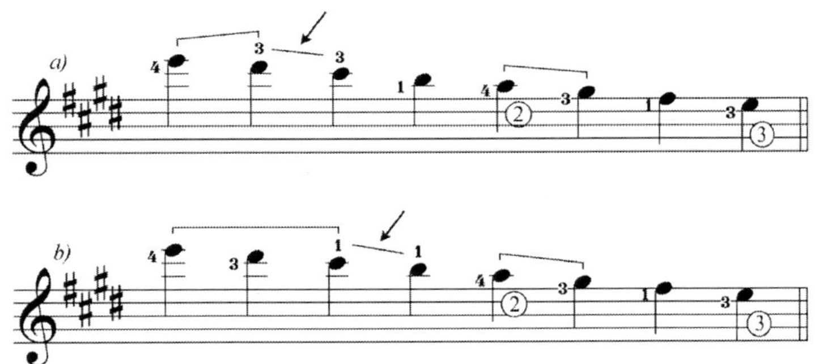

Progressive Placement and Release of Chord Positions

As an operation that is related to the positioning cycle, the gradual placement and release of chord positions –depending on the score– is another form of promoting the fluency of movements and economy of effort. Here are some examples:

• *Etude Op. 60 No. 1* of Mateo Carcassi: The release of finger 3 is slightly anticipated, since it will be the first one to move to the new position, aided by the rotation of the hand. The brief shortening of launch-notes in shifts indicates the moment to release the pressure on the remaining strings. Placement is accomplished in the following order: finger 3, 2 (with a superficial slide over the 3rd string in both directions), and partial barré. (Ex. 3.35)

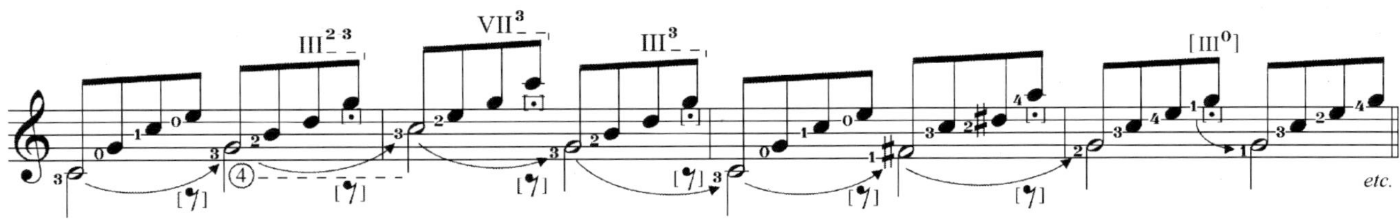

• In the chord progressions of *Etude Op. 38 No. 1* by Napoleon Coste and *Sonatina Meridional* by Manuel Ponce, it is possible to anticipate the barrés with a slight rotation of finger 1 during the shifts. (Exs. 3.36)

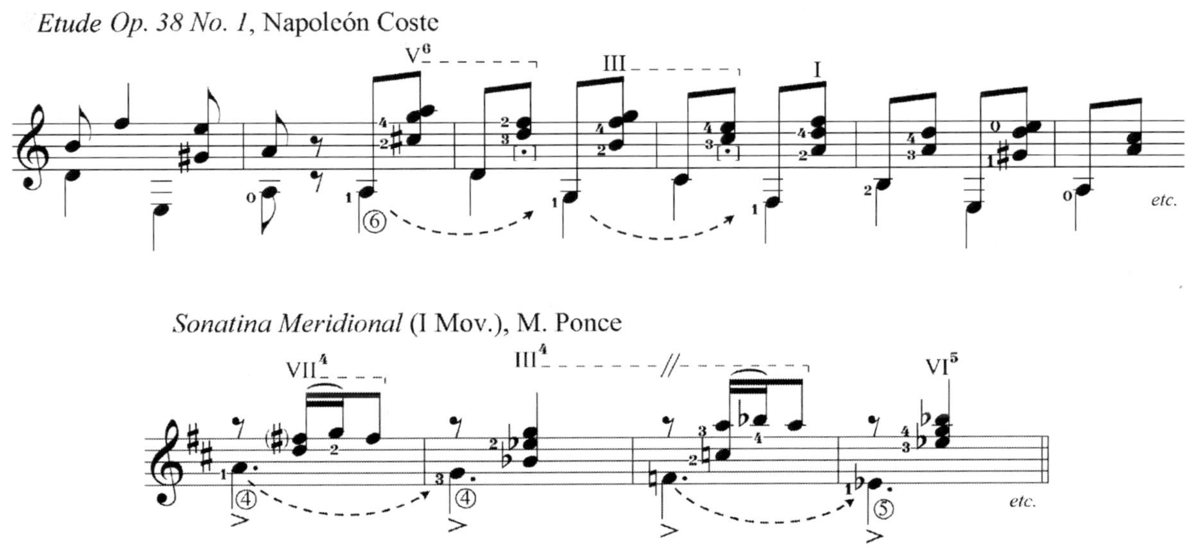

Performed as an *interpretive emphasis*, anticipating a note in an interval or chord with a fast shift is also a sort of progressive placement (See Ex. 3.51, *Etude No. 1* by M. Camargo Guarnieri, p. 91). Such gradual positioning can also work as a preparation for extensions.

Barré

One of the first references to the use of the barré dates from the late seventeenth century. The Mallorcan Francisco Guerau named it *cejuela* in his treatise *Poema harmónico* (Madrid, 1694).

From an anatomical and physiological standpoint, the barré is one of the most complex techniques, so both learning it and developing "endurance" in execution should be observed very carefully.

To play the guitar with an optimal use of our bodily resources, it is necessary to focus on efficiency and not on endurance, clearly a consequence of the former. This perspective requires a meditative approach to study, which prevents us from continuous overexertion when playing –the main source of injuries and technical deficiencies.

Engraving (detail) from *Instrucción de música sobre la guitarra española* by Gaspar Sanz (Zaragoza, 1674).

Roundness of the Hand in Barré

The traditional barré with the flattened finger interrupts the natural roundness of the hand, increases supination and requires significant pressure, which in turn restricts blood circulation.

The slanted placement of the instrument favors the use of an efficient "curved barré." Most of the work in playing a full barré is exerted by the metacarpal (proximal) joint of finger 1, thus the perception of comfort increases as we bring this joint closer to the 1st string, with the finger slightly arched and inclined slightly backward.

This technique offers several benefits:

• It reduces substantially the pressing surface, which in turn reduces the effort needed, resulting in greater precision and maneuverability.

• It contributes to the partial fixation of the middle and distal joints, and reduces the effect of their disproportions on the fretboard; in contrast to the traditional barré, it is often necessary to apply more pressure on the 3rd and 4th strings).

• It favors selective pressure in both chords and linear passages.

Using Selective Pressure in Barré Chords

Let's examine two applications of the curved barré:

In the F major chord (Photo A), the barré only presses the required strings: 6th, 2nd, and 1st (F, C, F), and in the B♭ major chord (Photo B) the barré only presses the 5th and 1st strings (B♭-F). (Exs. 3.37)

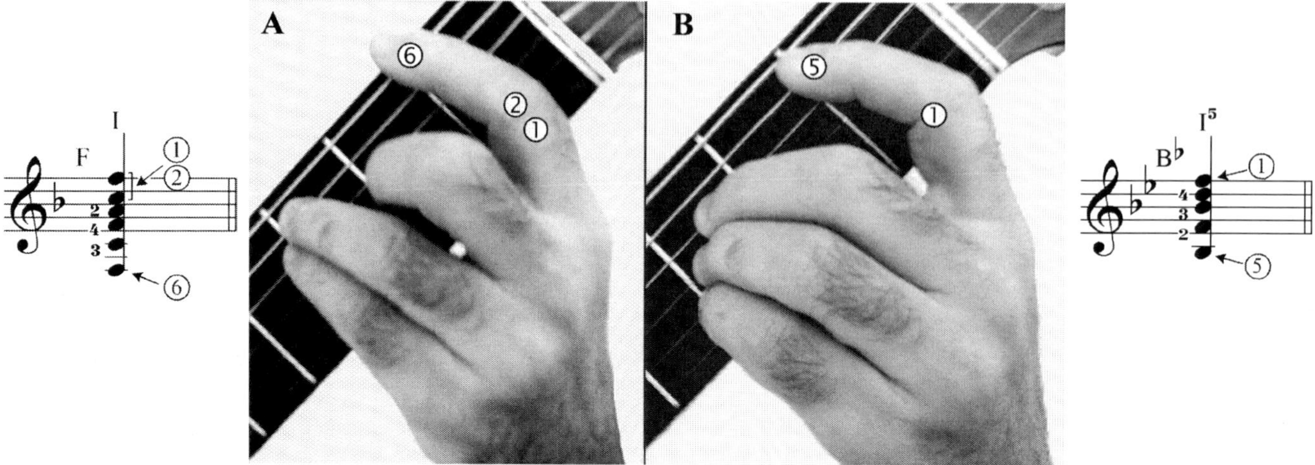

As analyzed, the position of the thumb determines the stability and economy of effort in pressing. Its normal placement in barré chords is towards the middle joint of finger 1.

It is not always possible to preserve roundness in barré chords. Extensions require a flattening of finger 1, which brings about all the mentioned disadvantages of traditional placement.

Reshaping the Barré

It is advisable to review the sensopostural pattern before beginning to use the curved barré, lightly placing it repeatedly with maximum relaxation and without exerting pressure on the strings. If this proves difficult, flip the guitar so that the strings are against your body, and practice placing "barré chords" on the curved surface of the neck, to which finger 1 can easily mold.

Another exercise consists of holding an imaginary baseball, and from this shape forming the round barré.

Full clarity of notes should not be required during the first attempts with normal pressure. Apply a small amount of pressure only at the very moment you pluck (as for a staccato). It will be necessary to control the position of the elbow to maintain hand-forearm alignment.

This practice can be initially structured in three steps. (Exs. 3.38)

After improving the barré position, and depending on the characteristics of each passage, additional resources can be implemented for better economy and graduated effort.

Increased Economy of Effort

Using the Weight of the Arm

Weight is especially useful in sustained chord positions. The flat barré makes this option difficult since it requires separating the elbow from the body, especially in the first positions. (Ex. 3.39)

Preludio No.2, F. Tárrega

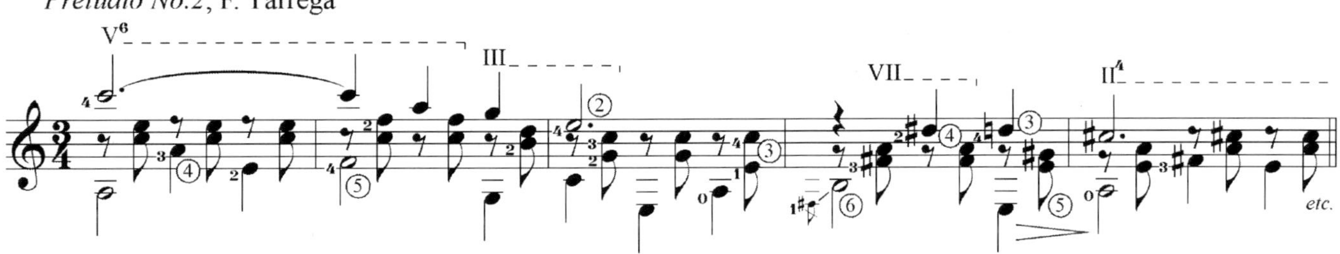

In the following fragments the use of weight guarantees free mobility of the fingers. (Exs. 3.40)

Sevilla, Isaac Albéniz

Danza Característica, Leo Brouwer

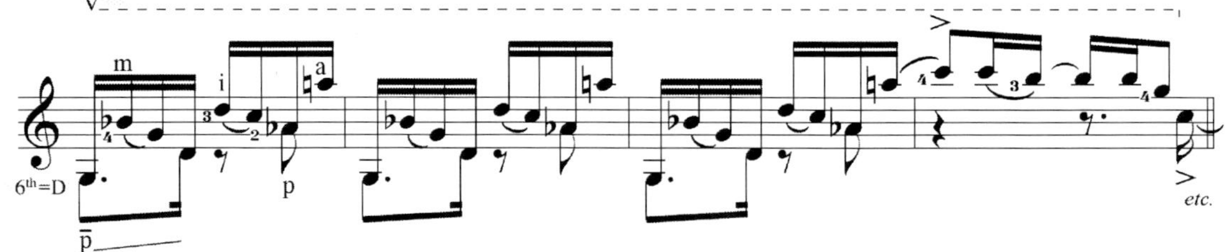

Intermittent Release of Pressure

Brief releases of pressure between strokes –without lifting the fingers from the strings– do not necessarily imply a staccato and prevent buildup of tension from the barré. The character and structure of each phrase define the effective moments to insert this imperceptible relief without affecting the musical discourse. A brief pause, a chord change or its repetition, may provide additional opportunities for readjustments of the thumb or elbow. (Ex. 3.41)

Gavotte BWV 1011, J. S. Bach

The use of weight and pressure breaks can reduce effort considerably in *Etude Op. 29 No. 13* by Fernando Sor, a score which demands a barré in 35 of its 58 bars. (Ex. 3.42)

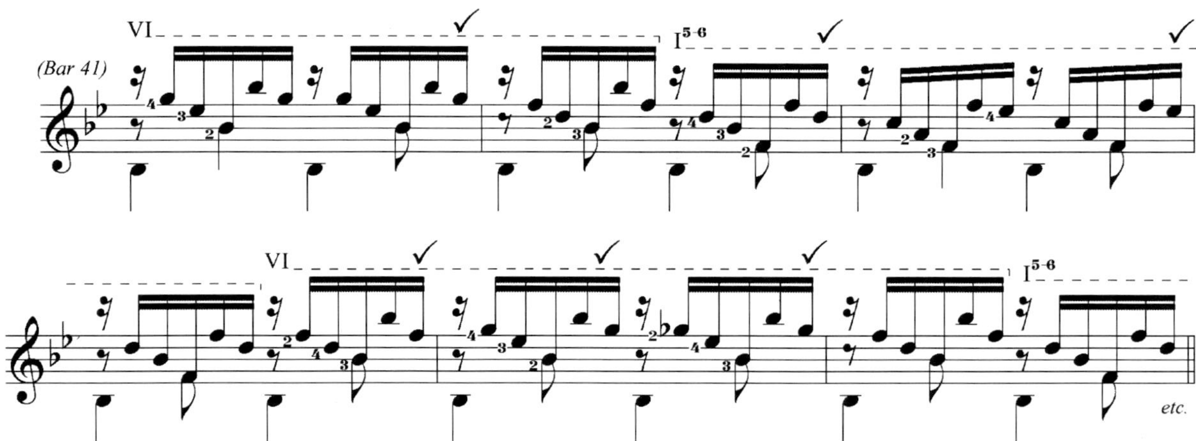

Selective Pressure in Linear Passages

As already mentioned, the curved barré makes selective pressure possible in linear passages. This contributes to balance and economy of transverse shifts with finger 1.

Execute a chromatic scale from a barré position, exerting pressure only when playing the notes that fall under the barré *(a)* As you approach the 3rd string begin to lift the tip of the first finger without reducing the pressure of the first phalange, until the finger remains only on the 1st string. To preserve the alignment, adjust the location of the elbow with a small turn of the hand. Later, repeat this procedure while playing a diatonic scale such as A minor in fifth position *(b)*. (Exs. 3.43)

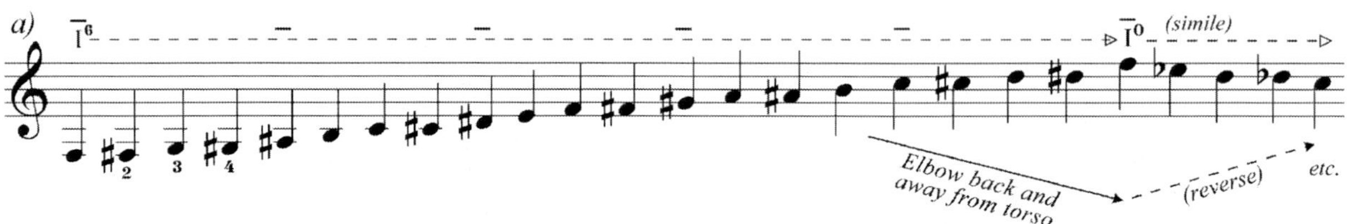

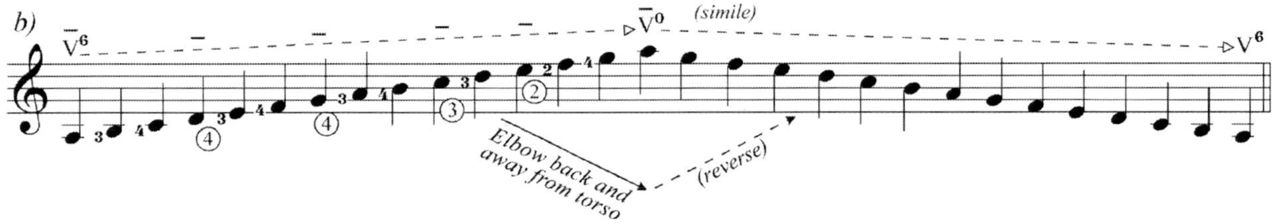

Selective pressure with the barré technique helps to balance the fast scale passages of Villa-Lobos' *Etude No. 7* (Ex. 3.44)

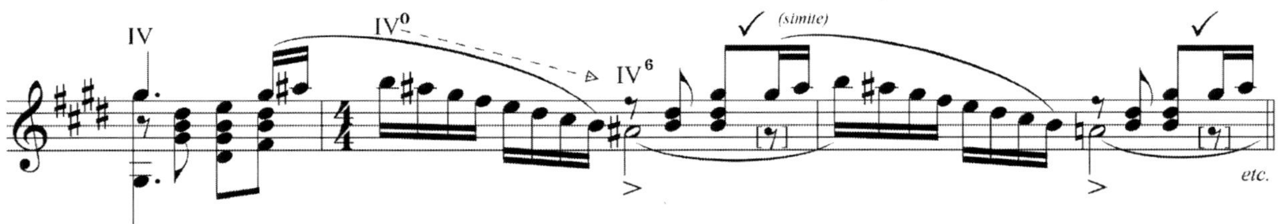

Barré in Advance

In certain cases, it is more effective to press the 1st or 2nd string with the first phalange of finger 1, rather than with the fingertip. This sort of preparation allows completion of a barré (*Pavana V*, by Luis Milán, and *Prelude* BWV 1006a by Bach), favors legato in shifts, and helps to avoid transverse extensions (1-2 between 1st and 6th in *Prelude* BWV 997).

It can be said that the barré in advance "keeps all the fingers on the fingerboard." A facile rotation of the hand speeds up the shift to second position in *Nocturno* by F. M. Torroba. (Exs. 3.45)

Pavana V, Luis Milán

Prelude BWV 1006a, J. S. Bach

Prelude BWV 997, J. S. Bach

Nocturno, F. Moreno Torroba

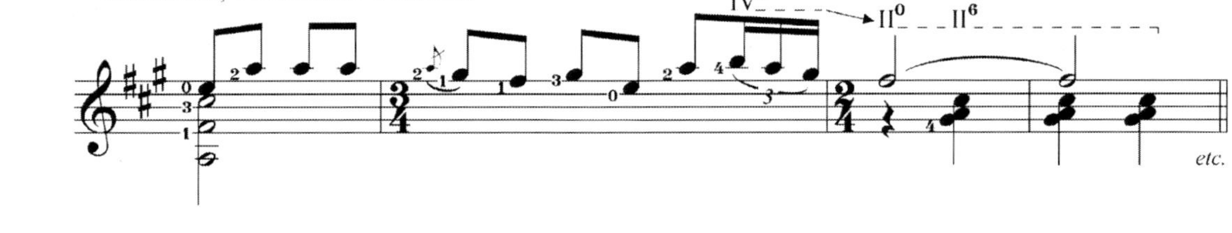

In the next example of progressive placement, the second note of each beat is produced with an anticipation of the barré, to be completed for the following note. (Ex. 3.46)

Sarabande (Double) BWV 1002, J. S. Bach

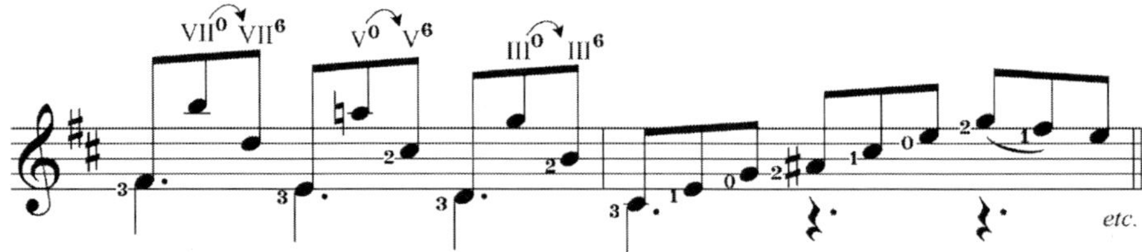

Let's examine the previous techniques combined in a single passage. The use of weight, selective pressing, and breaks are linked in a fluid management of energy on the fretboard. (Ex. 3.47)

Estudio No. 8, F. Tárrega

Partial Barré

Besides being used on chords, partial barrés help to simplify fingering in different ways, reduce movement and sustain notes for legato.

Whenever possible, flexing the middle finger joint on a barré up to the 3rd string requires less effort, and facilitates hand-forearm alignment. Additionally, and depending on the chord, supination can be slightly reduced.

Applying weight in partial barrés is not always functional, but selective pressure and breaks can easily be applied. (Exs. 3.48)

Estudio No. 10, F. Tárrega

Sonata Clásica (III Mov.), M. Ponce

Hinge Barré

An adult guitarist can cover up to three strings with the distal phalanx of finger 1. The A major chord in first position is a prototype of this procedure, where finger 2 assures stability. The use of the hinge barré is ideal in these two measures of *Etude No. 3* by Villa-Lobos. (Exs. 3.49)

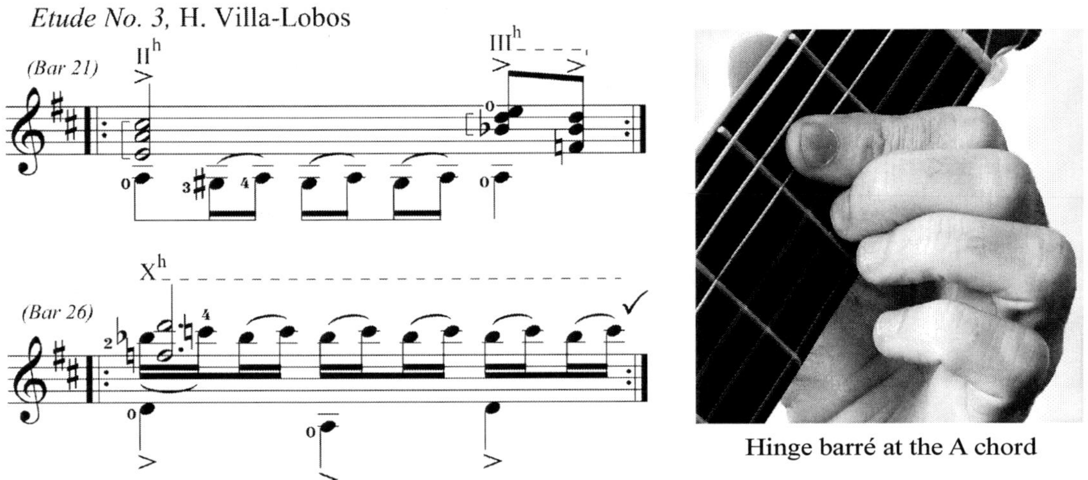

Hinge barré at the A chord

The "hinge" considerably reduces the pressure required, and therefore facilitates shifting. (Exs. 3.50)

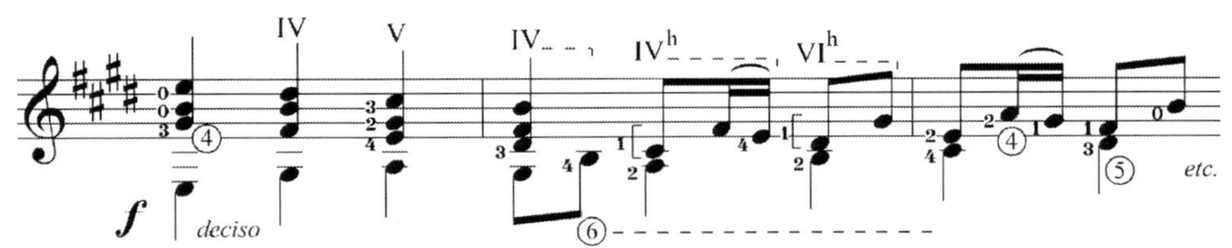

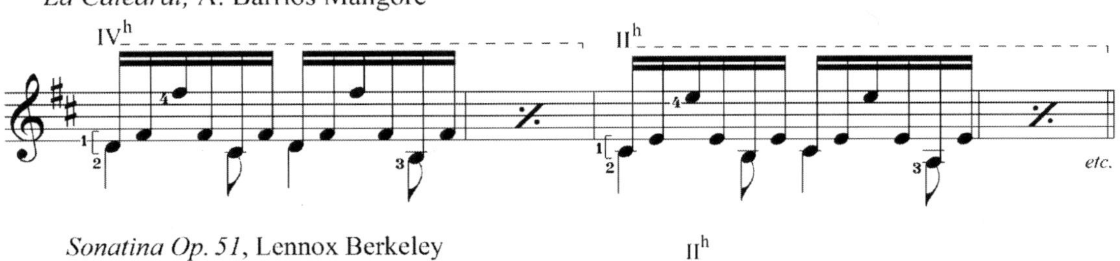

"Fourth-Finger Barré"

Often used in conjunction with a full barré, pressing several strings with finger 4 involves a complex extension. (Exs. 3.51)

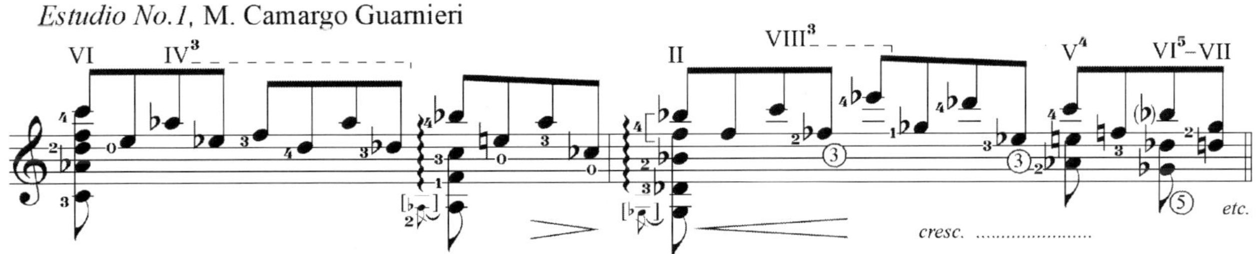

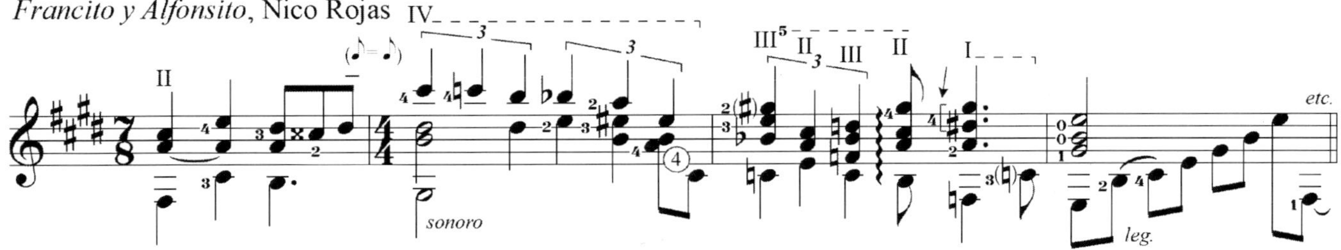

Extensions

Extension can be described as any open position of the fingers (abduction) that tests the flexibility of the hand, something that usually happens when the quadruple rule of one finger per fret is exceeded, which always implies greater muscle tension.

Let us recall that an effective handling of the instrument does not require compromising our physiology, but using it efficiently. Endeavoring to increase the natural elasticity of the hand through extension exercises is absurd and risky; it can cause more damage than good. It is essential to avoid continuous demand on the tendons, finger joints and the palm. Instead, a first aspect to consider is the hand-forearm alignment, since curving the wrist not only limits the mobility of fingers but also reduces the flexibility derived from the total length of the muscles, which includes tendons and joints.

This consideration does not exclude individuals with large hands, for whom the abduction of the fingers, i.e., extension, may obviously require less effort.

For a 1-4 extension on the 4th and 5th strings in the middle zone of the fretboard, such as the one required in Ponce's *Prelude No. 8*,[45] the torso tilts forward and slightly to the left (control of the arm angles for preserving alignment), and the guitar may be optionally raised with the heel. This process is simultaneous with a proportional approach of the elbow to the torso and a rotation of the hand. The photos show the joint arm-hand work, and the use of finger 4 as a support point for the shift. (Ex. 3.52)

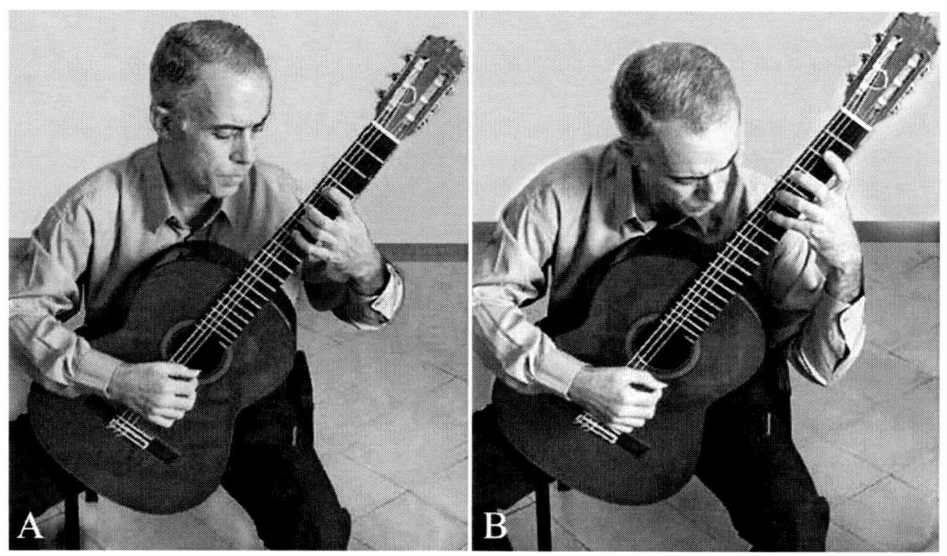

Preludio No. 8, M. Ponce
(Tranquillo)

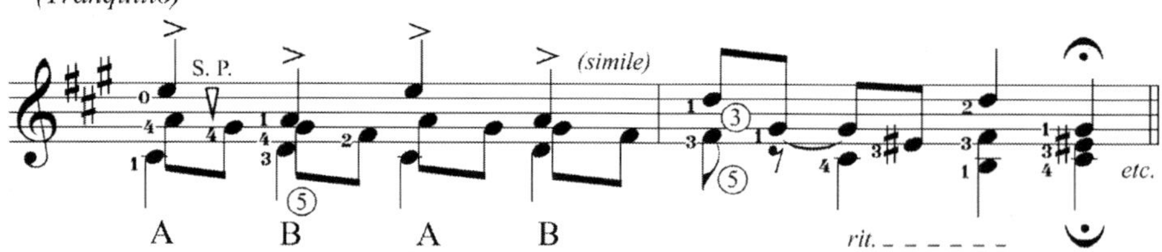

We have mentioned that decreasing supination –while maintaining the hand-forearm alignment– can mean more "functional capacity for extension" of the fingers, especially on the treble strings. *Las Abejas* by Barrios Mangoré, *Study IX (Homage to Llobet)* by Ricardo Iznaola, and the final movement of *Sonata Clásica* by Manuel Ponce have several moments where this technique is complemented with a readjustment of the elbow. (Exs. 3.53)

Las Abejas, A. Barrios Mangoré

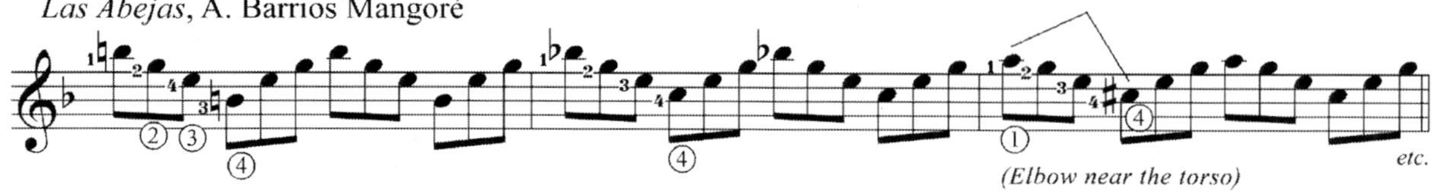

[45] Tecla Editions (Alcazar), *No. 1* in Schott-Eschig edition (Segovia).

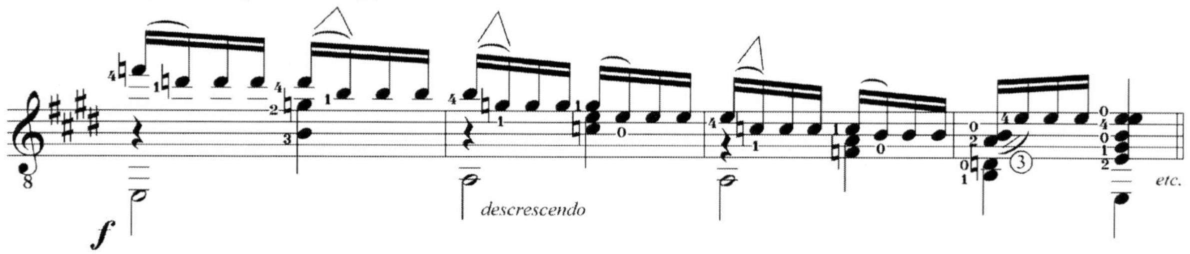

Preparing Extensions

In addition to physical conditioning (warm-up exercises), a relaxed placement of the hand should be established before executing extensions with a graduated use of effort (flexibility), and subsequent comfortable exit from the position. Otherwise, the fluency of movements will be compromised due to a physiological reason: the execution of precise movements becomes more difficult after an overload of tension. Some muscle groups remain momentarily limited or unavailable, an effect experienced as fatigue. This effect, more palpable in challenging works, also affects the fine motor skills of performers.

In the following segment of *Chôros No. 1* by Villa-Lobos, leaning toward the fretboard when playing F♯ with finger 2 favors alignment, and therefore the conditions for relaxation (roundness of the hand, rotation, fretting accuracy, etc.). By using finger 2 as a support point, and by moving the elbow "back and out," we begin the extension of finger 4 towards B on the 1st string simultaneously with the placement of fingers 1 and 3. (Ex. 3.54)

A similar preparation is recommended for this complex except from *Pavana* by F. Tárrega, where the mordent implies a simultaneous extension with the positioning of the full barré. (Ex. 3.55)

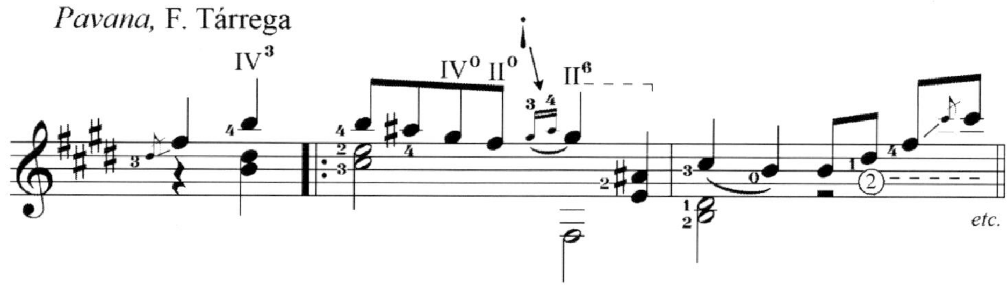

Alternatives

Clearly, modifying the notes should not be the first option to solve possible performing difficulties. To do so, even minimally, demands the most careful assessment from a defined interpretative criterion.

In *Mazurca* by Tárrega, the shortening of a bass note, and anticipating the barré allows avoiding the extension 2-4. (Ex. 3.56)

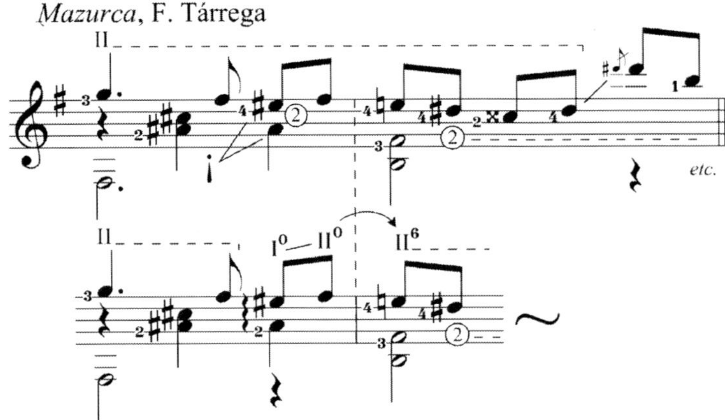

Extensions between fingers 2 and 3 are often the most uncomfortable. In the following fragment, an unnecessary doubling of D in the first chord is avoided, resulting in two possible fingerings. (Ex. 3.57)

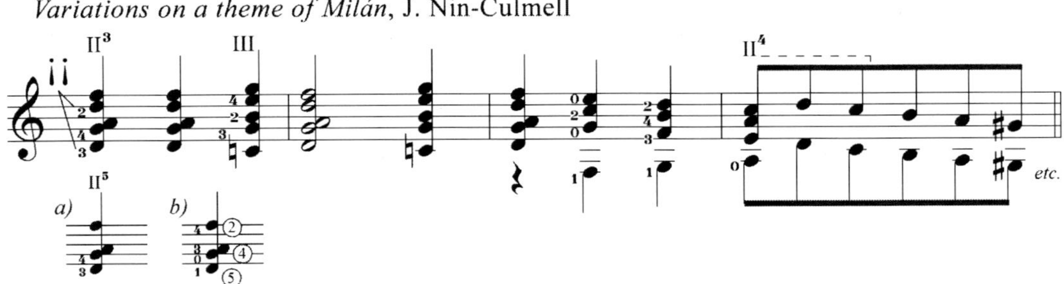

Some works by Barrios Mangoré present very difficult extensions, not always within the reach of markedly small hands. Extreme examples are *Mazurka Apassionata* and *Chôro da Saudade*. In this last piece, a possible solution is to use the thumb as a *capotasto* on the 6th string, a kind of barré with the external edge of the thumb, as used by cellists and double-bassists.[46] (Exs. 3.58)

[46] This fragment of *Chôro da Saudade* comes from Barrios' original manuscript (See Stover, 2010:271). The optional proposal is ours.

Left-Hand Articulation Techniques

Legato by Sustaining Resonance

In addition to a gentle attack toward the sound hole, legato articulation demands extending the notes as much as possible with sustained pressure. In this way, the resonance of the sustained notes in Villa-Lobos' *Etude No. 5* may suggest an overlapping of voices. (Ex. 3.59)

The second fingering of the following fragment presents more legato options. Planting allows prolonging of the notes that precede a string change, which in turn generates a fuller sonority. (Ex. 3.60)

Estudio No. 3, A. Barrios Mangoré

a)

b)

etc.

Let's examine fingerings for legato in two score passages by Bach:

Prelude BWV 997: Prolonging the notes creates a resonance effect that evokes the Baroque lute. (Ex. 3.61)

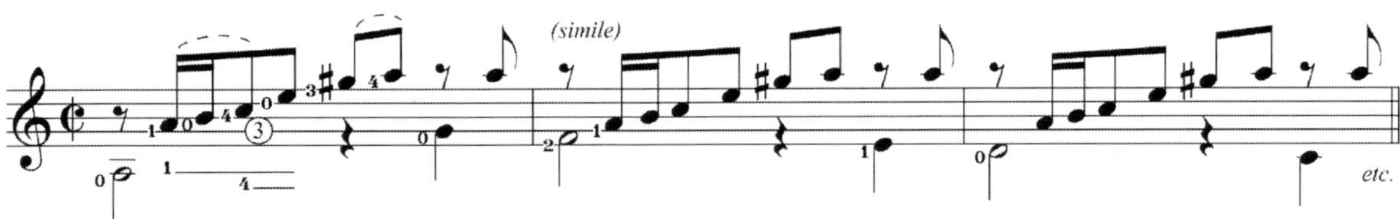

Gigue BWV 995: Legato is implied by means of a *campanella* fingering in the upper voice, and also by sustaining the B (finger 3 on 6th) while plucking A on the open 5th string. (Ex. 3.62)

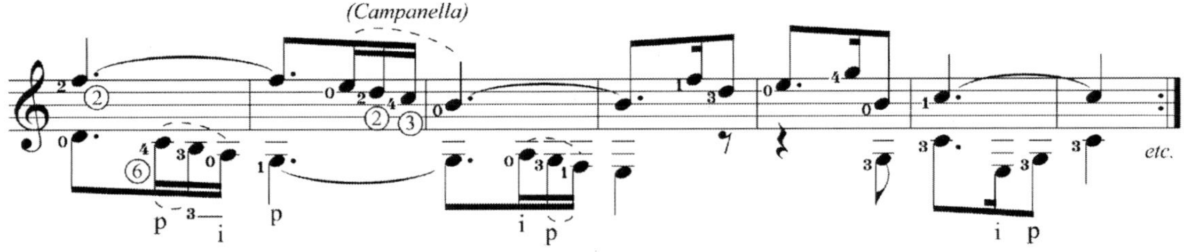

Campanella

Campanella consists of articulating a melodic line by combining open and fretted notes on two or more strings. The prolongation of some notes produces a pedal effect that resembles the sound of hand bells. Frequently executed with an arpeggio movement, campanella favors a rapid succession of notes, one reason why it is often overused.

The following examples offer two fingering options for the final measures of *Sarabanda* by S. L. Weiss. In the first one, excessive resonance and timbric imbalance (C on 4th followed by open E, etc.) diminish the clarity of the phrase. Shortening the duration of the open G (first measure) allows a clearer discourse *(b)*. (Ex. 3.63)

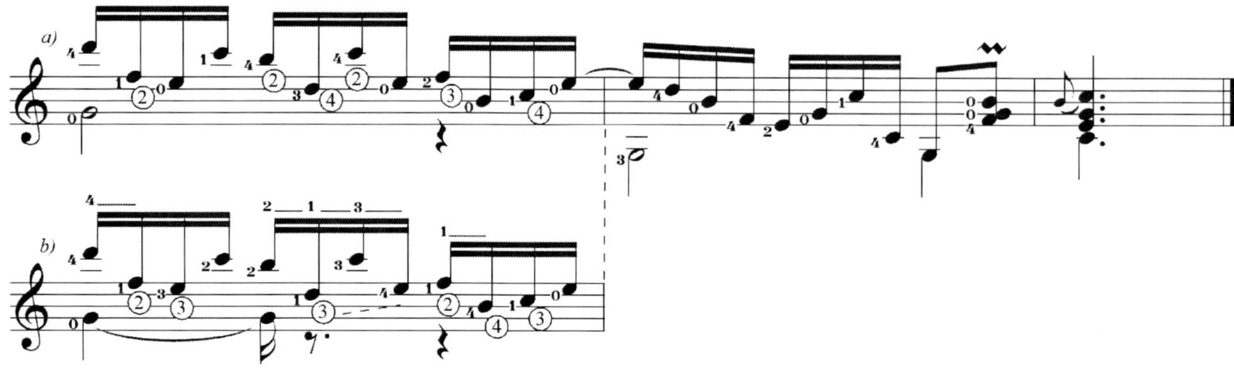

Campanella supports an imitation in *Fantasy X* by Alonso de Mudarra (Spain, sixteenth century), a piece with a suggestive subtitle: *... que contrahaze el arpa en la manera de Ludovico (... that imitates the harp in Ludovico's manner)*. (Ex. 3.64)

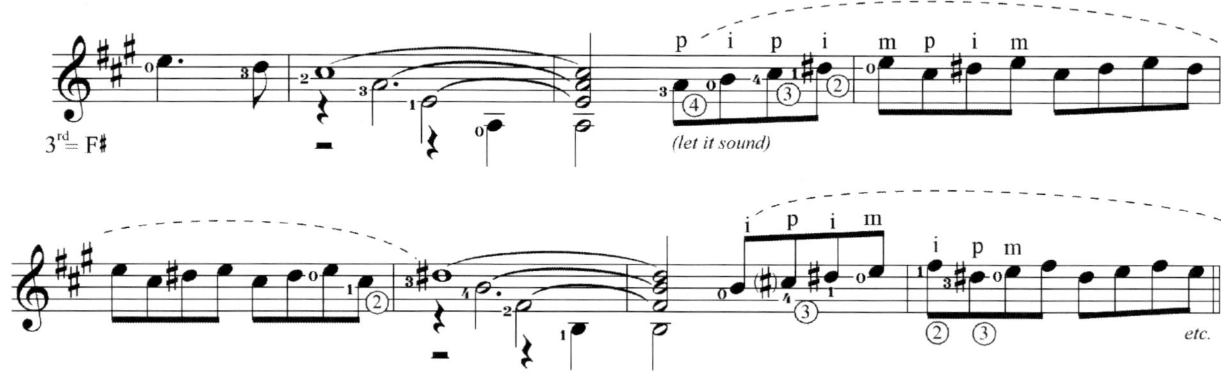

Because of its special effect, this fingering resource can also be employed as a motivic element in the contemporary music repertoire. (Exs. 3.65)

Aquarelle (I. Divertimento), Sergio Assad

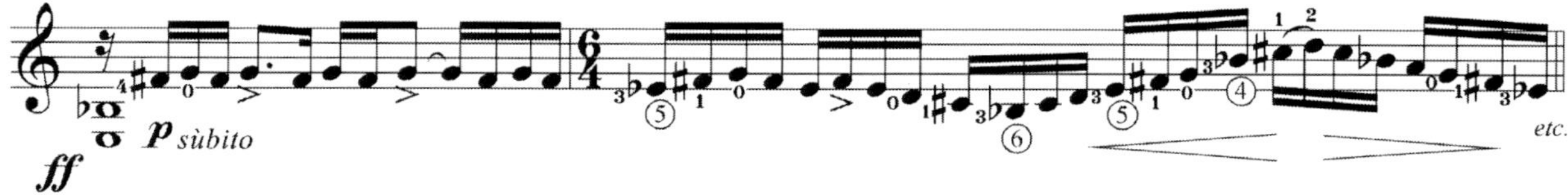

Acrílicos en el asfalto, Eduardo Martín

Direct Use of Sympathetic Resonance

In the first of the three final measures of *Julia Florida (Barcarole)* by Barrios Mangoré, A on the 2nd string activates a sympathetic unison harmonic on the open 5th string. A brief tenuto is enough to achieve this effect –optionally enhanced with vibrato– so that the shift to F♯ on the 6th string does not interrupt the melodic line. (Ex. 3.66)

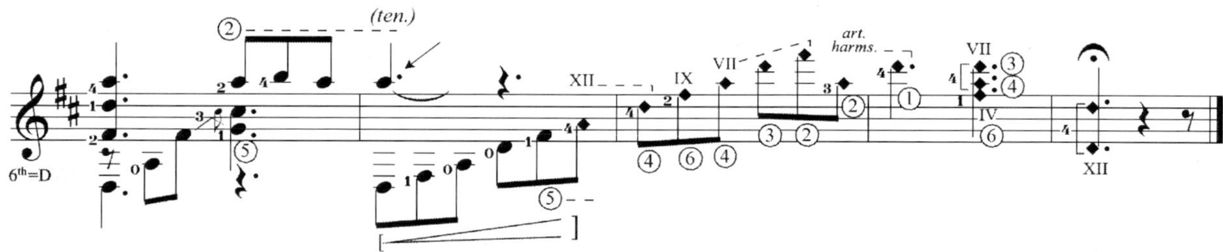

Agua e Vinho by Gismonti (Assad): A similar effect can be induced in the first note of this final segment, followed by a sustained campanella. (Ex. 3.67)

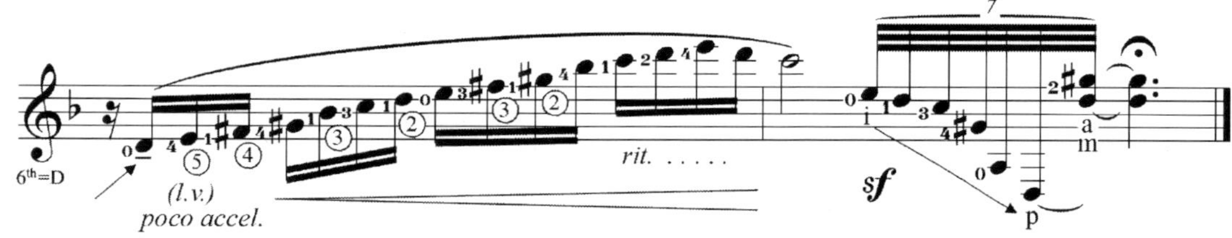

As we will see, prolonging notes through vibrato is another way to enhance legato.

Slurs *(Ligados)*

Achieving clarity, fluency and accuracy in slurs (ligados) demands complex muscle work, a reason why their practice must be undertaken moderately and progressively.

Ascending slurs are made by shortening the vibrating section of the string with a hammering of the finger –always vertically– with enough energy to generate a clear sound. With a relaxed hand, executing a two-note ascending slur with 1-3 (e.g., F-G on the 1st string, first position) does not necessitate a tensioning of fingers 2 and 4, which should naturally "follow" 3.

Descending slurs resemble plucking with the right hand. They can be performed in two ways: downwards (as in a right-hand rest stroke), resting the finger on the adjoining string; or upwards (as in a free stroke), which is mandatory in fast tempi ornaments (*Pavanas* by Gaspar Sanz), and overlapping voices (*Variations Op. 9* by F. Sor).

Although more complex, the upward slur provides a better sound quality since the string vibration is more vertical to the bridge. (Exs. 3.68)

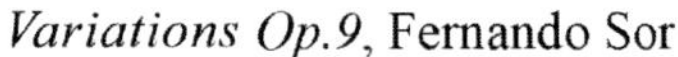

The sound-starting graph shows that greater resonance (sound duration) is produced by descending slurs. (Schaeffer, 2006:271)

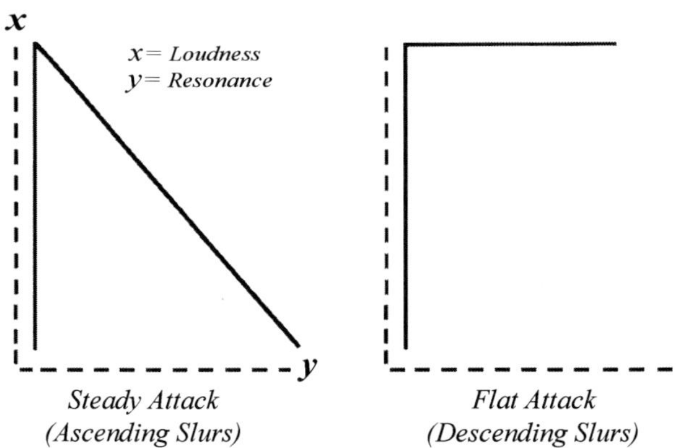

Both ascending and descending slurs must be performed with a balanced effort and precise movements. In descending slurs (as a rest stroke), a slow start can involve a surplus of force that modifies intonation by pulling the string, or generates noise, especially on the first string.

The "rest slur" produces a rather nasal timbre, more noticeable when repeated with the left hand alone (See Ex. 3.76, *Guajira*, by E. Pujol)).

It is possible to alternate both forms of descending slurs to achieve a balanced fluidity as in the following example: (Ex. 3.69)

Estudio Sencillo No. 7, L. Brouwer

From the 2nd string, the downward slurs guarantee stability before continuing with 1-0 upward slurs, favoring transverse displacements.

Planting when Playing Slurs

The balance derived from planting enables clarity and accuracy in slurring.

Descending slurs require a firm stability of the lower-note finger. A provisional practice to increase this perception is to reinforce planting with equal and simultaneous pressure of both fingers. (Ex. 3.70)

The sustained planting of finger 1 provides equilibrium in this fast sequence of descending slurs, where the hand-forearm alignment contributes to rotation in shifting. (Ex. 3.71)

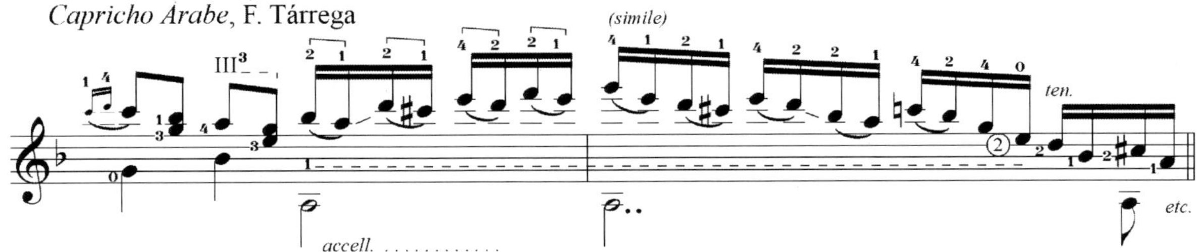

In *La Catedral* by Barrios Mangoré, the stability of slurs is reinforced by planting on string changes, which also facilitates legato. (Ex. 3.72)

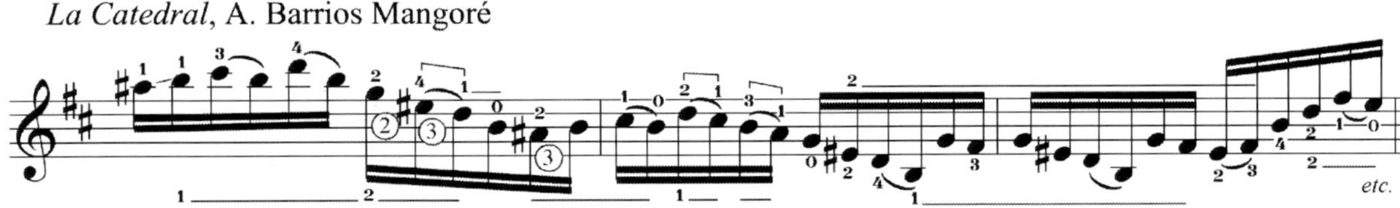

This section of *Estudio Sencillo No. 20* by Brouwer shows a tight sequence of slurs with open strings that leaves few options for planting. In this case, the palm coming into contact with the edge of the neck –with reduced supination– provides additional balance. (Ex. 3.73)

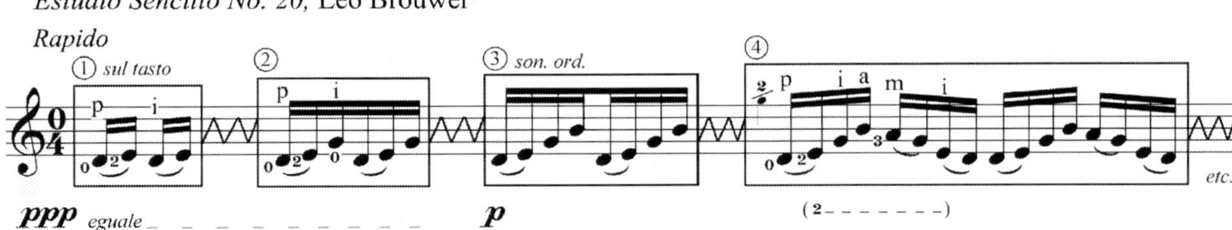

Cross-String Slurs

Basically used in fast passages, cross-string slurs are performed with "percussive hammering" on the inactive string. For greater balance they can be executed by using two or more fingers. (Ex. 3.74)

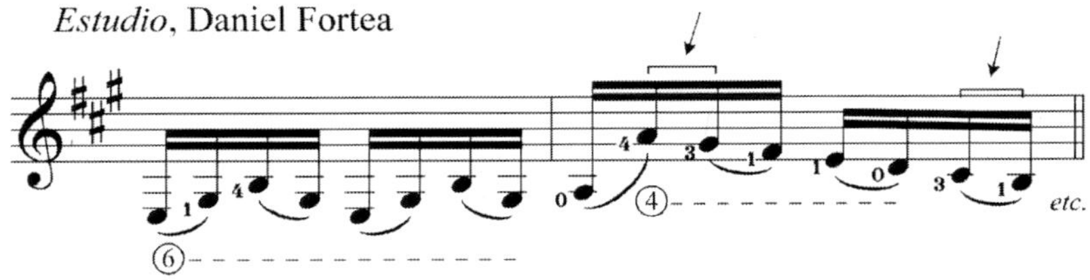

Observe this variant in another segment of *Capricho Arabe* (Tárrega) with a marked violinist style. (Ex. 3.75)

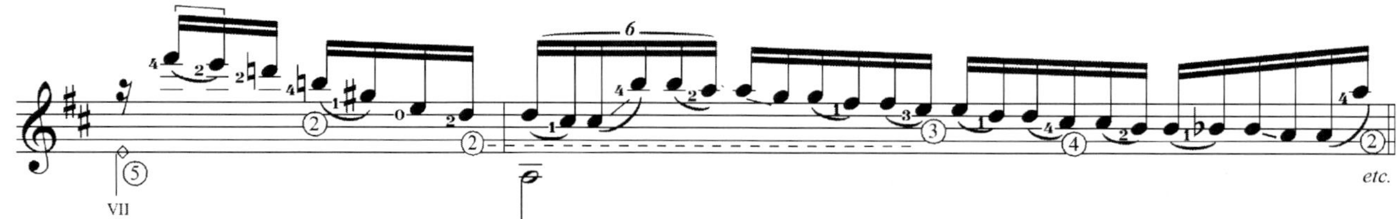

As in *Estudio Sencillo No. 20* by Brouwer, the contact of the palm with the side of the neck supports the security and balance of the descending slurs in *Guajira* by Emilio Pujol (left hand only). (Ex. 3.76)

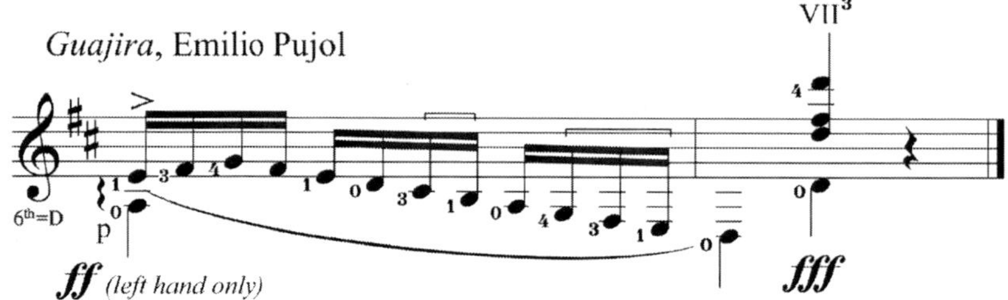

Rotation of the Hand in Slurs

A slight rotation of the aligned left hand, performed with a fixed wrist while maintaining hand-forearm alignment, can facilitate the execution of slurs, increasing economy of effort and agility. This option applies particularly to 1(or 0)-2, 1-3, and 1-4 fingerings. The increase in difficulty is noticeable as the fingering moves away from 1 to 2-3, 2-4, and 3-4. Although the action of the arm as a unit supports the execution of slurs, consideration of these factors is fundamental for an effective performance.

The use of hand rotation in slurs is characteristic of an advanced technical level. (Exs. 3.77)

Staccato

Besides its typical effect on phrasing, left-hand staccato offers a moment of relaxation –a quick release of pressure– that aids in the release from the position. (Exs. 3.78)

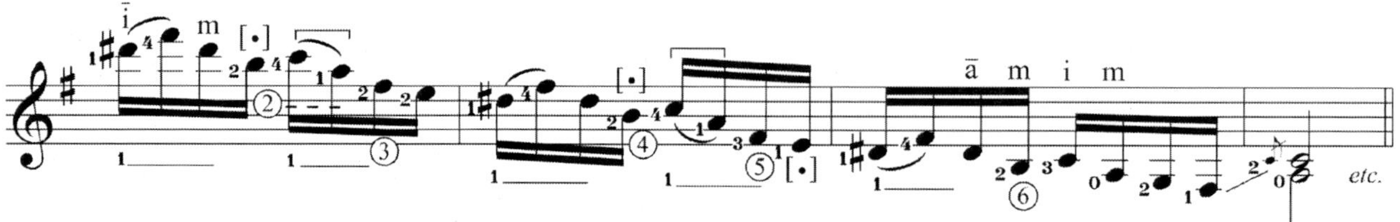

Remember that the "starting velocity" is greater when movements begin from a suitable muscle tone or comfortable position. In addition to providing a convenient lightness, executing a staccato on the note before a slur or ornament enhances the articulation contrast. (Exs. 3.79)

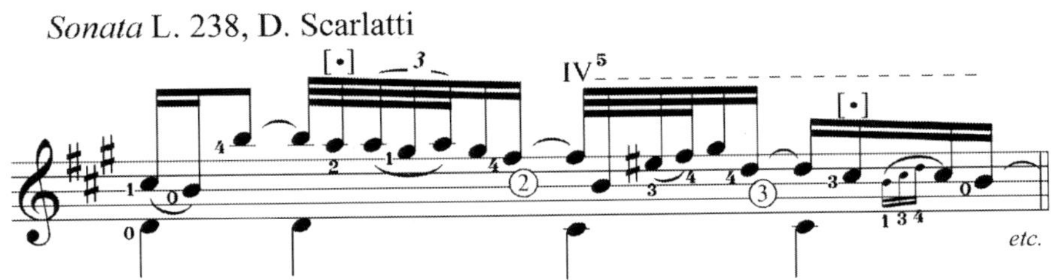

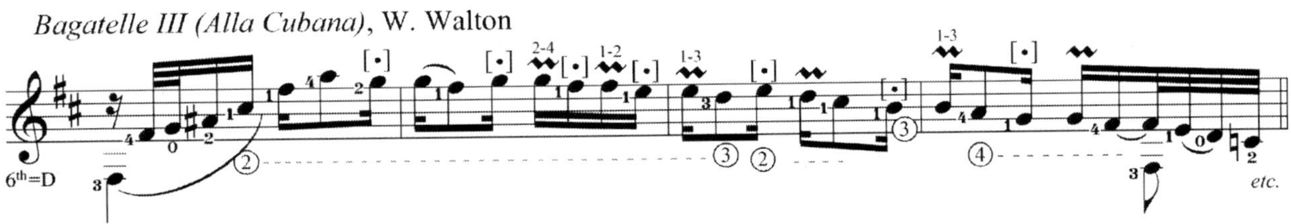

Slur-Staccato

Shortening the duration of slurred notes with a rapid release is another way to lighten shifts. In order to do this in ascending slurs, the pressure is removed from both fingers at once on the rebound; in descending slurs, the pressure is removed from the lower-note finger. Keep in mind that while ascending slurs on a single string are preceded by a vibration or active sound, in descending slurs the moment of pressing must coincide with the right hand plucking whenever possible.

During practice, insert a brief relaxation point after each slur-staccato. The slow and calm study of this technique allows a clear perception of the effort (tension) required, which is a basic aspect of achieving the muscle tone flexibility necessary for playing. (Ex. 3.80)

After performing these exercises you will begin to experience a greater fluency in fast passages. In the examples below, staccato signs have been added. (Exs. 3.81)

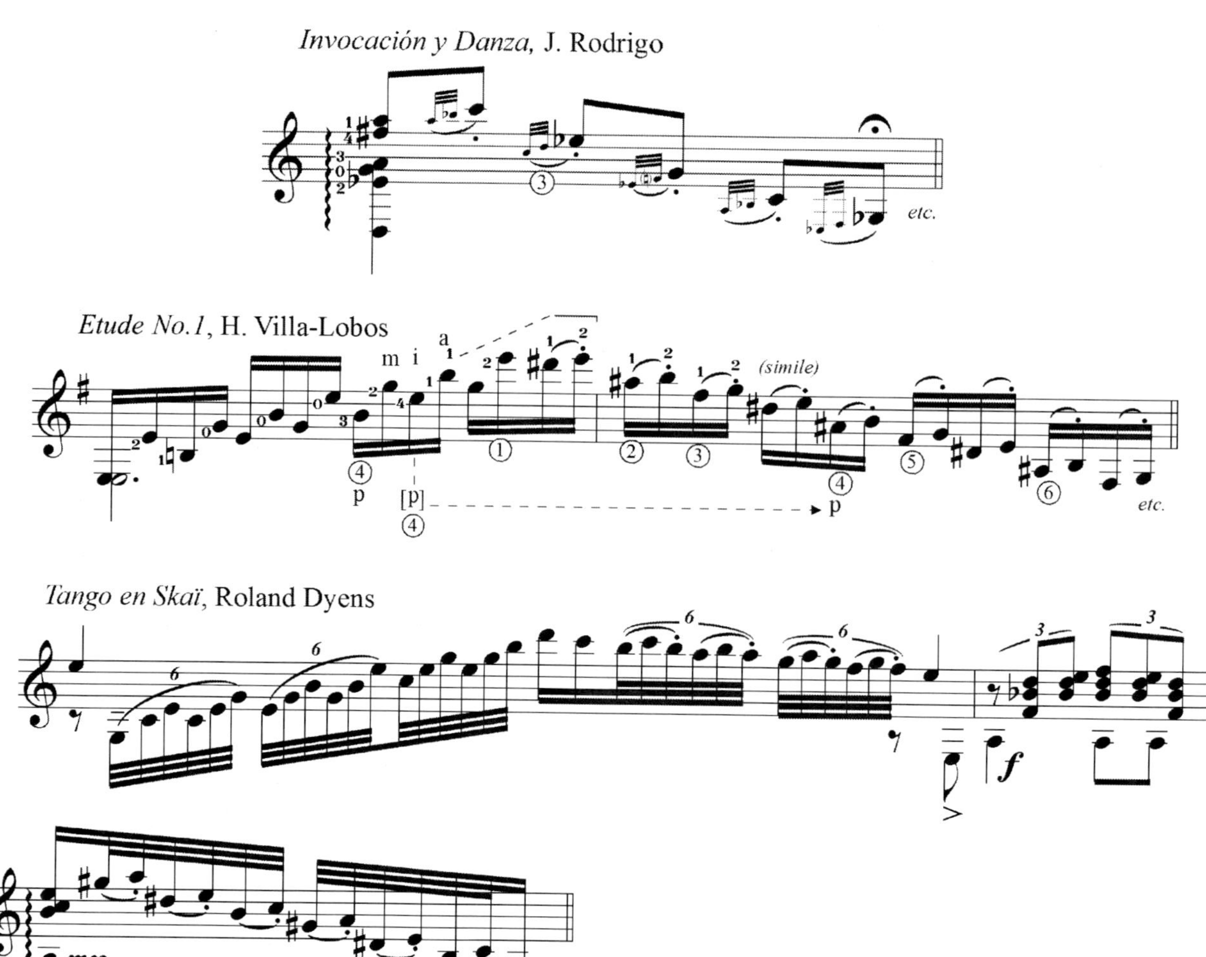

Let's analyze two examples of combined techniques, first by comparing fingerings.

In Example *b)*, barrés are inserted with progressive placement to gain resonance and stability. Once supination is reduced (favoring the 1-4 extension), hand rotation is applied to 1-4/1-0 slurs (first measure), on the second beat extension of the fingers (C-A, finger 4-barré), and shifts (symbolized by curved arrows). (Exs. 3.82)

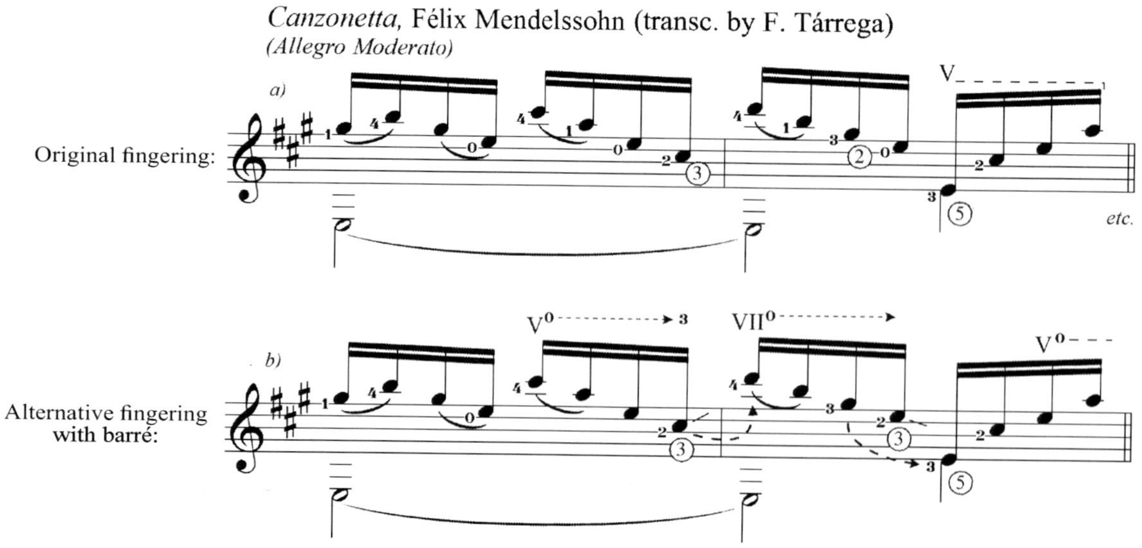

In the following rapid passage from *La Catedral* by Barrios Mangoré, position shifts are implemented with hand rotation, progressive placement, selective pressure (in barré), and slur-staccatos –all resources that promote a balance of work on the fretboard. (Ex. 3.83)

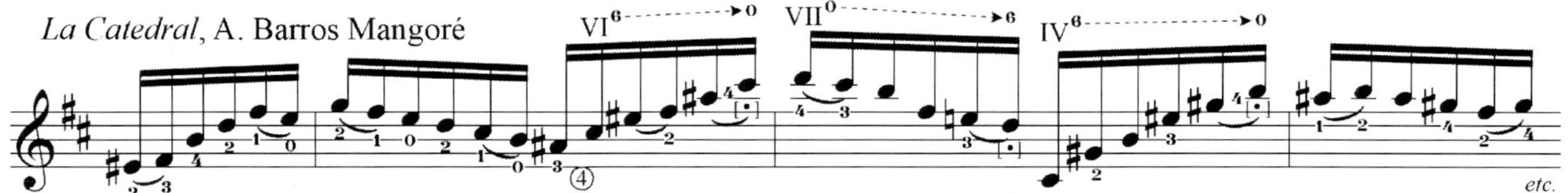

Glissando

A *glissando* (or *glissé*) is performed by sliding any finger along a vibrating string, to reproduce –depending on the score– all or part of the intermediate sounds. *Glissandi* can be classified as *fast* or *slow*.

Fast: With accent and force. Also used as a special effect.

Slow: Portamento (expressive glissando), characteristic of Romantic phrasing *(cantabile)*.

Glissandi are indicated with a straight line that goes from one note to the next. Depending on their type, glissandi notes can be written as a grace note "without fixed duration" because they do not represent a specific sound but rather the starting or ending point of the movement.

On the treble strings, glissandi must be carried out with light pressure, which favors movement and avoids the noisy friction produced by excessive pressure along the frets.

Fast Glissandi:

1. *From a note without fixed duration to another note with fixed duration:* 

Procedure:

After placing the finger on the fret specified by the note without fixed duration, pluck the string and simultaneously glide the finger quickly towards the note with fixed duration –which, without being plucked again, should sound for its full duration. (Ex. 3.84)

The reiterated descending glissandi in *Variations on the Carnival of Venice* (Paganini-Tárrega) suggests a vocal intonation, sometimes described as a "feigned sobs." (Ex. 3.85)

2. *Between two notes with fixed duration:*

Procedure:

Pluck the first note, allowing it to sound for most of its duration, and then quickly slide the finger until it stops on the second-note fret, allowing it to sound in tempo for its full duration, without being plucked again. This type of glissando is equivalent to a two-note slur. (Exs. 3.86)

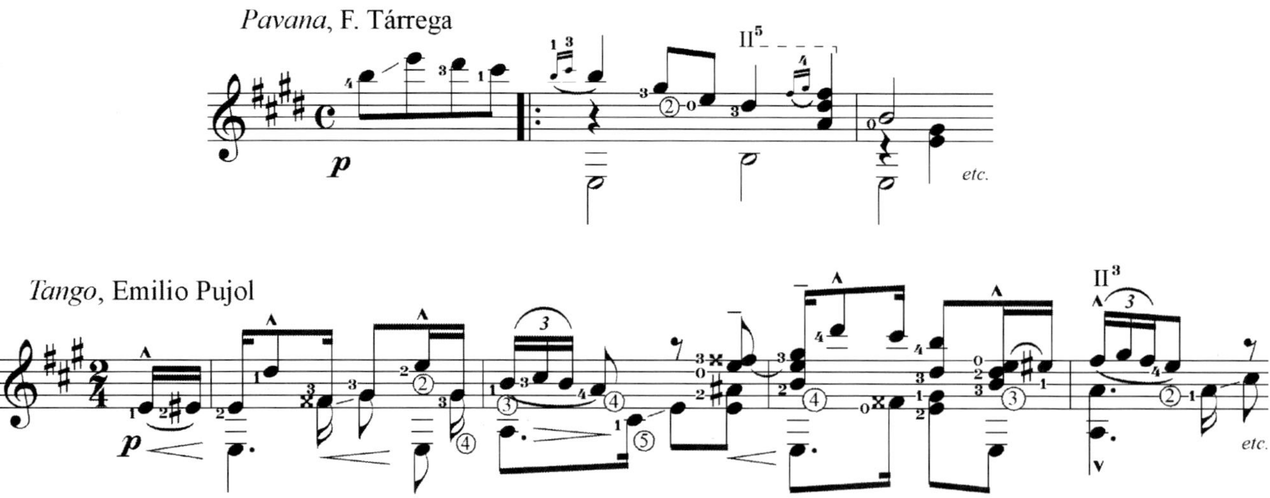

Portamento (Expressive Glissando)

From a note with fixed duration to another without fixed duration:

Procedure:

When the first note is plucked, it gets a part of its duration before the finger glides to the fret that corresponds to the note without fixed duration, reaching it in time to play the note with fixed duration that follows.

Portamento speed is determined by tempo, style, and phrase expressiveness. (Ex. 3.87)

Rotating the hand in fast glissandi supports fluidity and balance, while in ascending portamento it is possible to apply the weight of the arm. These shifts must be done with a relaxed gesture and light pressure.

Obviously, the finger or fingers that perform a portamento from a chord or interval will be the last ones to remain in place; this is facilitated by arpeggiated or disconnected plucking. (Segovia used to execute a fast arpeggiated chord lengthening the starting note of the portamento.)

In the following segment of *Sonatina Meridional* by M. Ponce, portamenti have been suggested which, in moderate to slow tempi, can culminate in a vibrato (+). (Ex. 3.88)

Sonatina Meridional, Manuel M. Ponce

Andante

6th=D

Performance:

Short portamento

Short Portamento

Unlike the expressive portamento –which could be named "long"– the short portamento consists of a small glissando at the start of the shift, which serves in achieving a subtle "impression" of legato. This technique gives a special finish to the phrase.

The brief portamento is particularly effective in large intervals. (Exs. 3.89)

This technique makes it possible to move the "round" and relaxed hand over two or more frets without the need for extensions. (Exs. 3.90)

Bourrée BWV 1002, J. S. Bach

Short or *brief* portamento applications in different contexts: (Exs. 3.91)

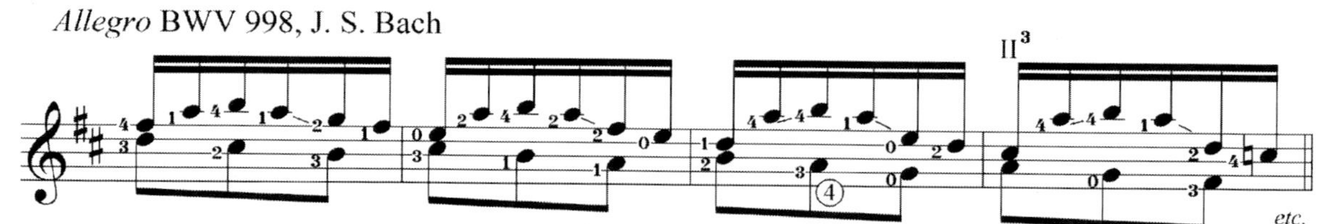

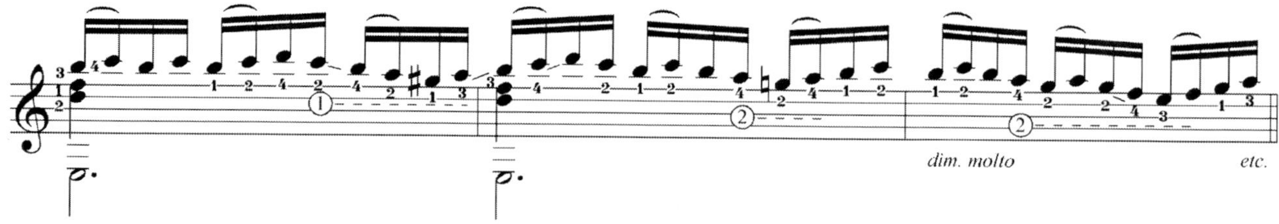

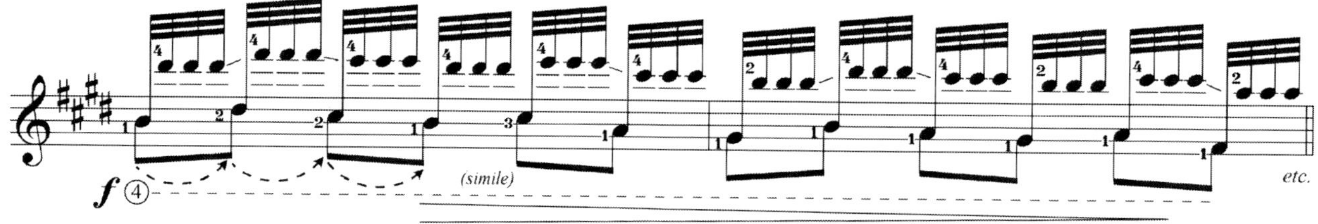

Here are examples of brief portamenti, either moving *from* a barré or *toward* placement of a barré. (Exs. 3.92)

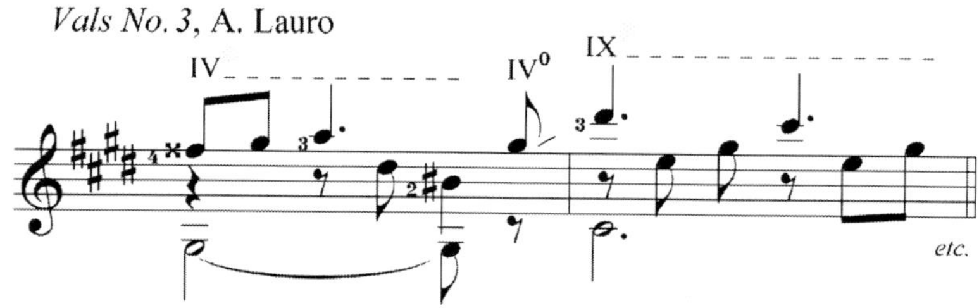

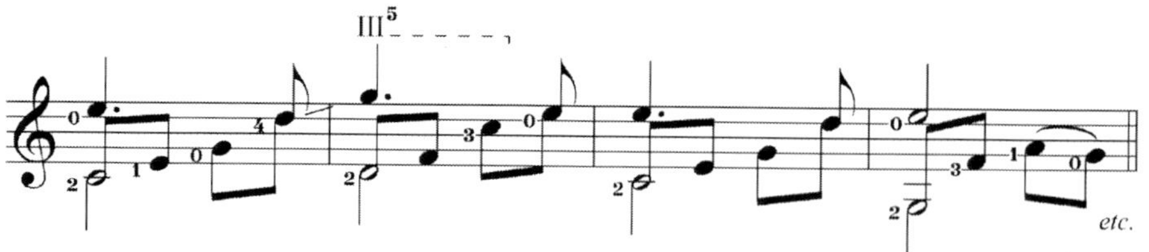

The following examples illustrate less common ways to apply legato through a short portamento: indirectly, from the penultimate note before the shift (*Sonata* by Antonio José Martínez), and in the opposite direction from the next note (*Sonata Clásica* by Manuel Ponce). (Exs. 3.93)

Sonata Clásica, M. Ponce

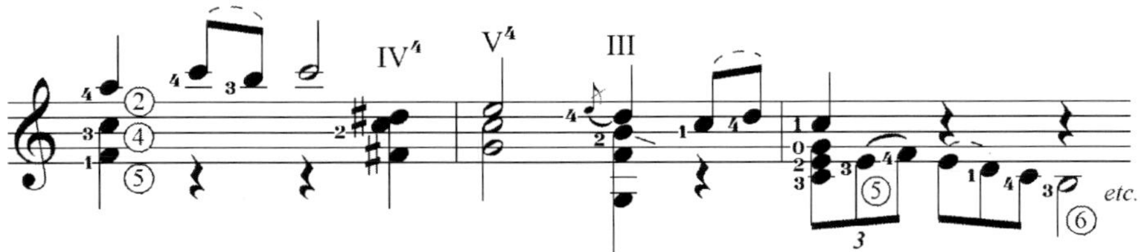

Let's examine two fragments that integrate several of the resources mentioned. The short slide favors shifts in both directions (*Decamerón Negro* by Brouwer), and preserves legato with an agile progressive placement (*Minué* Op. 11, No. 6 by Sor). (Exs. 3.94)

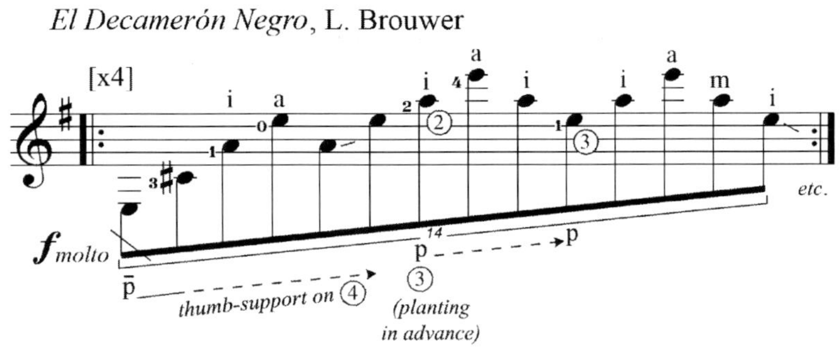

Practice of Short Portamento

Execute the following exercise on the treble strings. Chromatic intervals with 1-2, 2-3, and 3-4 present the greatest complexity. (Ex. 3.95)

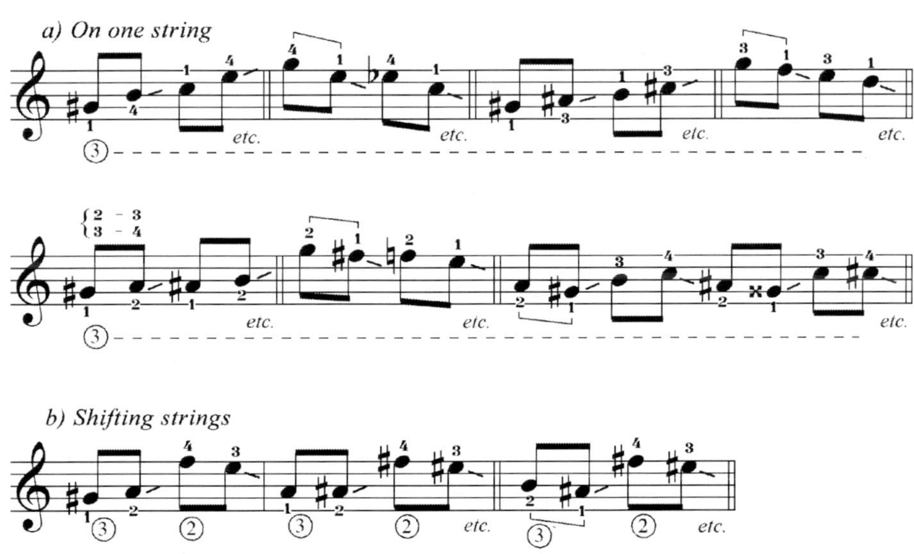

Vibrato

With its slight pitch oscillation, vibrato "humanizes" the sound, giving a warm emotional character to *cantabile*. Here Professor Isaac Nicola discusses this idiomatic technique:

> Possibly known even earlier, vibrato has been practiced, and its execution clearly explained since the seventeenth century in Gaspar Sanz's *Treatise*, who named it "temblor" (trembling). Later it is mentioned as "trémulo" by Aguado in his valuable method. For Sanz and his contemporaries, vibrato has as its main objective the lengthening of sound; only later did it acquire the character of expressive effect. From the second-half of the nineteenth century, and already with the name *vibrato*, it has been widely used by Tárrega and his followers until the present day.
> This resource produces the best results in expressive melodies, and usually is not indicated in a special way, thus depending on the player's criterion. For this reason it should be used moderately, since an excess would indicate bad interpretive taste.[47]

Once plucked, the string's oscillations do not reach their maximum amplitude immediately, so that vibrato applied simultaneously can interrupt its development (See Taylor, 1978:14). For the same reason, while vibrato on bass strings can be fast or slow, on the trebles it should be fast, in correlation with higher-pitched frequencies.

A relaxed disposition of the hand, its balanced placement, and economy of effort in pressing are essential for vibrato. Urshalmi points out:

> Vibrato is the best sign of our physical state (tension or relaxation). It can show us whether the player is aware of his body, and whether there is any collaboration between it and the instrument. (Urshalmi, 2006:135)

Taylor explains that the amplitude of the strings' vibration is defined by the fret, and vibrato is always performed by varying the tension of the strings, unlike on the violin, where it is executed by shortening and lengthening the string.

> ...Vibrato is normally made by keeping the fingertip firmly fixed to the string and moving the hand alternately towards and away from the nut slightly, so as to raise and lower the tension in the vibrating portion of the string.
> It is important to realize that in doing this, one is also raising and lowering the tension in the non-vibrating portion of the string between finger and nut. When playing a note at the twelfth fret, one's efforts are divided about equally between the two portions of the string, but in the lower positions the non-vibrating portion takes up more and more force. At the fifth fret, for instance, only about a quarter of the applied force actually goes to raise and lower the tension in the vibrating portion, while at the first fret, all but about one-eighteenth of the applied force is wasted. (Taylor, 1978:17)

This is clearly the reason why it is easier to execute a vibrato towards the middle of the strings than in the first positions.

The rapid movement of the hand in vibrato can be described as a fluid alternation of two moments: *thrust*, first and strongest impulse, which is carried out more easily towards the bridge (towards our body), and implies "loosening of the string" for a subtle lowering of its normal intonation; and *rebound*, accomplished by releasing the previous effort and continuing with a movement in the opposite direction, which tightens the string and raises its intonation.

Carlevaro classifies two types of vibrato: *longitudinal* and *transverse*. The former and most common, which is done following the string line and allows tone fluctuation in both directions; and the transverse, which allows only upward oscillations due to its movement direction and, therefore, with specific mechanical and sound features (See Carlevaro, 1984:95).

The longitudinal vibrato may be performed more intensively by planting of two or more fingers. (Ex. 3.96)

[47] I. Nicola, M. Pedreira, 2002:23.

Prolonging the Sound

Prolonging the sound with vibrato is achieved by gradually accelerating the oscillations to compensate for sound decay. It is a very useful resource if there are no sympathetic harmonics to support for resonance. While vibrato is more noticeable in slow tempi, it may not stand out expressively in fast tempi, but the energy applied induced to the string will briefly sustain its vibrations, supporting articulation of the melodic lines. (Exs. 3.97)

Cantilena de los Bosques, L. Brouwer

Danza Negra (Suite Venezolana), Antonio Lauro

In Romantic cantabile, vibrato can be emphasized by means of a discrete agogic accentuation. (Exs. 3.98)

Concierto de Aranjuez (Adagio), J. Rodrigo

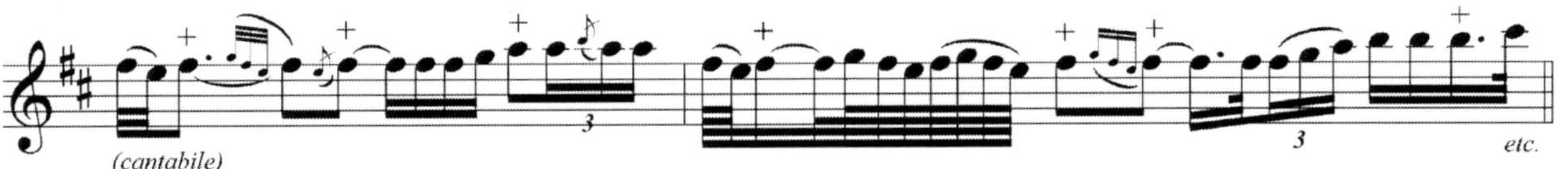

Prelude No. 4, H. Villa-Lobos

Lento

Paisaje cubano con tristeza, L. Brouwer

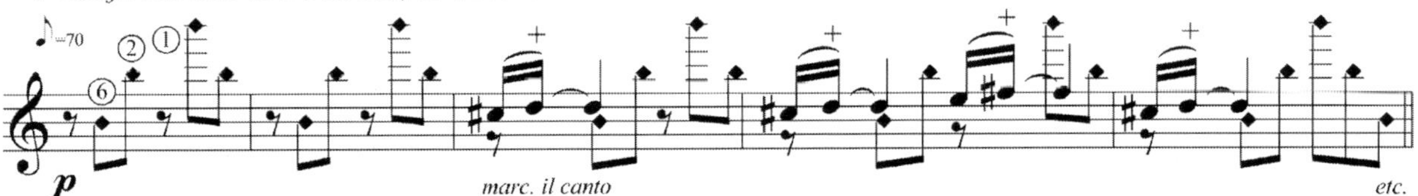

The vibrato of the voice and of bowed string instruments –especially the cello– are excellent references for guitarists. The outstanding cellist and pedagogue Lev S. Ginsburg wrote the following regarding the expressive application of this resource:

> When working on a musical phrase the student must establish which vibrato corresponds to the character of that phrase. In this case, the criterion is none other than the work's style, its contents, spirit, dynamic nuance, register, and timbre. Musical images of the performed score will suggest to the player whether the vibrato has to be excited, accelerated, slow or light, that is to say, what should be its amplitude and frequency. (Ginsburg, 1990:41)

Although the continuous use of this expressive resource is not essential, its total absence from interpretation represents an impoverishing limitation, and a probable sign of deficiencies in the performer's technical and musical training.

EPILOGUE

The following are some essential concepts that have inspired this book:

• Our bodies are the primary vehicle through which we realize artistic creation; in our case, with the aid of a musical instrument.

• Instrumental technique, with a physiological approach characterized by economy of effort and fluency of movements, can be applied to any score. This approach also implies a system of study focused on the best use of our psychophysical potential, which guarantees not only the avoidance of "professional injuries" but the achievement of greater results throughout a long-term career as performer.

• It is possible to adopt a work strategy that encourages a permanent enrichment of the perceptive experience, which is a primary condition of corporal awareness. This knowledge is tested during practice, a time during which we continuously discover and rediscover the *logic of the body*.

• Establishing an ergonomic link with the instrument helps to clear the path to spirituality in performance. Could it be possible to "experience the music" without feeling a free interaction with the instrument?

• The management of technical resources depends both on the development of psychophysical abilities and –substantially– on the player's artistic conception of the score. This is why technique will always be an individual matter.

• Authentic virtuosity implies a broad culture and a special balance of technical-expressive elements in performance. Ginsburg states:

> We would be unlikely to call a musician a Maestro if his/her qualities were reduced to only technical mastery of their instrument. ... A Maestro is the musician/artist who also possesses a deep intellect, brilliant emotional feeling, a creative personality, inspiration, and of course, virtuosic technique that is used as a powerful means of expression to deeply reveal the content of the music that he/she performs.(1990:5)

The music scholar Alexandre Lavignac summarized with poetic simplicity the performer's true mission:

> ...Enchant instead of astonishing the audience, [and] play more for the heart than for the eyes. (1950:109)

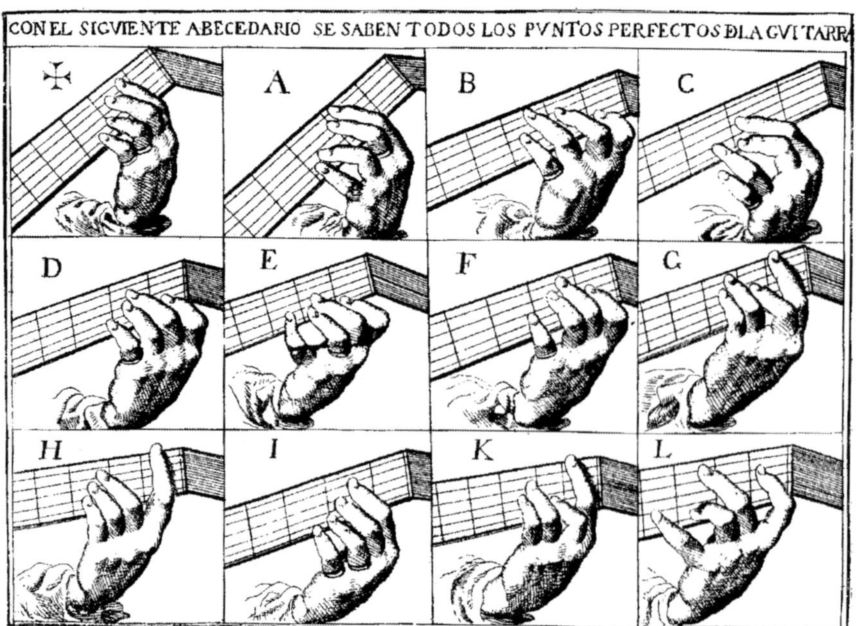

Engraving from *Instrucción de música sobre la guitarra española...*, Gaspar Sanz, Zaragoza, 1674.

Appendixes

I. A Brief Anatomical and Physiological Outline

II. Study of Symmetries of Body Posture with Profilometry

III. Pre-Warmup Exercises

I. A BRIEF ANATOMICAL AND PHYSIOLOGICAL OUTLINE

Skeletal Structure

From a mechanical perspective, the skeleton provides support, muscles are the engines of movement, and joints provide levers which allow an efficient use of energy.

The *carpus* (wrist) consists of a group of eight short small bones, ordered into two lines of four; the one closest to the wrist, which it is part of its articulation, is composed of the *scaphoid, lunate* and *triquetrum* bones. The *pisiform*, although is part of the first line, does not intervene in wrist articulation.

The second line of wrist bones is composed of the *trapezium, trapezoid, capitate* and *hamate.*

The palm (or *metacarpus*) consists of five elongated bones, the *metacarpal bones*. They are counted from the thumb onwards as the first, second, third, fourth and fifth metacarpal.

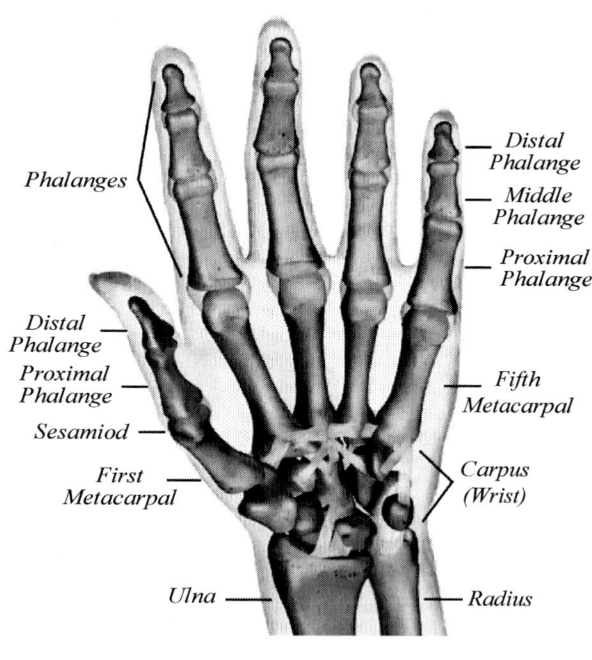

Hand Bones

Each metacarpal bone is articulated with a finger. The phalanges are the elongated ossicles that make up each segment of the fingers. The thumb has two phalanges: *proximal* and *distal*, the other fingers have three: *proximal* (or metacarpal), *middle* and *distal* (third phalanx).

We can move our fingers thanks to a complex group of muscles that extend from the elbow to the last phalanges.

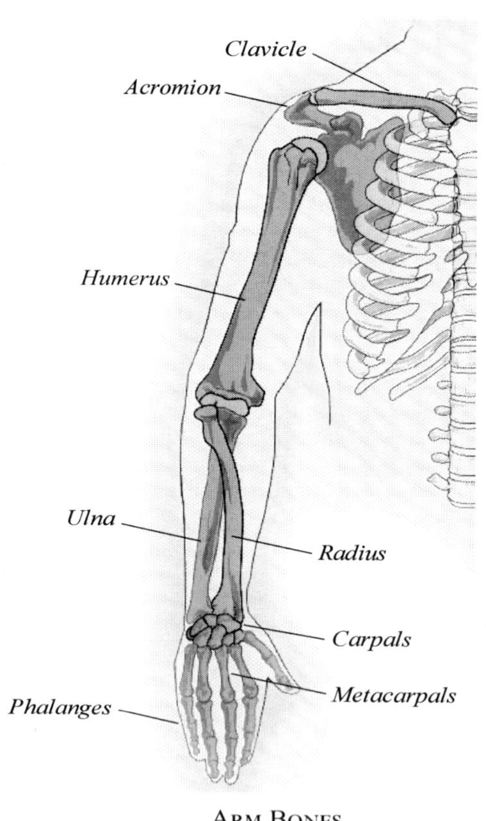

Arm Bones

Almost every muscle in the body acts in coordination to provide solid support for the hands to work. Any movement exerted by the fingers, hand or forearm demands the specific activity of one or more muscle groups in a coordinated effort.[48]

[48] All segments of the skeleton are interrelated. The arm, shoulder, thorax, spine and support on the seat of the *ischial* bones provide stability to the work of the hands. Although the flexion and extension movements of the fingers are performed by the muscles located below the elbow, the stability of the elbow joint itself by the arm muscles is not less important. At the same time, the arm must stabilize from the shoulder, and this involves the deltoid, trapezius, pectoral muscles, etc.

The bones of the arm *(humerus)* and the forearm (*ulna* and *radius*) present a different architecture. The humerus is an almost rectilinear bone, articulated with the *scapula* above (head of the humerus) and below with the ulna and radius.

The ulna and the radius are long bones, articulated together at their ends and separated in the rest of their extension by an elliptical space (interosseous space). The ulna is positioned towards the outer side of the forearm and the radius towards the inner. Both articulate with the *carpus*, which together with the metacarpus and phalanges constitute the bones of the hand.

Muscle Structure

All muscles have basically the same structure, from the smallest that move and stabilize the ossicles of the middle ear, to the huge *quadriceps femoris* on the front of the thigh.

Each muscle has a hook attachment at each of its two ends, called *origin* and *insertion*, and a fleshy and contractile part, known as the *muscle belly*. The origin and the insertion are usually composed of non-contractile tendons, and the hooks vary according to the mechanical needs of each joint.

Muscle groups are classified by their function in two general categories: the *dynamic musculature* (responsible for movement) and the *supporting* or *skeletal musculature* (providing structure).

The *agonist* muscles are the prime movers; they providing the force for flexion. *Antagonists* oppose the movements of the agonists. They contribute to the realization of gentle movements by means of their power to maintain muscle tone (*tonus* or residual tension), and also relax and allow movement of the flexor group. This natural mechanism of balance is called the *myotatic reflex*.[49]

[49]Reflexes are involuntary reactions to external or internal stimuli that generally tend to counteract the disturbance that gave rise to them. Common examples are coughing and blinking. In the so-called *myotatic* or *muscle stretching reflex*, the recipients send that information to the brain, which in turn directs the muscle (antagonist) to resist and contract. The time elapsed between the stimulus and the response (latency) is very short (25-30 milliseconds), so the process stops almost simultaneously with the triggering stimulus. A distortion of this reflex is clearly noticeable in focal dystonias.

A third set of muscles are the *synergists*, which aid the agonists and reduce undesirable activity or unnecessary movements.

Muscle Groups

The hand has a highly complex structure that enables its great motor versatility. Its muscles can be divided into two groups: *extrinsic* and *intrinsic* muscles. The extrinsic muscles are located in the anterior and posterior compartments of the forearm. They control crude movements and produce a forceful grip.

The intrinsic muscles are located within the hand itself. They are responsible for the fine motor functions of the hand. The main muscle groups involved in the mobility of the hand and fingers are the *flexors, extensors, adductors, abductors, supinators* and *pronators (deflectors)*. Let's examine a synthetic description of their functions.

Flexors and Extensors

Flexors allow bending the wrists and fingers. In the opposite direction, the extensors (antagonist group) move the fingers and palm to their normal rest positions.

These muscles are located on both sides of the forearm: the flexors on the anterior (palm side) and the extensors on the posterior. They are long, thin muscles that are connected to the *humerus*, covering the forearm bones, and most of them cross the wrist joints –also on both sides– through the *carpal tunnel* and palm until inserted again the phalanges of the index, middle, ring and little fingers through delicate tendons.

There are different typologies of these groups: *the common extensor of the fingers*, *the extensor of the index* and *extensor of the little finger*, *flexors* (*long* and *short*), and *the extensor (separator) of the thumb.*

Adductors and Abductors

The adductor muscles allow the fingers to be joined laterally, and the abductors extend from the center (middle finger). Both are groups of short muscles inserted between the parallel bones of the palm and its dorsal part.

The adduction of the thumb is performed by a transverse and deep muscle, located in the palm (passes below the thenar eminence),[50] which works along with other muscles of the back of the thenar. Both groups actively participate in the circular movements of the thumb.

Supinators and Pronators (Deflectors)

Rotation of the hand or *pronosupination* is performed by the muscles of the forearm. *Supination* occurs when we turn our thumbs outward to observe the palm, and *pronation* is the reverse movement. The middle zone between supination and pronation is assumed when the arms freely hang at the sides of the body.

Supination is performed by two muscles (the biceps in the upper arm and the supinator in the forearm) that connect the humerus and the radius. *Pronation* is produced by a quadrilateral transverse muscle *(pronator cuadratus)* that connects the two bones of the forearm near the wrist under the flexors, and also by a transverse muscle *(*the *pronator teres)*, which extends diagonally from the humerus and upper ulna at the elbow to an insertion point near the middle of the radius. Upon pronation, the radius rotates over the ulna, and restores the natural resting attitude of the hand and forearm.

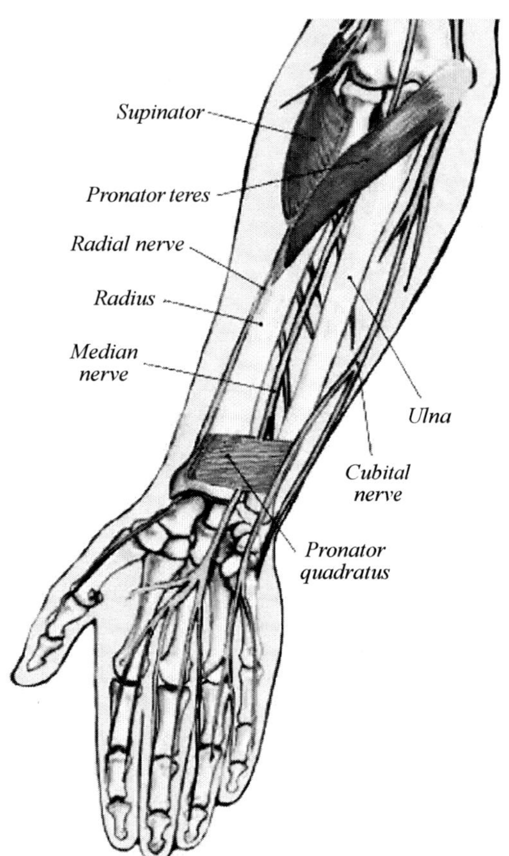

Supinator and Pronator Muscles (Palmar View)

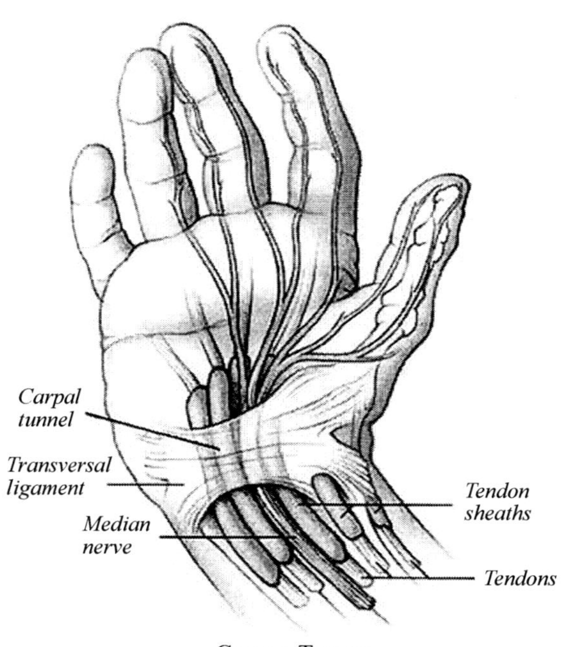

Carpal Tunnel

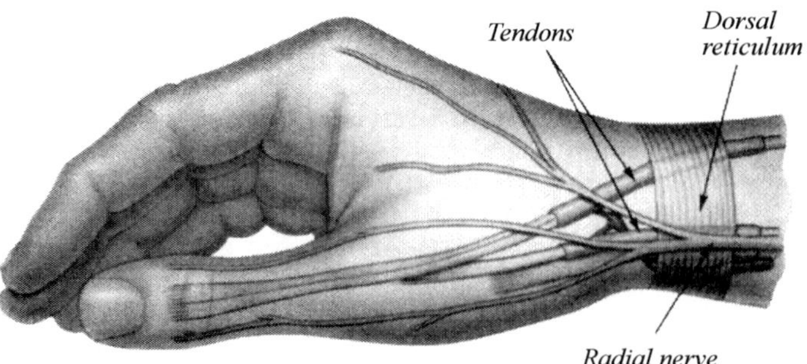

Extensor of the Thumb and Radial Nerve

[50] The thenar muscles are three short muscles located at the base of the thumb (*opponens*, *abductor* and *flexor*). The muscle bellies produce a bulge, known as the *thenar eminence*. They are responsible for the fine movements of the thumb. The *hypothenar* muscles produce the *hypothenar eminence*, a protrusion on the middle side of the palm, at the base of the little finger. These muscles have similar names and organization to the thenar muscles.

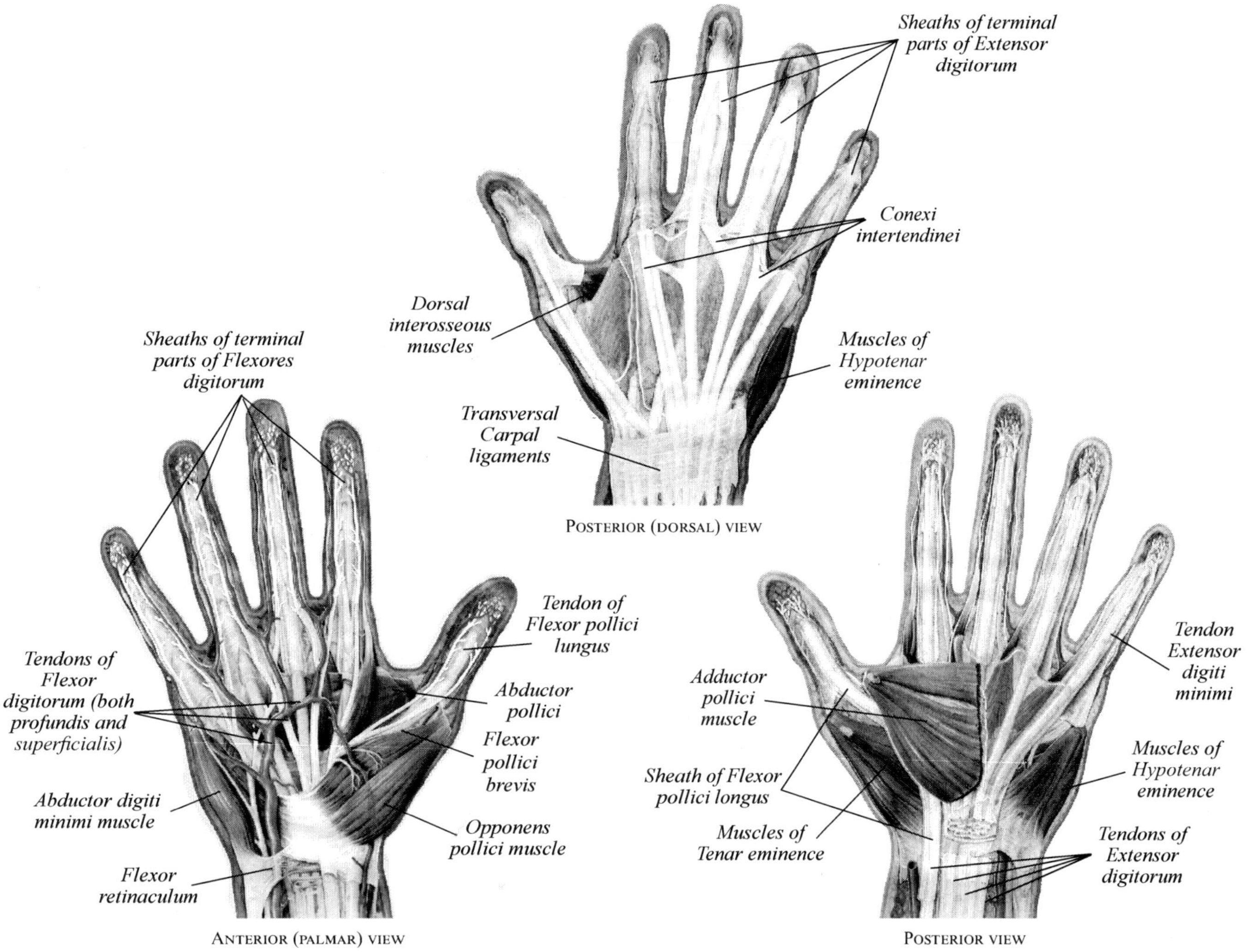

Sheaths of terminal parts of Extensor digitorum

Conexi intertendinei

Dorsal interosseous muscles

Muscles of Hypotenar eminence

Transversal Carpal ligaments

Posterior (dorsal) view

Sheaths of terminal parts of Flexores digitorum

Tendon of Flexor pollici lungus

Tendons of Flexor digitorum (both profundis and superficialis)

Abductor pollici

Flexor pollici brevis

Abductor digiti minimi muscle

Opponens pollici muscle

Flexor retinaculum

Anterior (palmar) view

Adductor pollici muscle

Tendon Extensor digiti minimi

Sheath of Flexor pollici longus

Muscles of Hypotenar eminence

Muscles of Tenar eminence

Tendons of Extensor digitorum

Posterior view

Hand Muscles and Tendons

Nervous System. Arteries and Veins of the Hand

Nerves

The nerves innervating the muscles of the hand originate higher up, from a structure called the *brachial plexus.* This plexus is formed from the combination of the anterior branches of the 5th to 8th cervical spinal nerves and the first thoracic nerve.

The branches of the brachial plexus going to the hand are the *median, ulnar,* and *radial* nerves. When referring to the hand, the radial nerve only provides cutaneous innervation along the outside of the thumb. In contrast, the other two nerves supply the hand muscles; the median nerve predominantly supplies the thenar muscles, while the ulnar nerve mainly innervates the hypothenar and other intrinsic muscles of the hand. The main branches projecting onto the hand muscles are from the median and ulnar nerves.

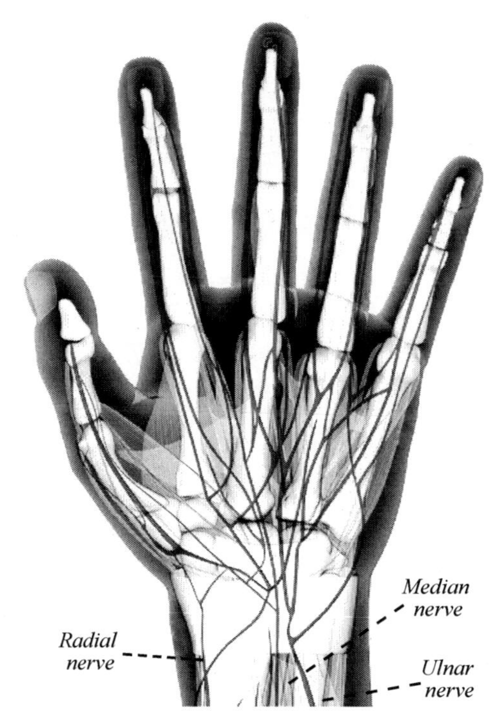

Hand Innervation

Nerves of the Hand.

- Median nerve
- Common palmar digital nerves
- Proper palmar digital nerves
- Ulnar nerve
- Superficial branches
- Deep branches
- Dorsal branches

Arteries

The arteries deliver oxygen-rich blood *from* the heart to the tissues of the body.

All arterial branches of the hand originate from the *radial* and *ulnar* arteries, the two major blood vessels that supply blood to the forearm and hand. After it travels across the wrist, the radial artery branches out to form a network of blood vessels in the hand.

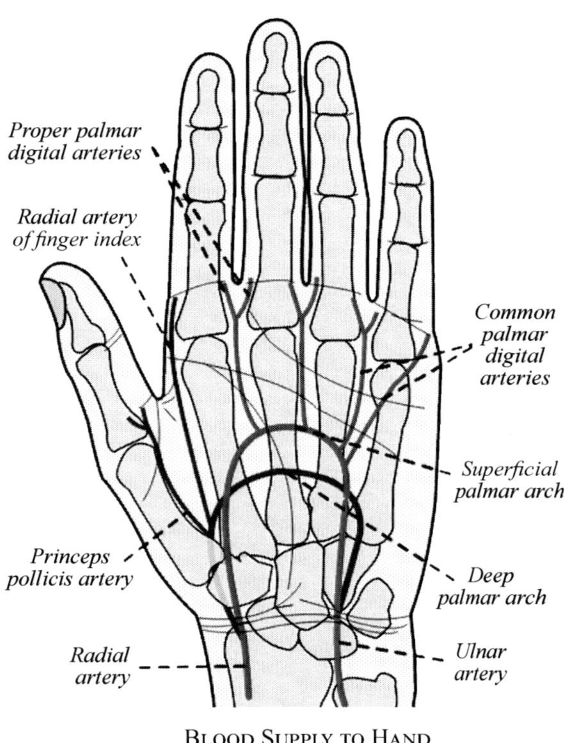

Blood Supply to Hand

Branches of Radial and Ulnar Arteries in the Hand.

- Superficial palmar arch
- Deep palmar arch
- Common palmar arteries
- Proper palmar digital arteries
- Dorsal carpal arch
- Dorsal metacarpal arteries
- Dorsal digital arteries
- Dorsal metacarpal arteries
- Principal artery of the thumb

Veins

Veins are blood vessels that carry blood *towards* the heart. Since the hand is the terminal region of the upper extremity numerous *anastomoses* take place here,[51] resulting in quite a complex vascular network.

Essentially, the veins of the hand drain into either the *radial* or *ulnar* veins and consist of the following:

- Superficial palmar venous arch
- Deep palmar venous arch
- Dorsal venous network of the hand
- Palmar metacarpal digital veins

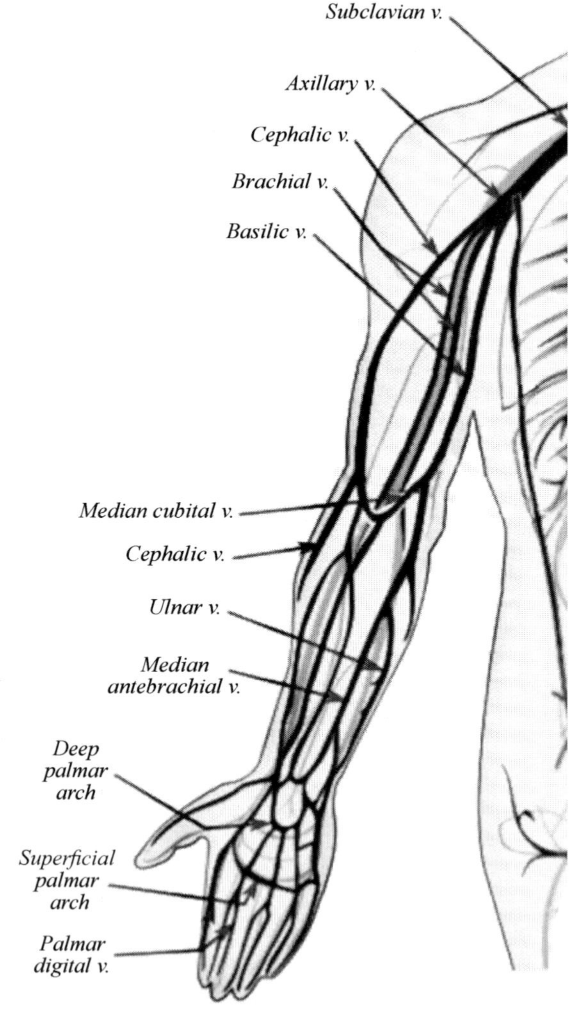

Arm Venous System

[51] A *circulatory anastomosis* is a connection or looped interaction between two blood vessels. Anastomoses occur normally in the body in the circulatory system, serving as backup routes for blood flow if one link is blocked or otherwise compromised.

Muscular Physiology

Muscles are composed of two types of fibers that are stimulated by nerve impulses: those of rapid contraction or *white fibers*, and those of slow contraction or *red fibers*.

White fibers are strong and fast but fatigue easily. They form approximately 50% of muscle tissue and are divided in turn into two types: *fast white* and *explosive white*. The rest of the muscle tissue is made up of slow (red) fibers.

For fuel, energy fibers use ATP (adenosine triphosphate), which is found in minimal amounts inside the muscle, so it runs out in no time. When ATP is exhausted, white fibers resort to burning glucose (sugar), which they metabolize anaerobically (without oxygen). This process creates lactic acid as residue, which acidifies the muscle and stops its contractile activity. This effect is called *transitory fatigue*, because once this substance is evacuated, the muscle returns to normal function.

White explosive fibers increase their potency in training but not their size. White fast fibers markedly enlarge their size with exercise, hence they produce hypertrophy (muscle enlargement), as seen in bodybuilders.

Red fibers are slow compared to white ones. Their color is due to the presence of *myoglobin*, a red protein that carries the oxygen used in their metabolism. Red fibers are weaker than the white ones but they never fatigue; theoretically, they stop working when the fuel runs out. The glucose they use is metabolized aerobically (with oxygen).[52]

The innervation of muscles presents a highly efficient organization. There are two types of nerve fibers: the *motor fibers*, which transmit impulses from the *central nervous system* (CNS) to regulate their contractions, and the *sensory fibers*, which transmit information about the state of the muscular contraction to the CNS.

The *kinesthetic sense* apparatus resides in the muscle tissues, tendons and joint capsules, where innumerable receptors *(neuromuscular and neurotendinous bundles)*, sensitive to the elongation and the tension of the muscles, record the variations of these parameters, allowing us to know in which direction and how quickly we must move.

Contraction is the physical process where, by means of a nervous stimulus, the distance between the ends of a muscle is shortened. This shortening can reach up to two-thirds of the total resting muscle size. Generically, *tension* is the degree of contraction produced by and for muscle activity.

Contraction can take place in a limb without its flexing, i. e., without changes in the length of the muscle *(isometric contraction)*, but usually a modification occurs that gives rise to the movement of its adjacent joint.

An insufficient contraction does not deploy the force required to provoke movement, while if it is excessive, it has an effect of loading or weight sensation derived from the resistance opposed to movement.[53]

Relaxation occurs at both neuromuscular and psychic levels. In the context of muscle work, relaxation is defined as a period of diminished tension between two moments of tension, the loosening of muscles in order to prepare for a new contraction (greater degree of tension). In this book we have used the term *functional relaxation* to denote a condition that allows fluid development of actions.

It is very convenient for the musician to not only perform physical exercises, but also to practice relaxation techniques (Schultz's *Autogenic Training*, Benson's *Relaxation Response*, etc.). Such training helps to balance physical and mental activity, conditioning the individual for efficient use of energy at all times.

[52] *Metabolism* is a balance between *catabolism* (destruction of structural components) and *anabolism* (plastic body building). When a muscle is exercised, the organism reacts by strengthening it, and therefore, increases its volume (hypertrophy) and strength. To do this, it synthesizes new proteins that will form part of the muscle (anabolism). If the person does not exercise, the body reacts by destroying part of the muscle and causing a decrease in size (catabolism). The sequence of construction and destruction is permanent, and the entire body's muscle mass is renewed in a constant equilibrium. The balance is in favor of the muscle when it is stimulated by training, but against it when it remains inactive.

[53] When a muscle or a certain group of muscles reacts under hyper-tension once in a while, no harm is done, but when a certain movement (particularly a specific or professional one) is repeated over and over for a long time during the day, an immediate slowing down of speed and fluency is felt. The decrease in speed causes deterioration in musical output. Insufficient output is not the end of the story… The long term consequence is physical damage, known as *professional disease*. This applies not only to playing music but also to other fields such as dance, sports and manual labor. (Urshalmi, 2006:32)

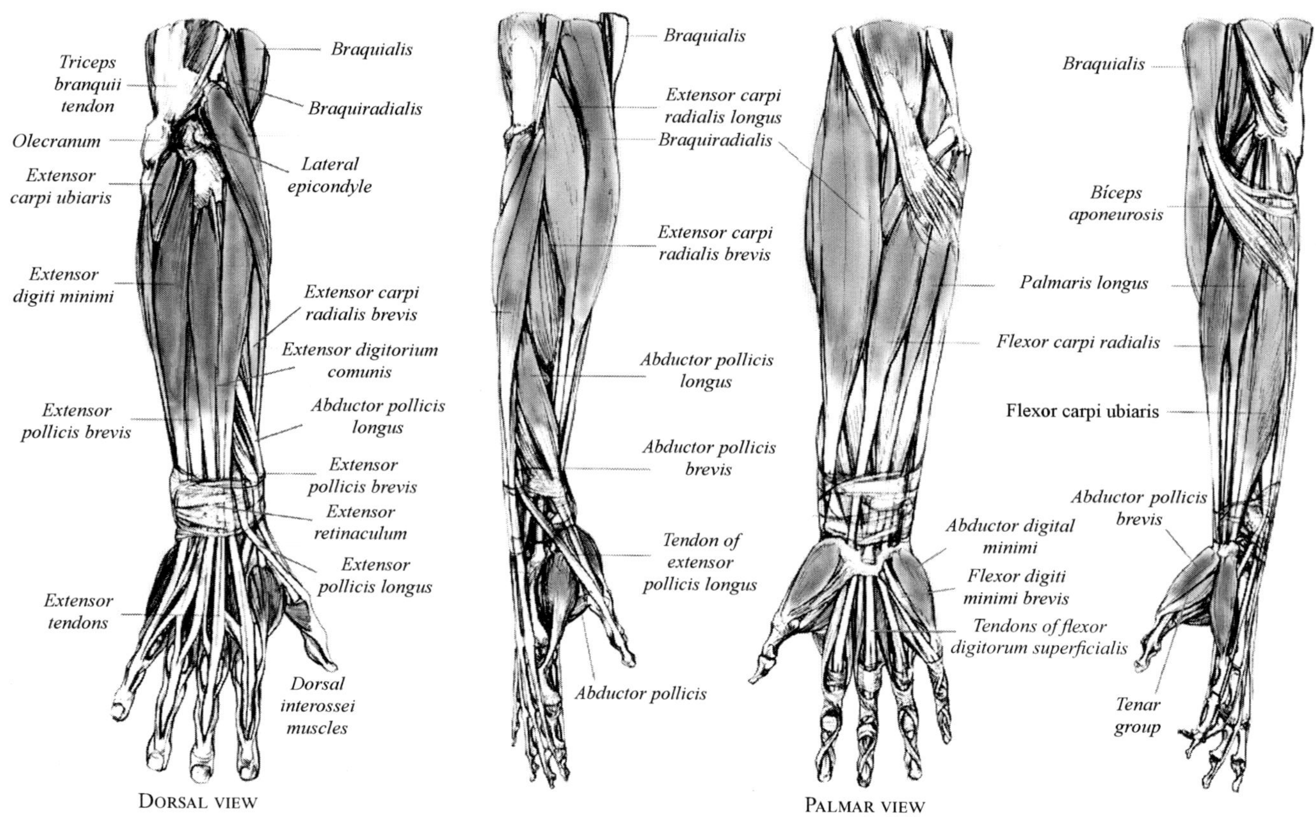

HAND AND FOREARM MUSCLES

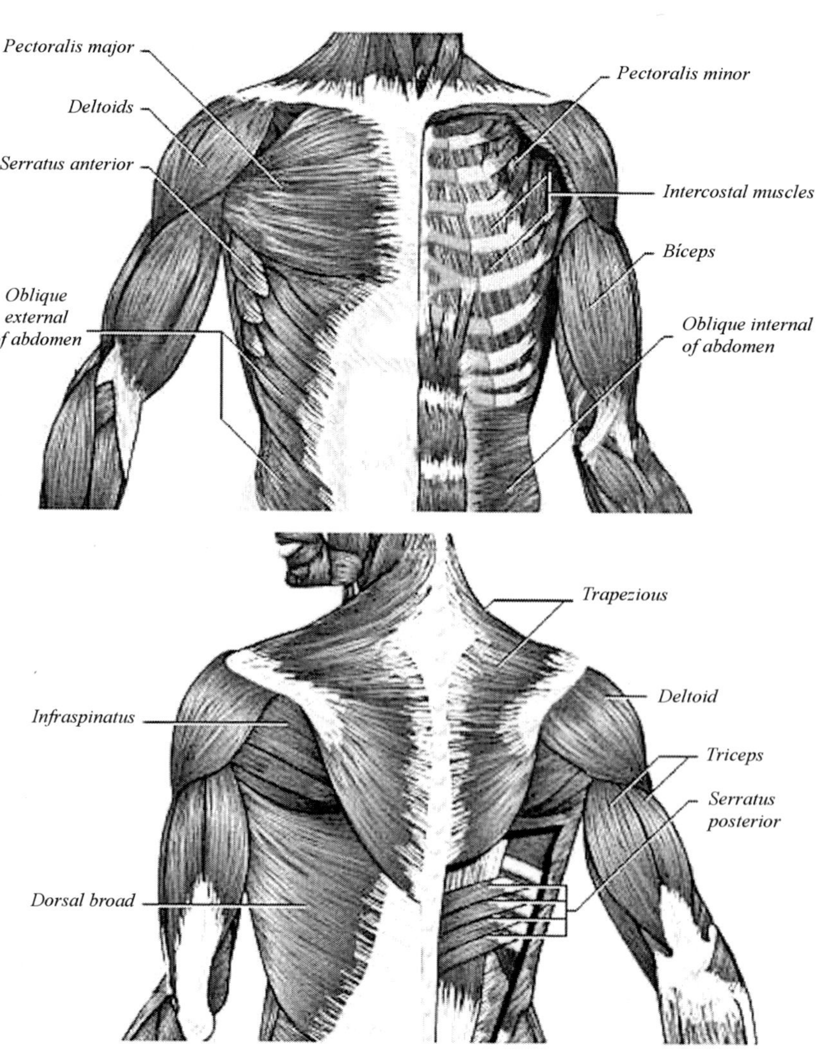

SUPERFICIAL CHEST AND BACK MUSCLES

The continuous muscle work of any modality is linked to a constant increase of tension. Each new action starts at a higher level of tension, although this can be cushioned by a specific ability.

Individuals trained in relaxation techniques can momentarily reduce their overall stress level so that new performance takes place more easily. This possibility is particularly useful for instrumentalists, allowing them to achieve in a shorter time the *eutony* or muscle tone suitable for an action, and to quickly resolve residual tensions.[54]

Muscle tone is the property of the muscle by which a partial and permanent contraction of varying degrees is sustained. It is the level of tension of muscle fibers, and by extension, of all the tissues of the body. This semi-contracted state, which maintains a constant length of the muscle, is automatically conditioned by the central nervous system.

Each situation requires a different muscle tone. Breathing, voice, posture and movement are closely linked to tone, which itself is modulated by our emotions and thoughts. *Emotions are communicated through muscle tone, as tone is one of the clearest expressions of the unity of mind and body.*

Psychophysiologists describe muscle tone as "the activity of an apparently resting muscle." This definition indicates that the muscle is always active, even if this does not translate into movements or gestures.

> ... This tonic function has the property of regulating the apparent activity of the muscle, which conditions our posture, and makes the body muscles ready to respond promptly to the multiple demands of life. (G. Alexander, 1989:25)

Eutonic movement is characterized by lightness of execution and by the use of the right energy for a good physical result.[55] Lightness presupposes releasing tone fixations and the integration of the muscles that do not participate as motors of the movement.

Tonic contractions in the skeletal muscles sustain the posture for long periods without signs of fatigue. The absence of fatigue is due to the fact that different muscle fibers contract separately, which allows alternate periods of rest and activity.

The antigravity muscles (neck retractors, back extensors, etc.) show the highest degree of tonicity, and during sleep, their lowest levels are reached.

Stress and anxiety increase muscle tone, but the muscles may shorten too much, causing annoyances, pains and, above all, an imbalance of forces between the agonist and antagonist groups.

Tone flexibility is found in sensitive individuals who are in touch with themselves and capable of establishing a conscious dialog within themselves and with others; such people display creative behaviors in their daily life, in their family and group interests in general, and in their artistic production and work.

> Muscle tone flexibility is a necessary condition for the optimal development of a means of expression: sculpting, painting, drawing, writing, singing, movement, etc., whose realizations are improved and enriched by a refined adaptation. (G. Alexander, 1989:35)

•

[54] Disciplines and methods of psychophysical work like Gerda Alexander's *Eutony*, M. Feldenkrais, M. Alexander, *Body Map*, Pilates, etc., as well as the practice of Yoga and Tai Chi, report an unquestionable benefit. On the other hand, *Body Expression* exercises stimulate personality growth through expression, suggestion, and self-realization. Efficient (or beautiful) movements are not always performed instinctively. It is necessary to develop them through specific training.

[55] Achieving Eutony in performance is equivalent to what Aaron Shearer describes as the deployment of a "productive tension," as "minimal muscular effort necessary to play the guitar" (Shearer, 1980:9).

II. STUDY OF SYMMETRIES OF BODY POSTURE USING PROFILOMETRY

Using a process called profilometry or Moiré Topography,[56] research was conducted comparing two ways of holding the guitar (postural dispositions) and their effect on the symmetry of the body.

The procedure consists of focusing a filtered light beam across the back of the subject through a thin net of strings; the light can also be projected through a slide for an equal effect.

The contrast produced by the stripes of light and shadow outlines a sort of "relief map" that represents skeletal-muscle shifts, and reveals the degree of tension in each posture.

Once photographed, the samples were processed with special software to determine the amount of asymmetry. Additionally, the test made it possible to detect spinal problems in several participants.

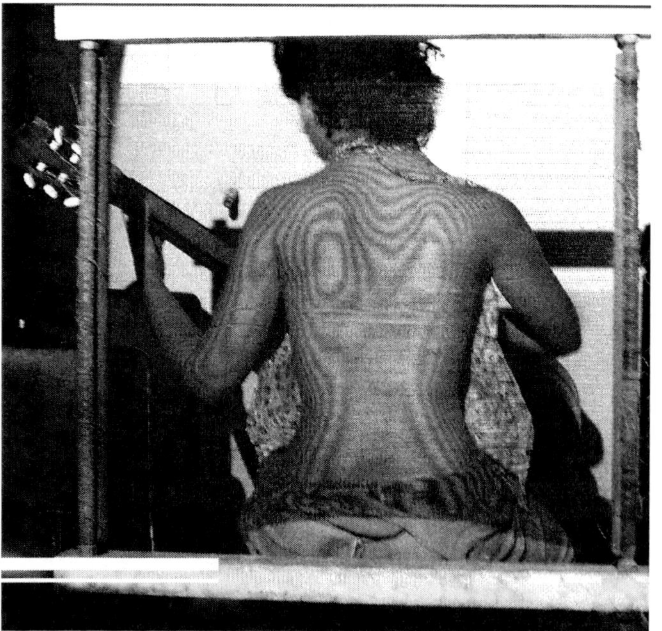

Improving postural symmetry is increasingly recomended in studies to prevent injuries, help relieve pain, reduce joint stress, and also improve balance, level of energy, functional motion, flexibility and breath capacity.

Results

In all the individuals studied (25 adults between 18 and 22 years old, and medium height average) a greater degree of muscle distortion was observed in the traditional placement of the instrument than in the slanted one, although the slanted one was not their usual placement.[57]

Even with the existence of a moderate scoliosis (B and C Photo series), asymmetries in the upper part of the back clearly decreased with the slanted placement.

The use of the footstool, which inclines the hip, always produces a degree of tension in the lumbar area (Photos 2 and 3). The fourth series shows the effect of a slightly round-shouldered or hunched-over posture.

Description of Samples

1. Normal standing posture, without the instrument.

2. Traditional placement of the guitar (with footstool).

3. Slanted placement *(adapting the guitar to the body ...).*

[56] See H. Takasaki: "Moiré Topography" in *Applied Optics, Optical Society of America*, vol. 9 No. 6, 1970). Profilometry has multiple applications. It has been used in the detection of pathologies of the back and thorax –mainly with children– replacing x-rays. The present study was carried out by Dr. Beatriz Moreno and the author with a group of guitar students at the University of Arts, and the National School of Music in Havana during a two-year course of study (2004-2006).

[57] See Chapter I, *Posture, Instrument Placement and Breathing.*

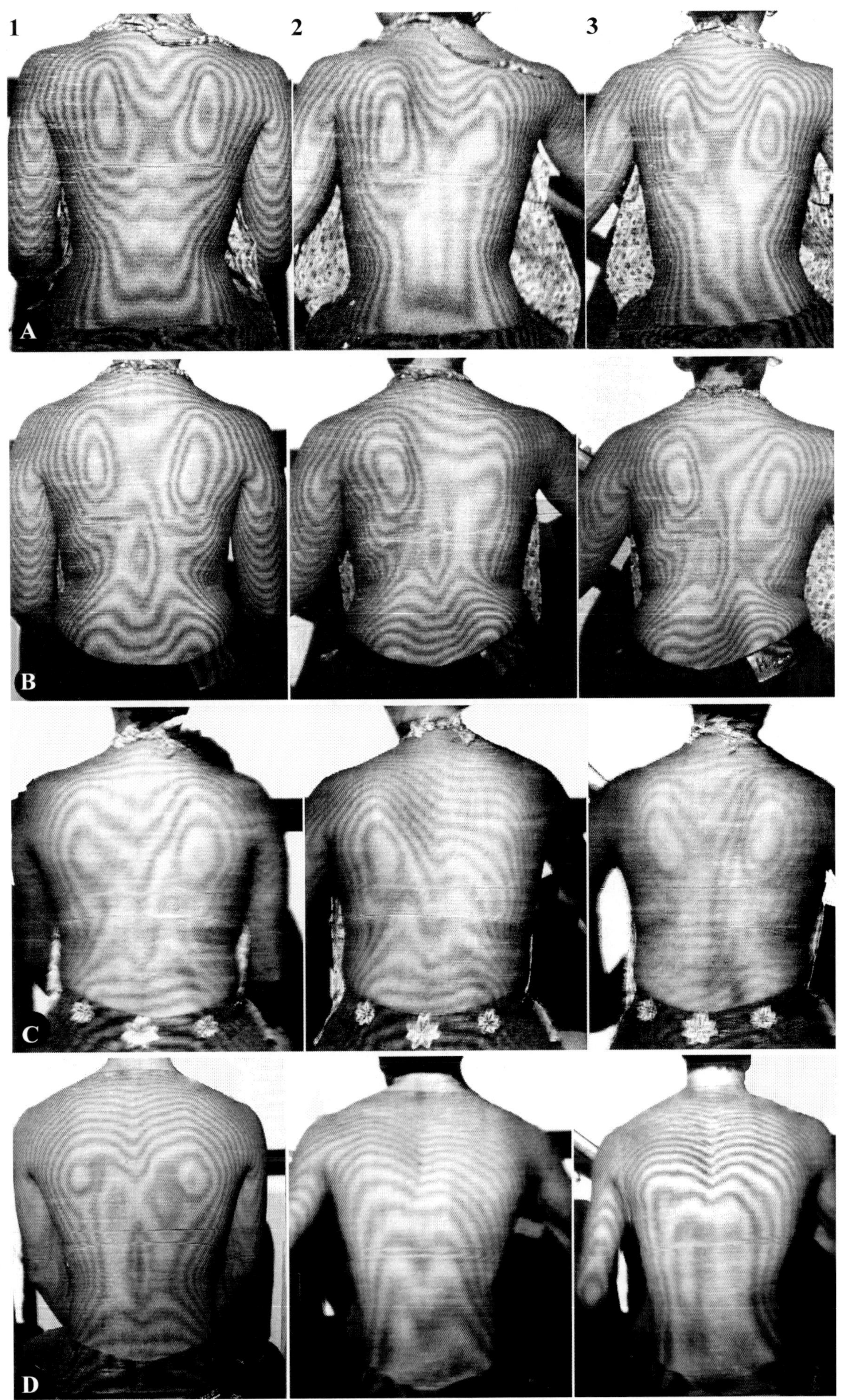

1. Normal standing posture / 2. Traditional placement of the guitar / 3. Slanted placement

III. PRE-WARMUP EXERCISES

It is usual to experience greater confidence in playing after a few minutes of smooth and progressive activity on the instrument, which together with the warming up of our hands and limbs also stimulates the speed of the reflexes "reconnecting" the body to the sounding means. This process is enhanced significantly if preceded by joint and stretching exercises that also promote warm up and flexibility.

Flexibility is the ability to efficiently carry out movements in their entirety. Flexibility exercises seek to maintain a correct degree of elasticity and muscle tone, a fluid and free mobility, and efficient muscle coordination.

Stretching the muscles and tendons increases blood circulation and prepares them for physical activity.

Flexibility can vary considerably from one person to another due to several factors like age, lifestyle, injuries, trauma, etc. Depending on these aspects or on an appropriate exercise plan, flexibility can be modified considerably in the same person. Its lack in one joint creates problems in other areas. For example, stiffness in the hips negatively impacts spine, knees and feet.

The main component of the connective tissue of the muscles is *collagen*, a contractile and elastic substance. If the muscles remain inactive for a long time, the collagen hardens and restricts mobility. Like an elastic band, the muscle groups stretch more easily at a higher temperature. For this reason stretching is best done after a hot shower or after performing gentle movements to raise body heat.

Joint Gymnastics[58]

Starting at the neck and ending at the ankles, this set of exercises provides a workout for the joints of the body.

General posture: Standing, eyes looking forward, body relaxed.

a) Smooth movements of the head forward and backward (four times).

b) Smooth movements of the head to right and left sides (four times).

c) Slow rotating movement of the neck, four times from right to left, and four times in reverse.

d) Circular movement of the extended right arm, making "blade" movements four times from front to back, and another four in reverse. Repeat with the left arm.

• Make the same movement with both arms simultaneously.

e) Extend the right arm in front of the body and, holding it firmly with the left hand, rotate the elbow so the forearm turns like the blades of a pinwheel. Repeat four times from right to left, and four times in reverse. Repeat with the left arm.

f) With the right arm extended in front of the body, relax the wrist and rotate it. Repeat four times from right to left and four times in reverse. Repeat the exercise with the left wrist.

g) Standing with legs slightly apart and hands at the waist, tilt the trunk to the front and rotate the waist, keeping the trunk out of the vertical. Repeat four times from right to left and four times in reverse.

h) With the feet together and the hands at the waist, perform circular movements of the hips, keeping the trunk erect. Repeat four times from right to left and four times in reverse.

i) While standing, lean with the left hand on a wall or support yourself on a chair, then lift the right thigh to the horizontal position and hold it with the right hand to perform circular movements of the knee and lower leg. Repeat four times from right to left and four times in reverse. Repeat the exercise with the left knee.

j) Standing, leaning on the wall or supported on a chair, lift your right leg slightly, keeping your balance on the left leg. Rotate the ankle from right to left four times and another four times in reverse. Repeat the exercise with the left ankle.

When executing each of the rotating exercises pay attention to the movement and intensely "feel" the motion of the joint.

[58] Exercises designed by Dr. Rafael Albisa. These movements can be accompanied by rhythmic breathing.

Stretching Exercises

Stretching exercises should be slow and sustained from 30 to 60 seconds, and more for stiff or longer muscles. You should experience a slight discomfort, not pain. Otherwise, you run the risk of damaging the muscles.[59]

All the muscles of the body should be stretched, not only the hands and the fingers. It is convenient to do at least one good stretch session early in the day, and then repeat it, perhaps more briefly, before and after study.[60]

Dr. Carlos Rubén Gómez recommends structuring the pre-warmup in three steps:
a) Stretching.
b) Calisthenics: Soft movements of the fingers at chest height for a few minutes.
c) Soft work on the guitar: play without overexertion so as not to become fatigued. The goal is to increase temperature and blood circulation

At the end of the study session, it is beneficial to perform the steps in inverse order, gradually reducing the actions to finish with simple movements and a minimum effort.

Pre-warmup and cooling prevent pain and ensure a convenient elimination of the lactic acid accumulated in muscles during exercise (See Gómez, 2000).

Tips for Preventing Injuries in Musicians[61]

1. Do not increase rehearsal or study hours dramatically (maximum of 20 minutes more per day).

2. Leave the most difficult passages and pieces for the middle of the study session, when the musculature is already prepared but not exhausted.

3. Start at a slow tempo and gradually increase the speed.

4. Do not become obsessed about repeating a passage or gesture that does not end up going well. Look for alternatives or other ways to achieve that goal.

5. Take breaks of 5-10 minutes every half hour. You can use them to stretch the overloaded muscles, gently move the more tense areas or simply walk a little.

6. Maintain correct posture with balanced foot support and a good sitting position. Pay attention to breathing; regulate the height of the music stand and footstool.

7. Work in good environmental conditions considering lighting, ambient noise and room temperature.

8. Respect sleeping and eating schedules.

9. Do some complementary physical activity, avoiding contact sports. This will allow you to compensate for imbalances and eliminate tension.

10. Never play if you are in pain. In that case, you should stop practicing and perform gentle stretches. If the pain reappears in future sessions you should seek professional help as soon as possible.

11. Perform stretching exercises before and after playing.
The goal of stretching is to reduce tension, improve performance and the coordination of movements, as well as to prevent the occurrence of injuries. When performing the exercises, one should bear in mind that:

- You should not experience pain, only tension.
- Each stretch should be held for at least 20-30 seconds.
- Do not force the stretching. Simply hold the stretch without *bouncing*.
- Stretch exercises can be repeated several times.

•

[59] The myotatic reflex maintains muscle tone and protects the body from injuries. It is for this reason that stretching must be maintained for at least 30 seconds for the muscle to become accustomed to the new length and "send the signal" that there is no danger of injury. From that moment the contraction and the tension in the muscle are reduced, and we can stretch a little more.

[60] See Norris, 1993:99. In addition, this practice helps to compensate possible imbalances in the use of different muscle groups during practice.

[61] Published by Institut de Fisiologia i Medicina de l'Art, (www.institutart.com, info@institutart.com), with the collaboration of Fundació Ciència i Art (www.fcart.org info@fcart.org).

Basic Stretches[62]

1

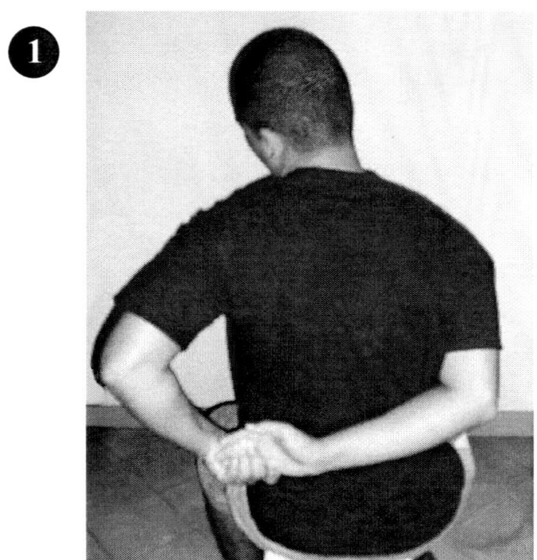

Stretch your arm down while tilting your head to the opposite side. Lean your head more or less forward to vary the tension zone, and repeat towards the other side.

2

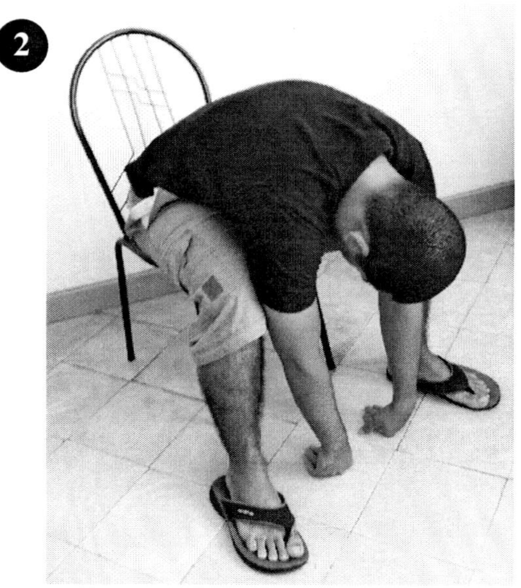

Bend the upper body over the thighs while keeping the back relaxed.

3

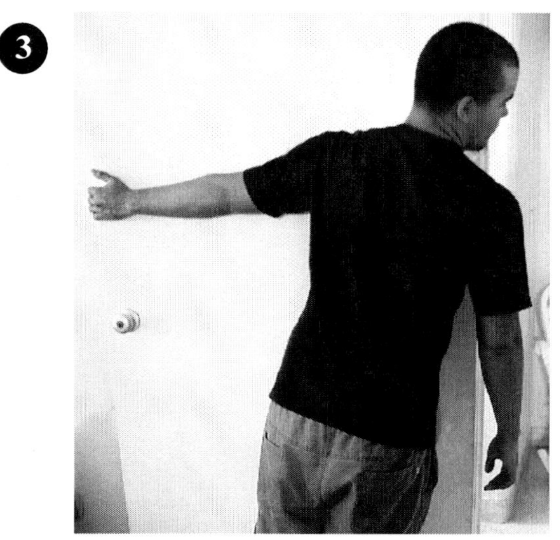

Apply tension to the arm, tightening the chest area. Repeat with the other arm.

4

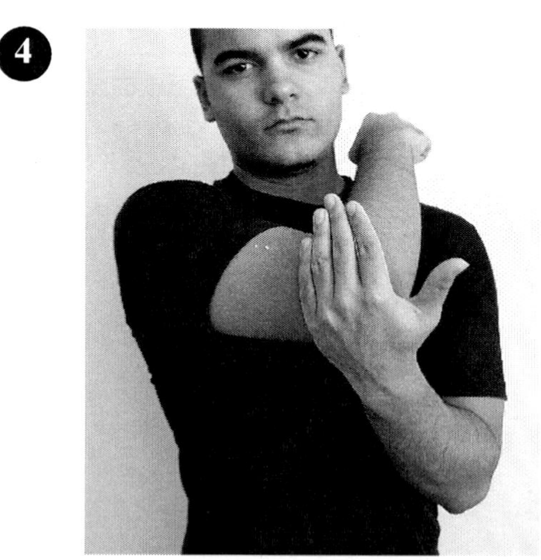

Pull the arm back leaving the shoulder relaxed so that it comes forward. Stress should be perceived between the shoulder blades. Repeat with the other arm.

---

[62] More information on special exercises for musicians can be found in *A tono. Ejercicios para mejorar el rendimiento del músico (Exercises to Improve Performance of the Musician)* by Jaume Rosset and Silvia Fábregas.

5

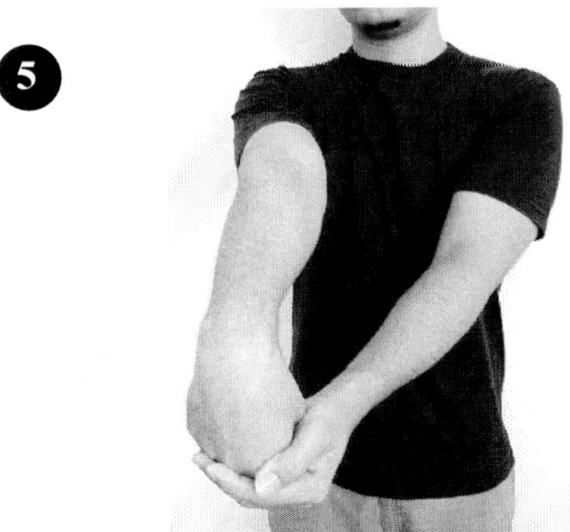

Close your fist, and aided by the other hand, flex the wrist downward while holding the arm outstretched. Repeat with the other arm.

6

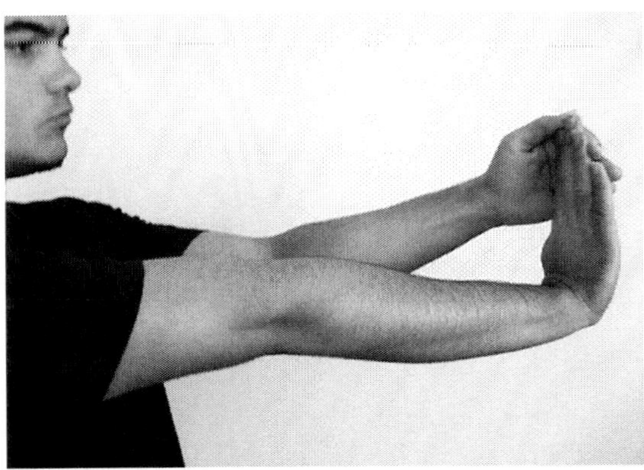

With your arm and fingers fully extended, pull back with your other hand. Repeat with the other arm.

7

Press to apply tension to the fingers of both hands, keeping the palms apart.

8

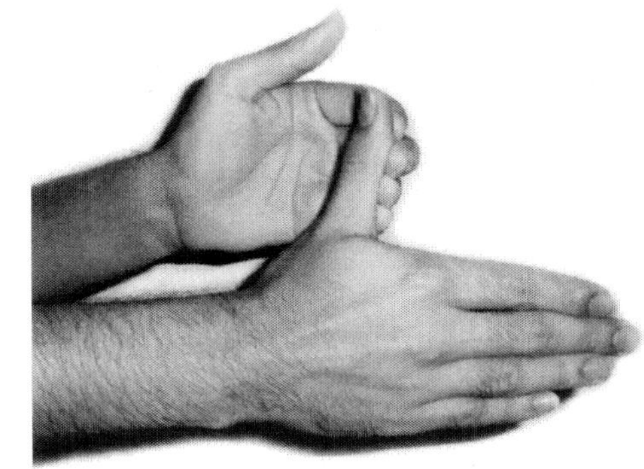

Bring your thumb back (extension), turning it inwards towards the body, not outwards the arm.

•

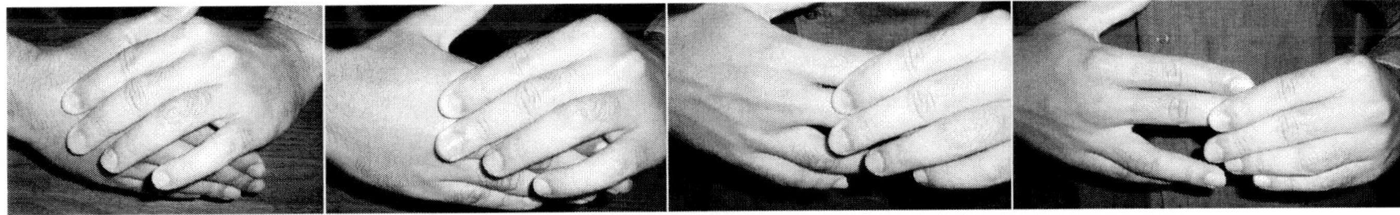

Following the practice session, immediate relief for the muscles of both hands can be gained by massaging and stretching each finger from the palm outward.

BIBLIOGRAPHY

AGUADO, DIONISIO: *Nuevo Método para Guitarra,* Printed by Aguado, Madrid, 1849.

ALEXANDER, F. MATTHIAS: *Aphorisms,* published by Jean M. O. Fischer. Mouritz, UK, 2000.

ALEXANDER, GERDA: *Eutony; The Holistic Discovery of the Total Person,* published by F. Murrow, New York, 1986,

AMAT, JOAN CARLES: *Guitarra española de cinco órdenes...* (Barcelona, 1596), Facsimile edition, Valladolid University, 2007.

BERKELEY, CHRISTOPHER: *The Musician's Hand: a Clinical Guide*, Taylor & Francis, London, 1998.

BERMUDO, JUAN: *Declaración de instrumentos musicales* (Osuna, 1555), Ed. Maxtor, Madrid, 2009.

BRAND, ULRICO: *Eutonía,* Ed. Abraxas, Barcelona, 1997.

CARLEVARO, ABEL: *Cuaderno No. 3 (Técnica de la mano izquierda),* Ed. Barry, Buenos Aires, 1969.
____: *Cuaderno No. 4 (Técnica de la mano izquierda),* Ed. Barry, Buenos Aires, 1970.
____: *School of Guitar. Exposition of Instrumental Theory,* Boosey & Hawkes, London, 1984.
____: *Técnica aplicada,* vol. I (Diez Estudios de Fernando Sor), Ed. Dacisa, Montevideo, 1985.
____: *Técnica aplicada,* vol. II (Cinco Preludios y Chôros No. 1 de H. Villa-Lobos), Ed. Dacisa, Montevideo, 1986.

CHIESA, RUGGERO: *La Chitarra,* EDT, Roma, 1990.

CONABLE, BARBARA: *How to Learn the Alexander Technique,* Andover Press, Portland, Oregon, 1995.
____: *What Every Musician Needs to Know About the Body.* Chicago: GIA Publications, Inc., 1998.

CRUZ, ELOY: *La casa de los once muertos (Historia y repertorio de la guitarra),* UNAM, México, 1993.

CURF, NICOLA: *Musician's Injuries: A Guide to Their Understanding and Prevention,* Parapress Ltd., Guilford, 1998.

DETHLEFSEN, THORWALD y RÜDIGER DAHLKE: *La enfermedad como camino,* Plaza & Janés Editores S.A, 1999.

ESCANDE, ALFREDO: *Abel Carlevaro, un nuevo mundo en la guitarra,* Ediciones Santillana S.A., Montevideo, 2005.
____: *Sor-Aguado-Carlevaro: continuidades y rupturas,* Ed. Barry, Buenos Aires, 2007.

FELDENKRAIS, MOSHE: *Awareness through Movement. Health Exercises for Personal Growth,* Harper & Row Publisher, NY, 1971.
____: *Body Awareness as Healing Therapy.* Frog Ltd., California, 1993.
____: *The Potent Self,* Frog Ltd., California, 2002.

FERANDIERE, FERNANDO: *Arte de tocar la guitarra española por música...,* (Madrid, 1799), Facsimile edition, Universidad de Valladolid, 2007.

FERGUSON, HOWARD: *La interpretación en los instrumentos de teclado,* Ed. Alianza S.A., Madrid, 2003.

FERNÁNDEZ, EDUARDO: *Technique, Mechanism, Learning (An Investigation Into Becoming a Guitarist),* Mel Bay Publications, Inc., USA, 2002.

GARDNER, HOWARD: *Arte, mente y cerebro. Una aproximación cognitiva a la creatividad,* Ed. Paidós, Argentina, 1997.

GENDLIN, EUGENE: *Focusing, proceso y técnica del enfoque corporal,* Ediciones Mensajero, Bilbao, 1988.

GINSBURG, LEV S.: *Del trabajo sobre la obra musical,* Ed. Pueblo y Educación, La Habana, 1990.

Gómez, Carlos Rubén: *Escuela fisiológica de la guitarra,* Ed. Fases, Argentina, 2000.

Grindea, Carola: *Tensions in the Performance of Music,* Kahn & Averill, Londres, 1978.
____: *Healthy Piano Technique,* Ed. Simrock, UK, 2000.

Guerau, Francisco: *Poema harmónico compuesto de varias cifras para el temple de la guitarra española* (Madrid, 1694). Editorial Alpuerto, Madrid, 2000.

Hemsy, Violeta y S, Kesselman: *Música y eutonía. El cuerpo en estado de arte,* Ed. Lumen, Argentina, 2003.

Hilgard, Ernerst R.: *Teorías del aprendizaje,* Instituto Cubano del Libro, La Habana, 1961.

Iznaola, Ricardo: *Kitharologus, The Path to Virtuosity,* Mel Bay Publications Inc., USA, 1997.
____: *The Physiology of Guitar Playing,* University of Reading, UK, 2000.
____: *On Practicing,* Mel Bay Publications, USA, 2001.

Käppel, Hubert: *The Bible of Classical Guitar Technique*, AMA Verlag, Germany, 2016.

Latham, Alison: *Diccionario enciclopédico de la música,* Fondo de cultura económica, Barcelona, 2010.

Lavignac, Alexandre: *La educación musical,* Ed. Ricordi Americana, Argentina, 1950.

Le Boulch, Jean: *La educación psicomotriz en la escuela primaria: la psicokinética en la edad escolar.* Ed. Paidós, Buenos Aires, 1986.

Le du, Jean: *El cuerpo hablado, psicoanálisis de la expresión corporal,* Ed. Paidós Ibérica, España, 1992.

Limón, Daniel: *Guitarra,* U.A.P., México, 1993.

Maisel, Edward: *La Técnica Alexander,* Ed. Paidós, Barcelona, 1995.

Matthay, Tobias: *The Visible and Invisible in Pianoforte Technique,* Oxford University Press, New York, 1947.

Meinel, Kurt: *Didáctica del movimiento,* Instituto Cubano del Libro, La Habana, 1977.

Menuhin, Yehudi: *Violin. Six Lessons with Yehudi Menuhin,* Viking Press, New York, 1972.

Merleau-Ponty, Maurice: *Fenomenología de la percepción,* Ed. Península, Barcelona, 1997.

Moretti, Federico: *Principios para tocar la guitarra de seis órdenes…,* (Salamanca, 1797), Facsimile edition, Universidad de Valladolid, 2007.

Neuhaus, Heinrich: *The Art of Piano Playing,* Preager Publishers, N.Y., 1973.

Nicola, Isaac - Martín Pedreira: *Método de guitarra*, Ediciones Atril-Abdala S.A., La Habana, 2002.

Norris, Richard: *The Musician's Survival Manual: a Guide to Preventing and Treating Injuries in Instrumentalists,* International Conference of Symphony and Opera Musicians (ICSOM), MMB Music Inc., USA, 1993.

Orozco Delclos, Luis y Joaquín Solé Escobar: *Tecnopatías del músico,* Aritza Comunicación, Barcelona, 1996.

Özgen, Mesut: *Designing Technical Training Programs for Classical Guitarists Based on Exercise Physiology Principles,* Turquoise Guitar Editions, US, 2006.

Pecchioli, Marco: *La Mano e la Chitarra,* Ed. Romana Musica, 2010.

Prat, Domingo: *La nueva técnica de la guitarra para la práctica de los cinco dedos,* Buenos Aires, Ed. Ricordi, 1921.

Pujol, Emilio: *Escuela razonada de la guitarra* (libro II), Ricordi Americana S.A., Buenos Aires, 1952.
____: *Escuela razonada de la guitarra* (Libro Primero), Ricordi Americana S.A., Buenos Aires, 1956.
____: *Tárrega (ensayo biográfico),* Ramos, Afonso y Moita, Lda., Lisboa, 1960.
____: *El dilema del sonido en la guitarra,* Ricordi Americana, S.A.E.C., Buenos Aires, 1960.
____: *Escuela razonada de la guitarra* (Libro Cuarto), Ricordi Americana S.A., Buenos Aires, 1971.

Riera, Juan: *Emilio Pujol* (biografía), Instituto de Estudios Ilerdenses, Lérida, 1974.

RISTAD, ELOISE: *La música en la mente,* Ed. Cuatro Vientos, Chile, 2009.

ROBBINS, ANTHONY: *Poder sin límites,* Ed. Grijalbo Mondadori, Barcelona, 1987.

ROMERO, PEPE: *La Guitarra,* Tuscany Publications, Tampa, Florida, 2012.

ROSSET, JAUME y SILVIA FÁBREGAS: *A Tono. Ejercicios para mejorar el rendimiento del músico,* Ed. Paidotribo, Barcelona, 2005.

ROUVIÈRE, HENRY Y ANDRÉ DELMAS: *Anatomía humana descriptiva y topográfica,* Instituto del Libro, La Habana, 1968.

RYAN, LEE F.: *The Natural Classical Guitar. The Principles of Effortless Playing*, Englewood Cliffs, Prentice-Hall, Inc., New Jersey, 1984.

RYWERANT, YOCHANAN: *El Método Feldenkrais,* Ed. Paidós, Argentina, 1985.

SANTOS, TURIBIO: *Heitor Villa-Lobos and the Guitar,* Wise Owl Music, Ireland, 1985.

SANZ, GASPAR: *Instrucción de música sobre la guitarra española,* Zaragoza, 1674, Facsimile edition.

SCHAEFFER, PIERRE: *Tratado de los objetos musicales,* Alianza Música, Madrid, 2006.

SCHAFER, ROBERT MURRAY: *Hacia una educación sonora,* Ed. Pedagogías Abiertas Musicales, Buenos Aires, 1994.

SCHULTZ, JOHANNES H.: *El entrenamiento autógeno,* Ed. Científico-Médica, Barcelona, 1969.

SEARBY, JOE: *Técnica Alexander,* Evergreen, Duncan Baird Publishers, UK, 2007.

SHOLES, PERCY A.: *Diccionario Oxford de la Música,* Ed. Pueblo y Educación, La Habana, 1973.

SOR, FERNANDO: *Méthode pour la Guitare,* Editado por N. Simrok, Bonn, 1830.

STANISLAVSKI, KONSTANTÍN S.: *Cómo se hace un actor,* Instituto del Libro, La Habana, 1970.
____: *La construcción del personaje,* Ed. Arte y Literatura, La Habana, 1986.

STIMPSON, MICHAEL: *The Guitar,* Oxford University Press, N.Y., 1988.

STOVER, RICHARD D.: *Seis Rayos de Plata. La vida y obra de Agustín Barrios Mangoré*, Ed. 200 Centenario, Paraguay, 2010.

SUÁREZ, CRISTINA: *Una aproximación al sistema de Fedora Aberastury,* Ed. Lumen, Argentina, 2005.

TAKASAKI, HIROSHI: *Moiré Topography,* Applied Optics vol. 9, No. 6, Optical Society of America, 1970.

TAYLOR, JOHN: *Tone Production on the Classical Guitar,* Musical New Services, London, 1978.

TENNANT, SCOTT: *Pumping Nylon*, Alfred Publishing Co. Inc., USA, 1995.

URSHALMI, JOSEPH: *A Conscious Approach to Guitar Technique,* Chantarelle Verlag, Music Media Investments Ltd., Isle of Man, EU, 2006.

USILLOS, CARLOS: *Andrés Segovia,* Ministerio de Educación y Ciencia, Madrid, 1973.

WILLIAMON, AARON: *Musical Excellence: Strategies and Techniques to Enhance Performance*, Oxfor University Press, New York, 2004.

ZÍNCHENKO, V. Y V. MUNÍPOV: *Fundamentos de Ergonomía,* Ed. Progreso, Moscú, 1985.

OTHER SOURCES

ALVISA, RAFAEL: "Para combatir el estrés," INIFUNCE, La Habana, 1982.

BEDEVIA, ARACELYS: "Dudar significa pensar," (interview) Dr. José Orlando Suárez Tajonera, *Juventud Rebelde,* La Habana, January 4th, 2008.

CHAIGNE, ANTOINE: "Acoustique et guitare," *Les Cahiers de la Guitare,* No. 4, Paris, 1982.

COOPER, COLIN: "Ricardo Iznaola and the Long-Term Approach," *Classical Guitar,* U.K., Agust, 1991.
____: "The Montes-Kircher Duo," *Classical Guitar,* vol.13, No. 12, U.K., 1995.

CONABLE, BARBARA: *How to Resolve Dystonias: A Movement Perspective*, http://bodymap.org/main/index.php.

EGUILAZ ARANGUREN, MARÍA JOSÉ: "La memoria en la interpretación guitarrística. Una aproximación a su problemática," http://musica.rediris.es/leeme.

ESTEBAN MUÑOZ, ELENA: "When Gesture Sounds: Bodily Significance in Musical Performance," http://www.performancescience.org/cache/fl0003540.pdf.

FELDENKRAIS, MOSHE: San Francisco "Quest," *Workshop*, ATM Recordings, Washington D.C., 1981.

GARCÍA TRABUCCO, ALEJANDRA y MARÍA A. SILNIK: "El plano corporal en la enseñanza de instrumentos musicales," http://eutonicamendoza.blogspot.com/p/investigacion.html.

GRINDEA, CAROLA Y FIONA CLAREY: "Focal Dystonia in Guitarrists," *ISSTIP Journal*, No. 12, U.K., 2004.

HEMSY DE GAINZA, VIOLETA y Susana Kesselman: "Introducción al abordaje eutónico de la música instrumental," http://www.guitarra.linkado.com/foros/showthread.php?t=2280.

HERNÁNDEZ, CLAUDINA: "La calidad del movimiento en la ejecución pianística" (tesis doctoral), biblioteca del Instituto Superior de Arte, La Habana, 2009.

JIMÉNEZ, ANTONIO y JOSÉ A. DE PAZ: "La periodización en el entrenamiento de la fuerza," http://www.efdeportes.com/efd72/fuerza.htm.

KEMBER, JANE and THÉRÈSE WASSILY SABA: "You and Your Guitar," *Classical Guitar,* vol.14, No. 5, U.K., 1996.

LEE HARPER, NANCY: "Don't Worry, Be Happy," *ISSTIP Journal,* U.K., autumn, 2005.

LISLE, RAE DE; DALE SPEEDY and JOHN THOMPSON: "The Role of Retraining in Rehabilitation from Focal Dystonia," International Symposium on Performance Science, www.performancescience.org.

NAREJOS, ANTONIO: "El taller de las manos," *Revista de la Lista Electrónica Europea de Música en la Educación,* No. 6, noviembre, 2000, http://musica.rediris.es/leeme/sumarios.html.

PELINSKI, RAMÓN: "Corporeidad y experiencia musical," http://www.pelinski.name.

POSTLEWATE, CHARLES: "Extending Right-Hand Technique to Include the Little Finger (Part I)," *GFA Soundboard,* USA, autumn, 2002.

____: "Extending Right-Hand Technique to Include the Little Finger (Part II)," *GFA Soundboard,* USA, summer, 2002.

PUJOL, EMILIO: "Pedagogía de Tárrega," *Guitarra,* año II, No. 2, La Habana, June, 1941.

REKAS, STEPHEN: "An Interview with Charles Postlewate," *GFA Soundboar*d, USA, 2003.

RIOU, ALAIN: "Rencontre avec Oscar Ghiglia," *Les Cahiers de La Guitare,* No. 33, Francia, 1990.

ROMERO, PEPE: "La preparación del guitarrista ante el concierto," http://www.orfeoed.com/guia/guia20.asp.

ROSSET I LLOBET, JAUME: "Independencia de los dedos,*" 12 Notas,* No. 34, Barcelona, diciembre-enero, 2002-2003.

____: "Problemas de salud de los músicos y su relación con la educación," XXVI Conferencia de la International Society for Music Education y Seminario de la CEPROM, Barcelona y Tenerife, julio 2004.

____: "Análisis clínico de la distonía focal en los músicos," *Clínica de Terrasa,* Barcelona, 2005, www.institutart.com/congress2005.

ROYLE, DOMINIQUE y NICOLA CULF: "The Perfect Technique?," *EGTA Guitar Journal,* No. 6, U.K., 1995, http://www.egtaguitarforum.org/ExtraArticles/../index.html.

SHEARER, AARON: *Learning the Classic Guitar (Part One)*, Mel Bay Publications, USA, 1980.

XIMENA, DIANA y DUILIO CRUZ: "Influencia de la respiración diafragmática en la motricidad fina," http://dialnet.unirioja.es/servlet/articulo?codigo=3181831&orden=247301&info=link.

GLOSSARY

abduction Separation of thumb, index, ring, and little fingers from the hand's midline (or middle finger). This action is performed by the four dorsal interosseous muscles, which assist in flexion at the metacarpophalangeal joints and extension at the interphalangeal joints. The opposite movement is called *adduction*.

acquired incapacity Negative learning whose limits to effective actions are evident.

anchoring A technique proposed by Neuro-Linguistic Programming (NLP), which advocates behavior development through the association of external stimuli with certain mental states or moods.

articulation Performance technique which affects the transition or continuity of a single note or between multiple notes or sounds.

attack Manner in which a note is initiated. Attack determines color, volume, and the sustain and decay of sound, depending on the type of stroke used (rest-stroke, free-stroke, fingertip, nail, etc.).

automatism A conditioned automatic response or habit.

autonomic nervous system Consists of nerves that connect the central nervous system (CNS) to the visceral organs such as the heart, stomach and intestines. It mediates unconscious activities.

biomechanics Science of movement of a living body, which studies how muscles, bones, tendons, and ligaments work together to produce movement.

campanella Produced by articulating a melodic line by combining open and fretted notes on two or more strings. The prolongation of some notes produces a pedal effect that resembles the sound of small bells.

corporal concept An individual's image of the body, built on the basis of sensations. It essentially determines the way in which we perceive and use our bodies.

damping Control of resonance (sounds) by stopping the vibrations of the strings.

ergonomic Physiologically functional in terms of comfort and ease of execution.

eutony A wholistic mind/body discipline created by Gerda Alexander which proposes a regulation of the muscle tone that adapts to every situation. The ideal is to achieve the right muscle tone, so that no more than the necessary energy is exerted. The term eutony comes from the Greek *Eu*: good, and Latin *Tonus*: tension.

extension Any open position of the fingers on the fingerboard that tests the flexibility of the hand, especially when the "quadruple rule" of one finger per fret is exceeded.

figueta *p-i-p-i* or *p-m-p-m* alternation on a string. The down-up motion of thumb and finger produces a sound similar to that of a flat pick.

fixation Refers to muscular integration, mostly in plucking. Carlevaro defined fixation as *the voluntary and momentary nullification or immobilization of one or more articulations for the purpose of allowing stronger and more capable elements to perform in a particular way.* (1984:22)

flotation Sensation of an apparent weightlessness of the arm which results from a sustained balance between various muscle groups, such as the arm abductors working together with the scapular muscles (mainly the trapezius and the rhomboid).

functional relaxation Degree of relaxation that allows a fluid development of actions.

glissando A technique performed by sliding any finger over a vibrating string, to reproduce –depending on the score– all or part of the intermediate sounds.

grip Degree of tension of the fingers on the strings before plucking.

hand-forearm placement Refers to the position of the plucking hand relative to the forearm. There are three biomechanical models that have a direct influence on sound production: *Aligned, Intermediate,* and *Curved Placement.*

kinesthetic sense Proprioceptive sensations/perceptions that receive and decode sensorial stimuli to guide us through space.

mechanism A set of conditioned reflexes that make execution possible; a primary component of technique. The development of a positive mechanism is conditioned by practice that takes into account the laws of physiology.

mechanism of support point Abel Carlevaro describes this resource as *a means by which one or more fingers on the fingerboard serving as a leaning point or fulcrum enable the arm to function as a lever of the first type to extend or join the other fingers in favor of greater mechanical ease* (1984:128).

motor coordination Coordination in general, the capacity or ability to move or handle objects, alone or with a partner, or work with a team in a game, etc.; the broadest form of coordination as the result of good development of fundamental motions.

muscle tone (or tonus) The property of the muscle by which a partial and permanent contraction of varying degrees is sustained. The level of tension of muscle fibers and, by extension, of all the tissues of the body. Too much or too little muscle tone can hinder sustained mobility. (See *Eutony*).

myotatic reflex (or stretch reflex) Essentially, it is the body's response to the stretching of a muscle, to protect it by keeping it at a constant length. In plucking it determines the automatic return of the fingers to their natural, relaxed position.

physiology The biological study of life processes, activities and functions.

picado Rapid scale-like passages characteristic of flamenco technique.

pivot finger A variant of the *mechanism of support point*, defined as a fretting finger that allows the hand to rotate to arrive at a new position, while sustaining –if necessary– the sound of the fretted note.

placement-release cycle A series of three left-hand fretting procedures –performed simultaneously with the right-hand *plucking cycle*:

1. Contact with the strings
2. Pressing (*Pisado*)
3. Relax and Release.

planting Preparing by placing two or more fingers on the strings at the same time, prior to their simultaneous or sequential use. Essentially, a resource for movement coordination.

plasticity Adaptive capacity; may refer to adaptability of technique, efficiency or remodeling of posture and hand positions.

plucking cycle A series of three events that comprise plucking, in which can be framed different right-hand technical procedures:

1. Contact with the strings
2. Grip/Thrust
3. Exit and Relax.

portamento Slow/expressive glissando, characteristic of Romantic phrasing (*cantabile*).

position or quadruple Fretboard area covered by the four left-hand fingers placed on consecutive frets. The position is determined by the fret played by finger 1. Therefore, finger 4 placed on F (thirteenth fret on the first string) defines the tenth (X) position.

positive inhibition A term from the Alexander Technique lexicon signifying "a voluntary interruption of tension." During performance, positive inhibition favors the work/rest rhythm necessary for the free mobility of both hands.

postural frame The relationship of all body parts to the guitar while seated in playing position.

postural symmetry Balance between the left and right sides of the body. The optimal posture for playing the classic guitar, achieved by using a guitar support and having both feet on the floor with equal weight distribution, and therefore, a straight spinal column with the shoulders aligned with the hips.

professional (or occupational) diseases Performance-related injuries like carpal tunnel syndrome or focal dystonia.

pronation (of the hands) Rotation of the forearm that turns the palm downward, opposite of *supination.*

pronosupination Hand rotation.

proprioceptive perception Relating to stimuli that are produced and perceived within an organism, especially those connected with the position and movement of the body. Proprioception is the awareness of joint position, whereas kinesthesia is the cognizance of joint movement.

psychophysical resources Relates to the relationship between one's internal (psychic) and external (physical) worlds.

pulsar/tañer Both Spanish verbs mean "to play" or "to pluck" the strings, but also "to feel" with the fingertips.

quadruple See *position*

rasgueado Right-hand strumming techniques characteristic of the flamenco style.

remodeling In general, any conscious change in terms of posture with the instrument or mechanism.

resources Generally refers to technical ability or options.

scapular girdle The scapular girdle is made up of the two shoulder blades and the two clavicles. It is divided into three regions: anterior or axillary, middle or deltoid, and posterior or scapular. It is a functional set that allows the union of the upper limbs to the thorax (spine, skull and rib cage). The scapular girdle is a sensitive zone of innervation, where the central nervous system CNS (brain and spinal cord) branches out to the *peripheral nervous system* (body parts), which is further subdivided into the *somatic nervous system* and the *autonomic nervous system*.

sensoperception The process by which we receive information from our senses so that it can be encoded and processed in our brain, and finally generate a conscious perceptual experience.

sensopostural patterns Sensations linked to postures which should be activated by establishing goals at the beginning of each practice session. Defining such patterns heightens the body's awareness of the instrument.

somatic nervous system Consists of nerves of the skin and muscles involved in conscious activities.

supination Rotation of the forearm that turns the palm upward.

support-planting Lightly resting the thumb on a string, generally after a rest stroke, or anticipating the next note to be played.

sympathetic resonance (or vibration) Harmonic phenomenon wherein a formerly passive string or vibratory body responds to external vibrations to which it has harmonic likeness. Sympathetic harmonics appear continuously in guitar performance and reinforce legato, mainly in the most common tonalities of the instrument.

ternary/quaternary fingering Refers to note patterns that allow the use of three or four right hand fingers for execution.

thrust Downward and inward motion of the plucking fingers, exciting the string in a more vertical elliptical fashion and producing a fuller, richer tone. Thrust is mainly applied in rest-stroke and with the thumb.

timbre Quality of auditory sensations produced by the tone of a sound wave. The timbre of a sound depends on its wave form, which varies with the number of overtones, or harmonics that are present, their frequencies, and their relative intensities.

twin-stroke Thumb technique that links timbre and accentuation (See Carlevaro, 1984:31). The plucking of two or more consecutive strings beginning with the fingertip and ending with the nail, emphasizing the last note.

visual-motor coordination Integration of visual perception and fine motor control. The execution of movements of the entire motor scheme (body) in which a visual perception of the occupied and free space is necessary to carry them out.

•

INDEX OF MUSICAL EXAMPLES*

*See publishing firms description on page 135.

Publishers:
(AL) Alphonse Leduc & Co.; (AV) Artaria, Vienna; (BA) Barry Editorial; (BE) Boileau Edition; (BF) Biblioteca Fortea; (BGE) Manuel Barrueco Guitar Edition; (BH) Boosey & Hawkes; (BMP) Belwin-Mills Publishing Corp.; (BP) Broekmans & van Poppel; (BSC) F. Birkel-Smith Collection; (CP) Chorus Publications; (CR) Cubafilin Records Ltd.; (CV) Chanterelle Verlag; (EA) Editorial Affedis; (EB) Edizioni Bèrben; (ED) Éditions Doberman; (EE) Ediciones Étoile; (EEE) Ediciones Espiral Eterna; (EG) Editions Gismonti; (EJR) Ediciones Joaquín Rodrigo; (EL) Éditions Lulu; (EMM) Ediciones Musicales Madrid; (EMU) Ediciones Museo de la Música; (ES) Ed. Schott; (ET) Éditions Transatlantiques; (EUE) Eulenburg Editions; (GG) Gendai Guitar Editions; (GSP) Guitar Solo Publications; (HL) Éditions Henry Lemoine; (IGW) Iznaola Guitar Works; (JWC) J. & W. Chester Editions; (JY) Juan Yané, editor; (MBP) Mel Bay Publications, Inc.; (ME) Editions Max Eschig; (ML) Deutscher Verlag für Musik Leipzig; (MMP) Master Music Publications, Inc.; (MO) Matanya Ophee Editions; (OT) Opera Tres; (OUP) Oxford University Press; (PMD) Prim-Musikverlag Darmstadt; (RA) Ricordi Americana; (RM) G. Ricordi Milano; (SB) Simrock, Berlin; (SEM) Soneto Editorial Musical; (SM) Schott Music; (SS) B. Schotts's Söhne; (SZ) Edizioni Suvini Zerboni; (TKE) Thomas Königs Edition; (UME) Unión Musical Española.

Martín Pedreira

Guitarist and composer, Martín Pedreira (Havana, Cuba, 1952) is currently Associate Professor of Music at the University of Arts in Havana.

He studied guitar with Isaac Nicola and Leo Brouwer, and has been teaching since 1975. He has conducted studies didactic and guitar technique in relation to physiology, in which he obtained a Masters degree in 2002, and later, a PhD in Arts (2007).

As a composer, he has also focused on the guitar. In 1987 he won the National Composition Prize of the Union of Writers and Artists of Cuba with his series of didactic pieces *Divertimentos I*. In addition he has written numerous didactic pieces, including *Music for David, 10 Studies, Brief Preludes*, and many others.

Pedreira has also published transcriptions and compositions of several Cuban guitarists, among them José Antonio Rojas ("Ñico" Rojas, 1927-2008), Roberto Gonzalez-Rubiera ("Guyún," 1908-1987), and Ildefonso Acosta (1939).

Since 2007 he has collaborated with the National Museum of Music performing analysis and digital transcription of scores of the Cuban heritage repertoire.

Pedreira is coauthor with his teacher, Isaac Nicola (1916-1997) of a *Guitar Method* in four volumes (Atril Editions, Havana, 2000), which is included in the syllabus officially adopted by the National System of Artistic Education in Cuba.

He is also the author of two theoretical books: *History of the Guitar* (Museum of Music Editions, Havana, 2018), and the present *Guitar Ergonomics: A Wholistic Perspective of Technique Through Repertoire* (2020).